Canadian COMPENSATION *Handbook*

DAVID E. TYSON
B.A., B.A.S., CHRP

Aurora Professional Press
a division of Canada Law Book Inc.
240 Edward St., Aurora, Ontario, L4G 3S9

National Library of Canada Cataloguing in Publication

Tyson, David E.
  Canadian compensation handbook / David E. Tyson.

Includes index.
ISBN 0-88804-384-8

1. Compensation management. I. Title

HF5549.5.C67T98 2002   658.3'22   C2002-905451-6

This book is dedicated to

Lorrie
&
Sarah
&
our future

Preface

In these early years of the 21st century, the traditional factors that provided a company with a competitive advantage have ceased to matter. Physical location, technical patents, bigger factories, proximity to natural resources, access to transportation routes and/or strong financing are not nearly as important as they used to be.

The difference between success and failure will be your ability to attract, retain and motivate the best people available. To do this you need the best "pay" system possible since pay is the essence of the contractual relationship between the employer and the employee. I use the term "pay" in the broadest sense to encompass all the rewards that the employee gains from the employment relationship.

I wrote this book for two reasons. First, I recognized a need for such a book among the owner/managers and human resource executives of small to medium-sized Canadian companies who are not compensation specialists but need a practical guide to establishing a comprehensive compensation program. While there are excellent textbooks on compensation in Canadian organizations, there is no book (to my knowledge) that is specifically written for the practitioner.

Secondly, the subject matter is the major part of my consulting practice and I felt that I could produce a book that, in addition to the usual attributes:

- contains workable (I know because I have seen them work) processes and procedures;
- is free of jargon and is easy to read;
- does not include the latest, or any, fad in compensation; and
- is logical and uses a "common sense" approach.

The book follows the approximate chronological order an employer should use when designing a compensation program from scratch. I have included checklists and other documents on the CD-ROM. These can be printed, modified and used at your convenience. The CD-ROM also includes spreadsheets that should prove helpful at various points in the process. Simply load them onto your computer and input your own data.

Finally, I have tried to include as much practical knowledge and as many tools as I could to make the process of setting up your own compensation system as easy as possible. I hope I have succeeded. I wish you well in your endeavours.

Toronto, Ontario   David E. Tyson
November, 2002

Table of Contents

Preface   v

1 Assessing Your Situation   1

Introduction   1
Analyzing Your Current Situation   1
Why Should You Have a Compensation Plan?   2
Who are Your Employees?   4
Employee Involvement   6
    Rationale for Employee Involvement.   7
        The Literature   7
        Personal Experience   8
        Legal Requirements   12
How to Involve Employees   13
    Focus Groups   14
    Employee Committee   14
    Opinion Surveys   17
    Use the Union   17
    Use a Consultant   18
Theories of Motivation   18
    Expectancy Theory   18
    Equity Theory   19
Employment Law in Canada   20
Checklist   21
Conclusion   23

2 Strategy 25

Introduction 25
Components of the Package 25
Pay the Job or Pay the Person 26
Internal Equity or External Competitiveness 27
Employee Groups 28
Who Should You Compare With? 29
    Occupational Group 30
    Geography 30
    Industry 31
    Size of Company 31
Setting Your Policy Line 32
Benefits Strategy 33
    Competition in the Labour Market 33
    Obligation to Protect or Help Your Employees 33
Organization of the Compensation Function 34
    Number of Human Resources Staff 34
    General Duties of the Compensation Function 35
    Structuring the Human Resources Department 35
Worksheet for Strategic Compensation Planning 36
Conclusion 37

3 Selecting a Job Evaluation Plan 39

Introduction 39
Types of Job Evaluation 40
    Whole-Job Ranking 41
    Point-Rating Plans (Point-Factor Plans) 45
    Classification 48
    Factor-Comparison 50
Advantages and Disadvantages of the Four Methods 51
    Whole-Job Ranking 51
    Classification 52
    Factor-Comparison 52
    Point-Rating 53
Setting Up a Job Evaluation Committee 53
Selecting a Job Evaluation Plan 54
Buy, Build or Adapt 55
Market Pricing — An Alternative to Job Evaluation? 56
Conclusion 58

4 Obtaining Information About Jobs 59

Introduction 59
Methods of Obtaining Job Information 60
Different Types and Uses of Job Descriptions. 61
Development of a Job Description Questionnaire 62
    Common Elements 62
    Questions in a JDQ for a Point-Rating Plan. 64
Distribution and Completion of JDQ. 67
Other Job Description Formats and Uses. 68
Conclusion 69

5 Conducting Job Evaluation. 71

Introduction 71
Selecting a Plan and Setting up a Committee 71
Rules for the Job Evaluation Committee 71
Rules for Conducting Job Evaluation 74
Selecting Benchmark Jobs. 74
Weighting the Factors 76
Developing a Point Table. 77
    Method A 78
    Method B 80
    Method C 80
    Choosing a Method of Building a Point Table. 80
Establishing Point Bands 80
Conclusion 83

6 Salary Surveys 87

Introduction 87
Why do Salary Surveys? 87
Types of Salary Surveys 88
    Published Surveys 88
    Executive Compensation Data 89
    Third-Party Surveys 90
Selecting and Interpreting Published Surveys 91
Ageing the Survey Data. 97
Consolidation Several Surveys 98
Conducting Your Own Salary Survey 100

Jobs to Include 100
Information to be Surveyed 101
Survey Data to be Requested 102
The Area in Which to Conduct the Survey 103
What Companies do You Invite to Participate? 103
Conduct of the Survey 104
Report to Participants 105
Using Survey Data to Build Salary Range Control Points............ 107
General.. 107
Increments Between Control Points....................... 108
Variations on Percentage Increments........................... 110
Conclusion.. 111

7 Putting it All Together — Basic Salary Administration 113

Introduction 113
Salary Ranges... 114
Step-rate System 116
General... 116
Adjusting for Inflation 116
Setting the Steps... 116
Reasons for Advancing a Step 118
Steps Above the Job Rate................................. 119
3M Salary Ranges 120
General... 120
Number of Salary Range Segments 121
Increases in Salaries..................................... 122
Timing of Salary Increases............................... 124
Variable Dates for Salary Increases 125
Changing the Number of Salary Range Segments 127
Administration of Salary Increases with a 3M System 128
Initiating the Increase 131
Levels of Approval Needed for a Salary Increase 131
Updating Your Salary Structure............................... 133
Changes in Jobs 133
New Jobs 134
Promotions and Demotions 135
Conclusion... 136

8 Benefits Basics 139

Introduction 139
Benefits Policy 139
    Obligation to Your Employees 140
    Why Provide Benefits? 140
    Sharing the Costs of Benefits 141
Costing Benefits 141
What are Benefits? 142
    Pensions and Other Retirement Income Plans 142
        Legislative Framework 142
        Company-provided Retirement Plans 143
        Other Retirement Plans 144
        Limits on Contributions to Retirement Plans 144
    Life Insurance 145
    Accidental Death and Dismemberment Insurance 146
    Primary Medical/Health Insurance 146
    Long-term Disability Insurance 146
    Short-term Disability Insurance or Sick Leave 147
    Dental Insurance 147
    Holidays 148
    Vacations 148
    Major Medical Insurance 149
Optional and Statutory Benefits 149
Benefits Surveys 150
Controlling Your Benefits Costs 153
Conclusion 153

9 Working Conditions 155

Introduction 155
Setting Your Policy 155
What are Working Conditions? 156
    Hours of Work 156
    Shift Schedules 157
    Lunch Periods 158
    Call-in Pay 158
    Shift Premiums 158
    Weekend Premiums 158
    Rest Periods 159
    Standby Pay 159

Lead-hand Premiums 160
Bereavement Leave 160
Jury Duty 160
Report-to-work Provisions 161
Statutory Minimums for Working Conditions.................... 161
Surveys of Working Conditions.......................... 162
Conclusion 162

10 Implementing and Costing Your New Salary Program 163

Introduction 163
Annual or Hourly Costs 164
Adding Statutory and Non-Statutory Benefits.................... 165
Costing Work-Related Pay................................. 165
Costing a New Salary Program 166
Step-rate System..................................... 166
3M System 168
Methods of Making the Transition to a 3M System............ 168
Conclusion 170

11 Designing a Group Incentive Plan 171

Introduction 171
Conditions Required Before Starting.......................... 172
Reasonable Employee Relations 172
Base Salaries.. 172
Expectation of Income to Share 173
Stability.. 173
Communications...................................... 173
Need for Additional Production 174
Management Commitment............................... 174
Membership 175
Occupation or Employee Group.......................... 175
Length of Service 176
Type of Plan 176
Leaving the Plan..................................... 176
Generating the Funds..................................... 178
Dividing the Bonus Pool 179
Earnings 180

Seniority of Length of Service 180
Equal Distribution 181
Merit Ratings 182
Attendance 182
Job Levels. 182
Contributions by Employees 183
Combinations 183
Choosing an Allocation Formula 183
Comparison of Plans 184
Conclusion 184

12 Team-based Incentives 185

Introduction 185
Why Team-Based Incentives? 185
Prevalence of Team-Based Incentives 186
What is a Team? 186
Traditional Design Issues. 187
Design Issues for Teams 187
No Profit. 188
Base Salary. 188
Number of Teams. 189
Dividing up the Team-Bonus Pool 189
Employees Who are Not Team Members 190
Models 190
Model A 190
Model B 191
Model C 191
Conclusion 191

13 Profit Sharing 193

Introduction 193
Definitions and Types of Plans 193
Cash 194
Deferred Profit-Sharing Plans 194
Employee Profit-Sharing Plans 194
Combination Plans 195
Group Registered Retirement Savings Plans 195

Objective(s) of Plans 195
Strategic Issues to be Decided by Management.................... 196
Major Design Issues.. 198
    Membership 199
    Allocation.. 200
Conclusion 202

14 Productivity Gainsharing 203

Introduction 203
Characteristics of Productivity Gainsharing Plans.................. 203
Scanlon Plans... 204
Rucker Plans 205
Improshare™ 205
Other Gainsharing Plans in Canada 206
Comparison of Gainsharing and Profit-Sharing Plans.............. 207
Efficacy of Gainsharing Plans 208
Conclusion 208

15 Employee Share Ownership Plans 211

General... 211
Types of ESOPs... 212
    Stock-Option Plans...................................... 212
    Stock-Grant Plans....................................... 212
    Stock-Purchase Plans 213
Effectiveness of ESOPs in Canada 213
Why Have an ESOP? 213
Disadvantages of an ESOP 214
Conclusion 215

16 Performance Management and Rewards... 217

Introduction 217
Major Purposes of Performance Appraisals....................... 217
Five Features Affected... 218

Role of the Supervisor 219
Timing of the Appraisal 219
Distribution of the Information 219
Appraisal Technique. 220
Type of Appraisal Instrument. 220
Appraisal Instruments 220
Employee Comparison or Ranking 220
Essay. 221
Direct Indices 221
Management by Objectives 222
Rating Scales 222
Behaviourly Anchored Rating Scales. 226
Critical Incident Method. 227
Developing a Rating Scale for Your Organization 227
Numerical Scale 228
Descriptions of Performance Levels 229
Performance Criteria 230
Possible Factors Used in Performance Appraisal. 230
Selecting Performance Criteria. 232
Writing Paragraph Anchors 232
Weighting of Performance Criteria and Summary Rating 233
The Performance Appraisal Process. 233
Timing. 234
Who Conducts the Initial Appraisal? 234
Review and Approval of the Initial Appraisal 234
Distribution of the Competed Forms 234
Advising the Employee. 234
Worksheet to Design a Performance Appraisal Form for
Reward Allocation Purposes 235
Points to Remember in Designing a Performance Appraisal Form 236
Performance Improvement. 237
Coaching Employees to Improve Their Performance 237
Conclusion 238

17 Pay Equity

17 Pay Equity 239

Introduction 239
History of Pay Equity in Canada 239
Pay Equity Jurisdictions in Canada 240
Pay Equity in Ontario. 241
Coverage. 241

Male and Female Job Classes. 242
Comparison of Male and Female Job Classes using a
    Gender-Neutral Comparison System 242
Identification of Job Rates 242
Identification of Comparator Job Classes. 243
Defensible Differences in Job Rates. 243
Determine the Required Pay Adjustments 243
Post the Pay Equity Plan. 244
Involvement of the Employees. 244
Maintain Pay Equity. 244
Enforcement 245
Pay Equity in Quebec. 245
Introduction 245
Specified Deadlines 246
Pay Equity Plans and Employee Committees 246
Development of a Pay Equity Plan. 246
Conclusion 249

18 Work/Life Balance 251

Introduction 251
Why Work/Life Balance? 252
Reasons for Developing a Work/Life Balance Program 252
General Principles for Selecting a Work/Life Benefit. 253
Responsibility for Work/life Balance 254
Components of a Work/Life Balance Program 254
Organization of Work Time. 255
    Work Design. 255
    Flexible Work Arrangements 255
Family-Related Leave 255
    Maternity Leave 255
    Other Leaves Related to Family 255
Child and Dependent Care Services. 256
    Dependent Care Resource and Referral 256
    Day Care. 256
    Special Leaves for Personal Business. 256
    Expenses for Dependent Care. 256
Employee Benefits 256
    Employee Assistance Program 256
    Flexible Spending Accounts. 256
    Financial Planning 256

Fitess Centre 257
Volunteerism. 257
Conclusion 257

19 Communication of Pay Programs 259

Introduction 259
What to Communicate 260
Communications During Design 261
Communications After Implementation of a New Program 262
External Recruiting. 262
Internal Job Postings. 263
Orientation 264
Supervisory Training 264
Joining a Group Incentive Plan 264
Employee Meetings 265
Cheques 265
Pre-retirement Planning 266
Communications Media. 266
Conclusion 267

20 Putting it All Together: The Design Process 269

Introduction 269
Developing a Classification Structure 270
Obtaining Salary Information from Published Data 274
Conducting your own Compensation Survey 276
Developing a Step-Rate Salary Administration Program 278
Developing a 3M Salary Administration Program 280
Developing a Group Incentive Plan. 282
Developing a Benefits/Working Conditions/Work/Life Balance Program 284
Developing a Performance Appraisal System 286
Conclusion 288

Appendices 289

Appendix A Human Resources and Related Professional Associations. 289
Appendix B Sources of Labour Market Information 293

Appendix C Glossary 299
Appendix D The Tyson-Totten Job Evaluation Plan 307
Appendix E Job Description Questionnaire 319
Appendix F Adapting and Using the Tyson-Totten Job
            Evaluation Plan................................. 329
Appendix G Contents of the CD-ROM......................... 337

Index 339

1

Assessing Your Situation

INTRODUCTION

Your employees are the best weapon that you have in your battles with your competitors. A compensation plan that will help turn your company into one that everybody wants to work for is worth your attention. In all the classic textbooks on compensation, the main objectives of a compensation program are to attract, motivate and retain qualified employees. The purpose of this book is the same. If you follow the prescriptions provided herein, you will turn your compensation program into a competitive advantage.

This chapter will take you through several analyses that will set the stage for designing such a compensation program. The chapter examines the following:

- analysis of your current situation;
- rationale for having a compensation program;
- establishing who your employees are;
- the question of employee involvement;
- theories of motivation;
- employment laws in Canada;
- assessment checklist.

ANALYZING YOUR CURRENT SITUATION

Unless you have a full-blown compensation and reward program and only bought this book to review it, there are a number of common symptoms that may indicate the need for a major reassessment. You do not need to experience all of these to justify establishing a new system.

1

These are the usual indicators of problems in the compensation field:

- frequent complaints about pay by employees;
- difficulty in attracting suitably qualified applicants to join because of pay levels;
- compression (*i.e.*, small differences in pay that do not reflect a difference in responsibility) between levels of employees such as first line supervisors and the highest paid employees under them;
- employees who quit, claim and can prove[1] that they did so because they were offered more money;
- supervisors or managers who are unwilling or unable to explain to employees the reasons for the size and timing of their salary increases;
- attempts by organized labour to obtain certification as a bargaining unit;
- internal job postings that go unfilled even though there are qualified internal candidates who would receive a promotion if appointed to such jobs;
- requirement to hire new employees at salaries greater than those being paid current employees in comparable jobs;
- lack of written policies or procedures for pay programs;
- disputes over job content;
- no written job descriptions; and
- in Ontario or Quebec, or if your company is federally regulated, a visit from an official of the Pay Equity Commission (federally it would be the Human Rights Commission).

These symptoms do not always mean that you need to develop a new compensation program. They can be indicators of other things, not necessarily even problems. For example, lack of written job descriptions may mean that your company is a young, highly flexible organization that does not wish to tie its employees to rigid, narrowly defined job descriptions. On the other hand, it can also mean that you have no clear idea of what you are paying employee A $75,000 a year to do. Since it is not written down, she can claim that what she is doing is what she is supposed to be doing and you have no way of proving otherwise. At the end of this chapter there is a brief checklist of these symptoms that you can use to assess your own situation.

WHY SHOULD YOU HAVE A COMPENSATION PLAN?

Many, if not most, small to medium-size enterprises ("SMEs") in Canada do not have a formal compensation program. Since you bought this book, you

---

[1] This is important; everyone claims they went to another job for more money but this is seldom true or accurate.

probably have felt the need for more structure than the "back-of-the-envelope approach" that you have been using so far. Here are the major reasons why you should have a formal compensation program:

- It will ensure that rewards are distributed fairly. Allocating rewards is a financial process much like purchasing raw materials or paying rent. However, it is different from these other processes in that the recipients, your employees, do not like it when they perceive that they are being treated unfairly. They have ways of making you suffer for your sins, such as: reducing the amount of effort they put into the job; quitting; organizing a union; or even stealing from you to make up for your poor reward system.
- A compensation program can support business or organizational goals. For example, you may be in the early stages of the corporate cycle and emphasizing growth in revenue beyond all other objectives. Your incentive plan(s) will therefore have growth in revenue as the criteria for establishing the bonus pool. You might determine that bonuses will only be paid if growth in revenue is at least 100% over the previous fiscal year.
- A program will ensure that your rewards package is competitive with similar organizations that employ similar occupational groups. This will enable you to persuade good employees to join your company.
- You will be able to control your costs. In the average Canadian company, payroll accounts for a major proportion of costs. In many knowledge-based industries such as information technology, management consulting and pharmaceutical research, the costs of people outweigh all other costs.
- It will enable your managers and human resources staff to make decisions about pay that are consistent with a corporate policy and with each other. Managers who have to continually fend off employee requests for raises or an explanation of the reward system will heave a sigh of relief when they are given some structure.
- A program will ensure that your company complies with the many pieces of legislation that are now impinging on the compensation field. Minimum wages have been around for a long time. Pay equity laws came into play in a major way in the late 1980s. There is an increasing number of legal cases regarding bonuses for executives who have been terminated. Executive compensation is being scrutinized more and more by securities commissions, pension investment advisors and major stock exchanges.
- Finally, a comprehensive and effective rewards program will give your organization a competitive advantage. It will enable you to attract the best employees, keep them longer and aggravate them less than your competitors. The quality of your human capital is the only true competitive advantage an organization can have these days. A formal compensation plan will provide a sound basis for keeping that capital.

WHO ARE YOUR EMPLOYEES?

At first, this may seem to be a silly question. An employee is anyone who is on your payroll. However, with the increasing use of alternative forms of employment, such as contract employees, telecommuters and job sharing, it is useful to look at some of the legal and other guidelines that govern which people who work for you are actually employees and which are not.

There are at least two ways of looking at whether a person is an employee or an "independent contractor". The first is according to income tax law or how the Canada Customs and Revenue Agency ("CCRA"), formerly Revenue Canada, views the situation. The second approach is to look at how the relationship is viewed by practitioners of labour relations or employment law. It is somewhat difficult to generalize about this since there are 11 sets of labour laws in Canada and much of the background material is actually found in case law and decisions by arbitrators and labour relations boards. However, I will give it a try.

A surprisingly large number of employers now hire "contract" employees. This means that the employee is hired for a fixed period of time such as one year or six months. Such employees are often not included in the benefits program. Their "term of employment" is considered to be fixed for the period established at the beginning and not renewable except at the wish of the company. Once the fixed term is over, there is usually no more obligation by either party to the other. More specifically, the employer considers the relationship ended and feels no obligation to provide severance pay or notice of dismissal.

The problem arises when the contract is renewed several times. Some so-called contract employees who are nominally employed for "one year" have had their contract renewed 15 times. In one such case,[2] the employer declined to renew the contract for the sixteenth year and the employee sued for severance pay. She was successful, although her employer tried to convince the court that she was not a permanent employee. Some of the factors that the court considered were:

- the person had been employed for many years;
- she had held a high-level job;
- she was given training and responsibilities that implied she would be with the employer for an indefinite period;
- signing of the contracts was often done after the "new" contract had started;
- the employee clearly considered herself to be employed for an indefinite period; and
- the conduct of the employer also indicated a long-term relationship.

---

[2]   *Ceccol v. Ontario Gymnasium Federation* (1999), 41 C.C.E.L. (2d) 312, 99 C.C.L.C. ¶210-014 (Ont. Ct. (Gen. Div.)), supplementary reasons 89 A.C.W.S. 938 (S.C.J.), affd 204 D.L.R. (4th) 688, 11 C.C.E.L. (3d) 167 (C.A.).

Another situation that can muddy the waters about the employment relationship occurs when a company hires staff as "contractors" who are supposedly self-employed. Such employees invoice the employer for their services and are paid by the accounts payable department. Unlike "contract" employees, they are not put on the payroll or paid through the payroll system. There are several advantages to both parties in doing this. The employer does not have to make Canada Pension Plan ("CPP"), Quebec Pension Plan ("QPP") or Employment Insurance ("EI") contributions for the employee. In Ontario, the payments to the employee are not part of the payroll so the Employer Health Tax does not apply. The employee can claim "business deductions" such as a home office, travel to the workplace, car lease and incorporation of the business. She also has all the advantages of being self-employed from an income tax point of view, such as deferment of bonus payments until 180 days after the year end of her business.

This practice is also extremely common. However, the CCRA takes a dim view of this practice if the "employee or contractor" works a full-time schedule for the employer organization. In most cases, the CCRA will maintain that the person is not an independent contractor but just an employee like all other regular employees, and therefore the company should be deducting and remitting, according to their relentless schedules, income tax, pension and employment insurance payments.

The CCRA applies a number of tests to determine whether a person who claims to be a contractor is in fact a full-time employee. They are:

- Does the person have other sources of revenue? In other words, is the employer her only client.
- Who supplies the equipment and materials used in the conduct of the alleged employment activities? Does the contractor work at the employer's place of business? Does she supply her own transportation and computer or other office equipment?
- Who decides when and where the work will take place? Can the employee choose what work to do on a project and when to do it or is she entirely subject to direction given by the employer?
- How is the person paid — at regular intervals (*e.g.*, every week) or when particular jobs or segments thereof are completed?
- What is the length of the relationship? Does it extend over many years or is the person only employed to do one assignment?
- Can the person realize a profit or a loss depending on how she conducts the work in question? An employee cannot do so.

You should be aware that, if the CCRA checks on the employee and finds that she is not an independent contractor, there are serious penalties for both parties. You, the employer, can be charged with:

- not deducting or withholding income tax;
- improper (*e.g.*, late) payment of CPP, income tax and EI;
- non-payment of income taxes; and
- non-completion of required documentation such as T4s.

There is a publication put out by the CCRA entitled "Employee or Self-Employed". It includes a list of questions to which you can answer yes or no. It is also possible to obtain a ruling on this question using a Form CPT-1 "Request for a Ruling as to the Status of a Worker under the Canada Pension Plan or Employment Insurance Act".[3]

Although there are apparent cost advantages to using contractors rather than employees, there are some disadvantages as well. Any contractor has to charge you the Goods and Services Tax ("GST") at 7%. This makes the price of avoiding the Ontario Health Tax of 1% quite onerous. In Chapter 10, "Implementing and Costing Your New Salary Program", we will take a more in-depth look at this question.

EMPLOYEE INVOLVEMENT

In designing any human resource system or program you basically have two choices. You can design the system yourself, at the management level. You may have a full-time human resources manager that you could bring into the process along with other members of your senior management group. You could just use a few trusted advisors from outside the organization such as your lawyer and your accountant. You could possibly hire an external consultant to help you with the design and then help you sell it to your employees.

The other way is to have your employees involved in the design from the start. This approach can be in addition to that described above or an alternative. In general terms, I would recommend using a combination approach but you can decide that after you read the rest of this section. The degree of employee involvement can vary widely, from total design to a quick look at the final draft of the program just before it is implemented.

In this section we will review:

- the rationale for involving employees;
- ways to involve them;
- when to involve them;
- methods of communication; and
- what not to do or what to avoid.

---

[3] This form is available on the CCRA website at www.ccra-adrc.gc.ca.

Rationale for Employee Involvement

I will summarize the rationale before giving you some of the voluminous evidence from the academic and professional literature that supports it.

You will have a better program with employee involvement than without it. Your employees will understand the program better. They will believe in it significantly more than if you don't involve them. In fact, if you don't solicit their participation it is more likely that you will not be believed at all about the merits, competitiveness, leading-edge characteristics or any other virtues that you claim for the program. Without involvement you will probably be accused of a variety of villainous acts that would put the robber barons of the 19th century to shame.

The evidence about the efficacy of employee involvement is divided into three categories: the literature; my personal experience; and legal requirements.

The Literature

In the early 1990s, management at Honeywell's Commercial Aviation Systems Division in Phoenix, Arizona, were concerned that their compensation system was not working to support a program to redefine and measure the behaviours and outcomes they wished from employees. On the one hand, division heads were pushing staff to focus on cost reduction and measurable productivity improvements. At the same time they were still granting pay increases based on time on a job. They progressed through their salary range on the basis of seniority.

In 1993, management formed the Participative Pay Team ("PPT") and called for volunteers. There was a large response and 25 employees were chosen,[4] including secretaries, machine shop workers, managers and engineers. The division employed 5,500 staff designing and manufacturing advanced avionics systems. There was only one person from human resources on the PPT and she acted as the team leader. The corporate human resources department in Minneapolis provided some initial training but otherwise left them to call when they felt the need.

Honeywell made a serious commitment in time (off the job) and money to bring the team members up to speed on the subject of compensation. They started with a two and one-half day training session on the basics and then assigned each team member responsibility to conduct specific research on their own. Over the next six months, each team member devoted about 20 hours[5] per month. Management made sure that their individual managers were clear about the necessity for this amount of commitment from their employee.

The PPT came up with a self-funded gainsharing plan introduced in 1994 which was phased in over four years. It has two components. First, a portion of

---

[4]   S. Caudron, "How Pay Launched Performance" (1996), 75:9 *Personnel Journal* 70.

[5]   *Ibid.*, at p. 73.

the available merit budget is allocated to fund a "risk-sharing amount". Employees start to receive payments if the division meets 80% or more of its financial objectives.

The second part of the plan is called a "success-sharing amount" and is paid out when the division exceeds its business goals. Employees can receive 5% of their base pay if the business goals are exceeded by 20% or more. The plan is also connected to the executive compensation program to ensure that rank and file employees and senior management are working towards the same, or comparable, objectives.

Communication, as usual, was vital to the success of the program and team members were an integral part of the communication program. Team members ran orientation sessions of two hours to give employees an overview of the new program and the measurements needed to generate a payment. The human resources department supported this effort by producing two booklets which were distributed during these sessions.

The company went further by also developing a business basics course which would enable employees to understand and utilize the high-level financial measurements (profit, working capital and economic value added) included in the new pay plan. This course was also conducted by members of the PPT.

Although it is difficult to separate the effect of employee participation from other quality improvement initiatives undertaken by Honeywell, the fact that the program was designed by employees for their fellow employees was a major factor in creating the buy-in necessary for a successful program. One team member said: "We had to have some reasonable justification for every decision we made because we had to face the people we work with every day."[6]

Personal Experience

My conviction about the merits of employee involvement began in the early 1970s. At the time I was working for S.C. Johnson & Son, better known as Johnson's Wax, at their Canadian head office and only manufacturing facility in Brantford, Ontario.

The company employed about 300 staff in Brantford and another 100 in the field sales offices and warehouses. It was not unionized and had been in Brantford for over 50 years. Even in the days before books such as *The 100 Best Companies to Work for in Canada*[7] it was considered to be an excellent employer.

The company policy was to pay at the nintieth percentile of the local labour market for clerical and hourly employees and at the third quartile of the packaged goods industry for management and professional staff. The superb

---

[6]   *Ibid.*, at p. 74

[7]   E. Innes, J. Lyon and J. Harris, *Financial Post 100 Best Companies to Work for in Canada* (Toronto: HarperCollins, 1991).

benefits package included both a cash and deferred profit-sharing plan and a pension plan. The company owned and operated a resort for employees and their families in Muskoka, a premier vacation spot in Ontario, and a hunting lodge in Northern Ontario. These were provided to staff at subsidized rates. The company was extremely proud of the fact that it had never laid off employees, even during the Great Depression. At the time, the fourth generation of the Johnson family was running the company. The corporate headquarters were in Racine, Wisconsin.

Johnson's Wax tried to keep on top of new developments in employee relations. In the early 1970s two phenomena developed regarding working time — the compressed work week and flexible hours. Until then the five-day, 40-hour work week had been the standard practice for generations. The compressed week changed five eight-hour days into four 10-hour days. Flexible hours simply meant that employees could, within limits, set their own starting and quitting times as long as they were on the job for certain "core" hours. This is now more commonly known as flextime.

Management became aware of these new and exciting options for structuring work schedules and appointed a five-member task force to investigate the possibilities. I was made chair of the group. The other members were representatives of management in manufacturing, finance, sales/marketing and quality control.

The task force took several months to complete its work. Among the many activities undertaken were:

- review of the literature of the time;
- development of a questionnaire to document the flow of information and/or material from department to department (these were completed by department heads);
- visits to other companies in the area; and
- research into relevant legislation, especially regarding hours of work.

The one thing we did not do, which is probably obvious to you given the subject of this section, was to ask the employees what they thought. We assumed, without any question at all, that we represented the management of an extremely enlightened, leading-edge company and the compressed work week was an exciting, progressive development. The employees will love this idea, and even more, will love us for bringing it to them. We were wrong!

We recommended to management that they conduct a nine-month test, for the whole company, which would cover most of the fluctuations in business we were likely to encounter.

The management committee accepted the length of the test but restricted the scope to the complete manufacturing and warehouse operations, the manufacturing offices, quality control and research. An essential part of our recommendations was that the employees be allowed to vote on starting the test with follow-up questionnaires to be administered each month thereafter. The

Vice-President of Manufacturing was to announce the start of the test at a mass meeting of the employees in the company cafeteria.

The reaction of the employees was the complete and total opposite of what we predicted or expected. They were outraged and extremely hostile. They accused the vice-president and management of every imaginable, and some not so imaginable, lousy motive for instituting this terrible idea. The poll taken showed just over 50% of the employees even willing to try the test. If only the hourly staff had been polled, we would not have received the 50% and the test would not even have started.

The task force members, including me, were stunned. We literally did not have the faintest idea what we had done wrong. Here was an exceptional employer, with a long history of outstanding employee relations, trying to institute a new program that had been well received by employees of other companies and we were being treated like we had the plague. It was totally incomprehensible and we did not know what to do.

However, since we had no alternative and the vote was just favourable for starting the test, we went ahead and did so. Then, it got worse. It seemed that nobody, except the members of the task force, thought the four-day work week was even close to a good idea.

As planned, we conducted an employee opinion survey after the test had been underway for one month. We asked the employees if they were in favour of converting to the four-day work week permanently after the test was completed. The question had five possible answers as follows:

Are you in favour of converting to the four-day week – please check one:

❏ Strongly in favour
❏ Somewhat in favour
❏ Neutral/no opinion
❏ Somewhat opposed
❏ Strongly opposed

Overall, about 60% of the employees said they were either strongly or somewhat in favour of converting. But when we released the results of the first survey, things got really frustrating for the members of the task force. First of all, the employees who were willing to talk said that they did not believe the results of the survey. They accused us of cooking the results. Then, adding insult to injury, they said that the use of the five possible answers was a trick on our part and that we should use only two possible answers — yes or no.

We had endless discussions at task force meetings about how to handle the situation. We were totally stumped about what to do. The only thing we could agree on was to continue the test since we were committed to it and there really hadn't been enough time to evaluate it from viewpoints other than the opinions of the employees, such as productivity and costs. We continued the test and also conducted the same survey for the next few months.

Basically, nothing changed. The complaints continued, although the votes in favour of converting full-time to the four-day week at the end of the test crept up a few percentage points. Our frustration at the task force meetings also stayed very high.

Personally, I was probably having more difficulty with the reaction of the employees than the other task force members. I was in the human resources department and knew, from a professional point of view, just how good an employer Johnson's Wax was (and still is — they are in a list of the 50 best companies to work for published in 2000 by Hewitt Associates, a major management consulting firm). I also knew, since I was in the executive team meetings that decided to investigate the feasibility and to conduct the test, that there was no devious scheme to cheat the employees and trick them into increasing productivity.

Finally, I came up with an idea. I cannot claim that this was a flash of brilliance. It was an act of desperation. I consulted with management and the task force and proposed that each of the five departments involved in the test be asked to elect a non-management employee who would become a full-fledged member of the task force.

Management accepted the idea and the elections were duly held. I was not at the meetings when the elections took place but I understand they were quite lively. It is reasonably accurate to say that the employees who were elected were generally suspicious and opposed to the idea of the compressed work week.

As soon as possible after the elections we held the first meeting of the new, enlarged task force. The new members had a million questions. We were totally honest and showed them all the files, including the completed survey questionnaires from previous monthly employee opinion surveys. One of their main concerns was the five-part answer just discussed. We spent a lot of time explaining that it was much more useful than a simple yes or no option. We requested that the employee representatives go back to their respective departments and hold a general meeting at which they would tell their fellow employees what they had learned. Shortly thereafter we had another monthly opinion survey.

The proportion of employees who were strongly or somewhat in favour of permanently converting to the compressed work week shot up to over 80%. It was absolutely astounding. The test continued and we had periodic meetings of the new, enlarged task force during which we continued to receive and deal with employee concerns. It was during this process that another astounding development occurred.

The elected, employee representatives started to sound and talk like management. When somebody raised a concern expressed by an employee that was somewhat frivolous or indicated suspicion of management's motives, the employee representatives would respond with comments like: "What's the matter with them?" or "Don't they realize what a good idea this is?" The transformation was truly amazing. If one could have recorded the meetings and then listened to them without knowing who the speakers were you would not be able to tell the management staff from the non-management employees.

We completed the test and took a final vote of all employees, including those who were not part of the test group, and over 90% voted in favour of switching to the four-day week on a permanent basis.

Somewhere in that process that I have just described I became a convert to the concept of employee involvement in the design and implementation of any human resource programs, including compensation plans. The lesson I learned was that even a company with an outstanding record of employee relations cannot introduce major change without consulting and involving the employees. Employee involvement made the difference in instituting the compressed work week at Johnson's Wax. There was no other intervening variable. If we hadn't involved the employees in the process, the compressed work week at Johnson's Wax would not have happened.

Legal Requirements

There are various situations in which you may be legally required to involve employees to some extent in the development of a compensation program.

Obviously, if any of your employees are unionized you are legally obligated to negotiate in good faith about the items that are included in either the recognition clause or the preamble of your collective agreement. The preamble is usually the first clause in the agreement. The recognition clause is usually the second. Here is an example of one of each taken from the agreement between Northern Telecom and the Canadian Auto Workers ("CAW"):[8]

> The general purpose of this agreement is to establish mutually satisfactory relations between the Company and the employees covered by this agreement, and to provide a more formal procedure for the prompt and equitable disposition of grievances, and to establish and maintain satisfactory working conditions, hours of work and salaries.

The union recognition clause identifies the type or location of employees included in the agreement and which the union can represent. Here is an example from an agreement between CAW, Local 124 and Titan Proform Company:[9]

> The Company recognizes the Union as the sole collective bargaining agency for all its employees employed in Metropolitan Toronto, save and except supervisors, persons above the rank of supervisor, office and sales staff, plant clerks and students employed during the school vacation period.
> Employee as used in this agreement shall mean those persons described in the bargaining unit set forth above.

---

[8]   J. Sack and E. Poskanzer, *Contract Clauses – Collective Agreement Language in Canada*, 3rd ed. (Toronto: Lancaster House, 1996), at p. 6-2. (Quotes reproduced with permission.)

[9]   *Ibid.*, at p. 7-4.

Between these two clauses, you will normally find the items, like wages, benefits and working conditions, which are subject to negotiation and the employees who are affected. However, it is important to recognize that an item not mentioned in the recognition clause, such as profit sharing, does not necessarily have to be negotiated. Companies have imposed profit sharing on a unionized workforce without negotiating the plan with the certified bargaining agent. This may not be a good labour relations practice but it is possible.

The Ontario *Pay Equity Act*[10] makes it mandatory that the employer negotiate pay equity with the bargaining agent for any unionized employees. Although the Act does not require the employer to negotiate pay equity with non-union employees, the Pay Equity Commission strongly recommends that employees be involved in the process. It is quite clear that the Commission considers job evaluation committees, with non-management employees as members, to be much more capable of comparing jobs in a gender neutral manner than committees comprised only of management staff.

The Quebec *Pay Equity Act*[11] is even stronger. All organizations with 100 or more employees must set up a Pay Equity Committee. Smaller employers have the option of doing so.

Under the Quebec Act the committee must consist of a minimum of three members. One-third of the members must be employer (management) representatives and two-thirds of the members must be employee representatives. Further, 50% of the employee representatives must be women.

The Quebec *Pay Equity Act* also gives the employee representatives significant clout. The representatives of the employer, and those of the employees, are treated as a group with each group having a single vote. If the employee group cannot decide, the employer group can make the decision required.

HOW TO INVOLVE EMPLOYEES

There are a variety of ways to get your employees involved in the process of designing a total compensation program or any component of it. You may have your basic salary administration system in place and want to install a productivity gainsharing plan. If you did not consult the rank and file for the basic program, do not feel that you cannot do so with the design of the gainsharing plan. It is never too late to introduce a high level of employee input. It might be a tougher sell at a later stage but it is still achievable.

There is one important caveat to my enthusiastic support of employee involvement. Involving employees does not mean abdicating your managerial discretion or authority. It might, but that is up to you. No matter what method

---

[10]   R.S.O. 1990, c. P.7.
[11]   R.S.Q., c. E-12.001.

you choose for obtaining input you can, and probably should, make it clear that you are the final decision-maker. Most organizations are not democracies and most employees will not want the responsibility of making the final tough decisions about who gets what. Remember, in the final analysis, compensation plan design is about allocating a finite resource, *i.e.*, money. It is a zero sum game and some tough decisions will have to be made. Very few staff will object when you make it clear that you reserve the right to make those decisions.

Here are some methodologies for getting employee input:

- hold focus groups;
- set up an employee committee;
- conduct a climate survey;
- use the union;
- use a consultant;
- interview individual employees.

Focus Groups

Focus groups are an extremely effective way to get opinions about compensation program design from a lot of employees. Basically, you gather a small group of employees (five to ten) who represent a cross-section of the company and ask them a series of questions about various aspects of compensation design. There are certain rules that you should announce to the employees before starting, which are:

- everything said stays in the room; and
- whoever is leading the group will not report individual opinions.

Focus groups are best used as a preliminary way to investigate the background to a possible new program. They are not as effective in actually designing a program since they are usually only brought together once. Their purpose is to answer a series of background questions about underlying attitudes and assumptions regarding compensation issues. They are not as useful at working on the design of a program.

Employee Committee

In my opinion, the most powerful method to get employees involved in the design process is to set up an employee committee or team. Some employers that I have worked with call these Cross-Functional Teams. In Chapter 4, "Obtaining Information About Jobs", the use of an employee committee for the purpose of selecting a job evaluation plan and actually conducting the process of job evaluation is discussed. That is an example of a limited use of an employee committee. However, at this stage, you need to consider broader possibilities than just job evaluation.

How do you go about setting up a committee? In Chapter 2, "Strategy", the issue of whether to divide your total employee population into two or more employee groups which will be treated separately in the new compensation plan is discussed. For example, you may have decided that, since you have about 120 employees, there will be one compensation plan for the whole company except for the top three jobs at the Canadian head office. An alternative would be to have a compensation plan for the unionized plant workers.

Having made that decision the following issues are involved in setting up a committee:

- size of the committee;
- whether the members are elected or appointed;
- characteristics of the members; and
- functions of the committee.

Five to seven members is a good size for a committee. Certainly, no more than 10. You have to balance the number of members against the other criteria, which can be conflicting. I highly recommend that you appoint the members of the committee. You will see from the list of characteristics which follows that it is necessary to be quite discriminating in the choice of committee members. If you have elections, you lose control of this process. This may sound contradictory. Here I am advocating large-scale employee involvement but opposing what may be the ultimate level of involvement, the right of employees to choose the people who will represent them. My experience tells me that this is not a problem. I have set up many employee committees, or they were already set up before I was called in as a consultant, but have never encountered opposition to the idea of the committee members being appointed by management. In fact, the idea that the committee members should be elected has never been suggested to me by any member of any committee that I have worked with.

A compromise between these two points of view was developed by a company in southern Ontario that manufactured metal hinges. The owner and president wanted to establish a profit-sharing plan and was enthusiastic about using a committee. He asked for employees to volunteer to be on the committee and then chose the members from the volunteers. This worked quite well.

When you are considering people for membership look for the following characteristics:

- representative of all sections, levels, departments and divisions of the company;
- a cross-section of the demographic profile of the organization in terms of age, seniority, gender, education, ethnicity, etc.;
- considered to be "opinion leaders" by their respective constituencies, they should be sufficiently well respected that their peers will feel comfortable being represented by them;

- willing to act as spokesperson for their group;
- reasonably articulate, they must be able to express the concerns of the employee group that they are representing;
- objective, in that they can separate the needs of the organization from those of the employees, especially themselves;
- capable of understanding the concepts involved; and
- ethical and responsible to the point where the information made available to them during the committee's work will not be used for personal gain or to the disadvantage of the employer.

There are a number of possibilities for the responsibilities of such a committee, such as:

- identify problems with current system;
- write the terms of reference for a consultant (see later section on using consultants);
- assist in the selection of a consultant or consulting firm — this could involve activities such as assessing proposals, interviewing consultants or doing reference checks;
- set overall corporate compensation strategy;
- select the components of the compensation mix;
- select the type of salary administration system;
- select the characteristics of the salary range system chosen such as width of ranges, number of steps, etc.;
- determine the type of incentive plan — profit sharing, gainsharing, other;
- determine the type of performance appraisal system;
- select characteristics of the performance appraisal system;
- make decisions about salary or bonuses for specific individuals;
- determine size of incentive plans relative to total cash compensation;
- select custom-designed or published salary surveys;
- determine which published surveys will be used;
- determine companies, jobs and/or industries to include in any custom survey;
- determine benefits surveys;
- interpret benefits surveys.

As you can see, there are a large number of possible responsibilities which can be assigned to any committee. However, there are some decisions that management should reserve for themselves. It is perhaps easier to describe the type of decision that should not be given to an employee committee. In general, the type of decision that most people would describe as policy should be reserved for owner/managers. It is always difficult to draw a precise line between policy and practice but here are some examples of what I consider to be policy issues:

- the level set for your compensation package vis-à-vis the labour market, *i.e.*, average, third quartile, etc.;
- with a profit-sharing plan, the percentage of profits to be contributed by the corporation to the profit-sharing fund;
- whether an incentive plan will be cash or deferred;
- the mix of elements in the compensation package such as all salary, base salary plus profit sharing or base salary plus gainsharing plus an employee share ownership plan ("ESOP").

The important thing to remember about this process is that, once you have given a committee an issue to deal with, you have to deal with their recommendations. Notice that I did not say that you have to accept them; just deal with them. That means explaining, and selling, your rejection of their recommendations. If possible, before you assign particular decisions to any employee group, identify their possible recommendations or the options they are likely to come up with. Then, if there is a possibility that you would not accept under any circumstances, do not give them that choice.

For example, you may have decided that you want your compensation package to include a base salary plus an incentive plan which, theoretically, could be profit sharing, productivity gainsharing or an ESOP. However, you absolutely will not consider an ESOP. Therefore, tell the committee that their choices are between profit sharing and a gainsharing plan.

Opinion Surveys

You can obtain a great deal of information about what employees think by conducting an employee opinion survey. There are a large number of consulting firms that will do customized surveys for you or you can purchase software to do one yourself. The advantages of opinion surveys include:

- most, if not all, employees will be asked their opinions;
- results are very quantified; and
- results can be easily analyzed and combined in a variety of ways.

The disadvantages include:

- costs can be high, especially using consultants;
- it can be time-consuming; and
- surveys can only capture opinions of employees about subjects they are familiar with — they cannot deal with hypothetical issues such as the design of an incentive plan.

Use the Union

If any of your employees are unionized, you may be able to legally consult with the employees without going through the union (see the earlier legal requirements section in this chapter) but I do not recommend it. One of the reasons you have a union is that the employees, at some time, felt that they needed someone to represent them. Even though they may not all still feel this way, they are used to being represented and probably expect it. I believe that you bypass the union at your peril.

Use a Consultant

Although I have written this book to enable you to set up your compensation program without the use of a consultant, here is one limited area in which an outside consultant can be useful. In general, there are three reasons for hiring a consultant.

The first is that they know how to do something you need done and you don't know how to do it. If this book does the job I intended it for this should not apply. The second reason is that you just don't have the time to do what needs to be done. The third is that you need an outsider with no vested interest to carry out the task. For example, most executive compensation work is done by consultants because boards of directors will not believe that an internal compensation manager has the necessary independence of action regarding the compensation package for the Chief Executive Officer ("CEO"). This third reason may justify the use of a consultant for this limited role.

THEORIES OF MOTIVATION

When discussing compensation, I have found that people love to expound theories about who is motivated by what rewards under what circumstances. Virtually all of these theories are merely extrapolations of personal experience, born of prejudices and half-baked theories. You probably have your own theories which, unfortunately, are unlikely to be based on sound psychological theory.

There are two generally accepted theories of motivation that I have found to be useful in designing compensation programs: (i) the expectancy theory; and (ii) the equity theory. You cannot build whole programs just on these two theories (you also need a lot of technical expertise and common sense) but I have found them to be extremely useful. I keep them in the back of my mind and use them as a sort of reality check when I am setting up a new program. Here is a brief description of each.

Expectancy Theory

Expectancy theory contains three major propositions or "expectancies" that must exist before an individual can be motivated to perform specific activities or undertake certain behaviour. The first is that the individual must value the reward that is being offered. Most compensation programs offered by employers in Canada use money, in one form or another, as the primary reward that is offered. The "pay" in "pay-for-performance" programs is virtually always money. There is nothing wrong with this. More money has very wide appeal, partly because it can be used for so many other purposes. People are not necessarily motivated by the money itself; more by what they can do with it — take a vacation, send their daughter to university or build that special home in the country that they have always dreamed about. On the other hand, many people are not motivated by money. Members of religious orders eschew the worldly goods that could be bought with money. The first astronauts were motivated by many things, such as scientific curiosity, patriotism or even danger and adventure.

The second part of the expectancy theory is that the individual or group must believe that he or she is capable of performing the tasks required. You can offer the sales representative a bonus of $10,000 for doubling the sales volume in his territory but, if he believes, validly or not, that it cannot be done, he will not be motivated to try. His behaviour will not change. It will not change even if he desperately needs the $10,000.

Thirdly, the expectancy theory holds that the reward offered will actually be delivered. When you offer merit raises for good or outstanding performance you have fulfilled the first two parts of expectancy theory. However, most merit programs are shrouded in secrecy. Employees do not see performance ratings of other employees; nor are they told the size of increase that the good employees received. Therefore, they have no proof that they will actually receive an increase in their salary if they perform well. All they have is your assertion. Unfortunately, this is usually not sufficient.

Equity Theory

The equity theory is somewhat simpler than the expectancy theory. It holds that each employee assesses the total of what he brings to the employment relationship (education, experience, training, skills, personality, effort, motivation, values and so on). He also sums up what he receives from the relationship (salary, bonus, benefits, career opportunities, skill development, training and such) and compares the two quantities.

If they are not roughly equal the employee will seek to re-establish balance. It is the balance that is important. There are two approaches the employee can take. He can sever the relationship and try to establish a new, more balanced one with another employer. Although you can lose a good employee this way, this situation can be the easier one to deal with.

The other way the employee will seek balance is by lowering his side of the equation. This is usually done by reducing his effort and/or motivation. This can be very difficult to observe and that is why it is the more problematic of the possible actions by the employee.

I use both expectancy theory and equity theory as the theoretical foundation for virtually every recommendation in this book. I will not always point this out as it could become quite repetitive. However, you should be aware that these are the two theories of behaviour that I have found most useful and that I use them continuously. I strongly recommend that, anytime you develop an approach to compensation that is not explicitly covered in this book, you test it using these two theories.

EMPLOYMENT LAW IN CANADA

Canadian labour law is divided between the 10 provinces and the federal government. Under the *Constitution Act, 1982,*[12] certain industries are governed by federal legislation and this includes all aspects of labour and employment law. The industries include banking, railroads, telecommunication and interprovincial transportation. All other industries are governed by provincial legislation.

This means that a software development company with headquarters in Ottawa and branches in Montreal and Vancouver is subject to three sets of labour legislation — respectively, Ontario, Quebec and British Columbia. On the other hand, the Canadian Imperial Bank of Commerce is governed by one set of laws — those of the federal government, even though it has employees in all provinces and territories.

Companies that operate in one or more of the three Canadian territories are subject to federal labour law unless the respective territorial legislature has enacted other legislation.

Here is a list of the compensation items that are usually covered by labour law:

- minimum wages;
- overtime pay;
- call-in pay;
- vacation;
- public holidays;
- severance pay;
- pay equity;
- health taxes;
- workers' compensation;
- employment insurance; and
- other payroll taxes.

It is important to recognize several features of this situation. First, the legislation specifies only minimum standards. The average or median in virtually all subjects, in all industries, exceeds the legislated minimum. They

---

[12] Being Schedule B of the *Canada Act 1982* (U.K.), 1982, c. 11.

can also be exceeded by collective agreement with a union or through an individual employment contract.

Secondly, there are 14 sets of rules that employers may need to follow — for the 10 provinces, the federal government and three territories.

Thirdly, there is not enough space in this book to provide detail regarding the provisions of employment standards Acts in the various jurisdictions. There are several excellent reference books, in a looseleaf format with several updates per year, that you can use for this purpose.[13]

Fourthly, this type of legislation and its attendant regulations are continually changing. You should be continually monitoring the situation either through subscribing to or purchasing one of the reference books just mentioned or attending seminars or conferences. These are provided by a wide variety of private conference organizations, boards of trades/chambers of commerce, professional associations (see Appendix A, "Human Resources and Related Professional Associations") and industry groups such as the Conference Board of Canada.

Finally, it is important to recognize that there are always exceptions to the so-called minimum standards. Professionals in law, dentistry, medicine and accounting are not covered by minimum standards regarding overtime, minimum wages, public holidays and vacations. Employees in construction are also frequently exempted from these rules.

CHECKLIST

Here is a checklist you can use to assess your current compensation program and determine the extent of your development needs.[14] You may find it useful to have other executives in your organization complete it as well. Comparing notes on your answers can generate a very useful discussion.

To use this checklist, review the question and in the second column put yes or no. The third column contains a "good" answer. By this I mean that, if your answer matches, there is probably not a problem. However, if your answer is different put a checkmark in the last column.

Obviously, not all of these questions indicate problems of the same magnitude. However, any checkmark does indicate a possible area of concern and should be investigated. As a very rough rule of thumb, if you have more than 10 checkmarks, read this book very quickly and get to work.

---

[13] See, for example, Carswell's *Compensation Guide* (Toronto: Carswell, 1996), and *Canadian Labour Law Reporter* (Toronto: CCH Canadian Ltd.).
[14] This checklist is available on the accompanying CD-ROM.

ASSESSMENT CHECKLIST

Item	Yes/ No	Good Answer	✓
1. Do you have a formal method of establishing a salary grade or level for a job?		Yes	
2. Are there written descriptions for most jobs?		Yes	
3. Are there salary ranges established for each job?		Yes	
4. Have you compared your salary levels with those in other companies (using a formal salary survey) within the last year?		Yes	
5. Have you compared your benefit package with those offered by other companies within the last year?		Yes	
6. Have you prepared and posted a Pay Equity Plan for employees who are regulated by federal, Quebec or Ontario law?		Yes	
7. Do you have a formal system for evaluating the performance of employees?		Yes	
8. Is there a central control for all salary actions (hire, promotion, merit increase, cost of living increase) in the organization?		Yes	
9. Do you have any written material that is given to employees describing the compensation program?		Yes	
10. Have there been any recent attempts to have a union certified at your organization?		No	
11. Have you had problems hiring new staff at salaries below that of current employees in similar jobs?		No	
12. Have you had many complaints from employees about salaries relative to those in other companies?		No	
13. Was the last payout from your bonus/incentive plan well received?		Yes	
14. Have you had any employment standards complaints regarding such items as overtime or vacation pay?		No	
15. Have any employees been getting paid excessive amounts of overtime?		No	

Item	Yes/ No	Good Answer	✓
16. Have significant numbers of employees complained about their pay levels relative to other employees in similar jobs?		No	
17. Have you adjusted your salary or wage scales in the last year to reflect changes in the labour market?		Yes	
18. Do you find that managers and supervisors are very reluctant to conduct performance appraisals?		No	
19. When an employee has received a negative performance appraisal, does his or her performance usually improve?		Yes	
20. Does the average employee understand why they received their last increase in base pay?		Yes	
21. If you have conducted a recent employee opinion survey, does it indicate dissatisfaction with pay levels?		No	
22. Do employees recognize why they received their last bonus?		Yes	

CONCLUSION

This chapter has explained why you need a formal compensation program, provided two general theories on motivation, and explained the legal jurisdictions for employment laws in Canada. I have also provided you with a rationale for, and guidelines on using, employee involvement in the process. Finally, you have a checklist that you can use to assess your current situation.

2

Strategy

INTRODUCTION

This chapter will take you through the process of developing an overall policy for your compensation program. You will set your policies regarding:

- the components of your rewards package;
- job or person-based pay;
- internal equity versus external competitiveness;
- different packages for different groups of employees;
- the definition of your labour market (employers, industries and/or geographical region);
- your policy line;
- the type and amount of benefits to be included; and
- the organization of the compensation function.

There is also a worksheet at the end of the chapter which you can use to organize your strategic decisions.

COMPONENTS OF THE PACKAGE

Every employer that ever existed, or will exist in the future, had a "package" of rewards that was used in various ways to attract, retain and motivate employees. The usual components of the package are:

- base salary or wages;
- short-term incentives (usually a time frame of one year or less), with the payout in cash;

- long-term incentives, such as multi-year bonus plans or stock plans;
- benefits such as dental insurance, pensions and income protection;
- premiums for non-standard hours worked, such as weekends, night shifts and standby; and
- other "rewards" that comprise the "work experience", such as training opportunities, promotions, the culture of the organization or compressed work weeks.

PAY THE JOB OR PAY THE PERSON

This issue is brilliantly summarized by the old saying (with apologies to taxi drivers): "You pay the taxi driver for driving the taxi, not for having the Ph.D."

In all the time I have been in the human resources field, the absolutely fundamental principle of compensation management has been that you start with paying employees for doing a specific job. There were many exceptions to this rule, such as when a person was demoted and his salary was "red-circled". New graduates from colleges and universities were hired at the going rate for their particular discipline but were usually soon placed in a specific job, other than trainee, for which a salary range had been established.

Nevertheless, the principle remained — a person is paid for the job that they are performing. This is often called job-based pay. In recent years, however, a new concept has developed. It is called person-based pay. Other terms used are skill-based pay, pay-for-knowledge, and competency-based pay.

Using this approach, employees are paid according to the skills, competencies and abilities that they bring to the workplace. One's first reaction to this idea is that you will pay staff more than you would under a job-based system since they might have, or acquire, skills that are above those needed for the job. Lawler maintains that it "does not necessarily produce pay rates that are dramatically different from those produced by paying for the nature of the job".[1] He reasons that the skills people possess are normally closely aligned with the job they are performing. However, he also recognizes that two scenarios are possible — employees can be paid more than they would be under a job-based system, or they could be paid less if they don't have the necessary skills. I do not accept this second scenario, since such employees are unlikely to be placed in the job if they do not have the necessary qualifications.

Skill-based pay systems are often used in new plant start-ups, so called "green field" operations. It is considered to be especially applicable in organizations that are seeking to establish a high-involvement, team-oriented style of management. Proponents of skill-based pay maintain that it provides

---

[1]   E.E. Lawler, *Rewarding Excellence: Pay Strategies for the New Economy* (San Francisco: Jossey-Bass, 2000), at p. 41.

for more employees who can perform multiple tasks. This makes the workforce more flexible, fewer staff are required, and absenteeism and turnover are lower.

There are a number of problems with skill-based pay. A major one is that, in my opinion, it does not comply with pay equity legislation anywhere in Canada. Since the two largest provinces, Ontario and Quebec, have pay equity laws that apply to the private sector, this is a major concern. In the other provinces, with the possible exception of Alberta, it is likely that such legislation will eventually be passed. Other problems include determining the market value of a particular skill and assessing the skills actually possessed by individuals. For these reasons, I do not recommend the use of person-based pay.

INTERNAL EQUITY OR EXTERNAL COMPETITIVENESS

Internal equity exists when two different jobs are considered to be of equal value and have the same compensation package. The incumbents do not necessarily have to be paid exactly the same salary or receive the same bonus as long as both have the same opportunity. The relative value of jobs is established by the use of a "job evaluation" system or plan. This is discussed in detail in Chapter 3, "Selecting a Job Evaluation Plan". However, the main point here is that if you want internal equity, you have to use some sort of job evaluation plan.

An employer is considered to be externally competitive when jobs in the organization are paid comparably to the same jobs at other employers. If you want, or believe that it is absolutely necessary, to be competitive with other companies, you must seriously consider using "market pricing" instead of job evaluation to set up your pay scales. Market pricing is reviewed in Chapter 3.

These two concepts are often in conflict. For example, the job evaluation system may determine that job A and job B are of equal value and therefore should be in the same salary range. However, your market surveys clearly indicate that job B should be paid $10,000 more, per year, than job A. This means that you have three major options if you want to be both internally equitable and externally competitive:

- pay job B at market and overpay job A;
- pay job A at market and underpay job B;
- split the difference and underpay job B by $5,000 and overpay job A by $5,000.

Internal equity is usually more important in large, mature organizations than it is in new, start-up operations which are rapidly growing and need to recruit large numbers of employees from other organizations.

EMPLOYEE GROUPS

Organizations often tailor the compensation package to a particular category of employees. For example, Company X is an importer of costume jewellery with one facility encompassing all 40 Canadian employees in Toronto. It has one package for its four executives and another one for everyone else. Company Y, with 1,000 employees, and a manufacturing facility in Calgary, a head office in Montreal and a distribution centre in Toronto, has four packages: executives; middle management at all three locations; first line supervisors; and non-management at both Calgary and Toronto. Here is a comparison of some of the components of the rewards packages for Companies X and Y:

Component	Company X Executive	Company X Non-Executive	Company Y Executive	Company Y Non-Management Calgary
Base salary	Compared with small importers across Canada	Compared with local employers in North Toronto	Compared with executives of Canadian companies of comparable size	Compared with all large employers in Calgary and area
Pension	Defined benefit – company pays 50%	Group RRSP – no employer contribution	Defined benefit – company pays 100%	Defined contribution – company pays 50%
Stock plans	None – private company	None	Options up to 3 times salary	Stock purchase plan – payroll deduction

A word of warning here. A little more than 15 years ago it was common practice to have separate plans by occupational groups such as "clerical" or "factory/hourly" or "secretarial" or "nurses" or "engineers". This practice was based on the belief that the "market" treated these groups differently and therefore employers had to tailor their pay programs accordingly. To do otherwise would be to have a mixed bag of rewards which may or may not appeal to the targeted group.

This approach worked for many years. In fact, it was quite effective. However, the problem was that the so-called occupational groups tended to be dominated by one gender or another. Secretarial/clerical jobs were almost exclusively female. Factory jobs and engineers were generally mostly male. The result was that females were paid less than males. In Canada, the gap was estimated to be about 30%, and 10% of that was due to this type of systemic discrimination. The answer to this problem is pay equity legislation, which is covered in Chapter 17, "Pay Equity".

The point is that you have to be careful how you separate employee groups for the purpose of designing a pay package. Here are some guidelines that will assist you in determining whether to have one or more compensation plans in your organization:

- If you have a unionized group or groups of employees you will obviously need a plan for them — that will be called the collective agreement.
- You have to differentiate between different compensation plans and the dollar amounts in different plans. For example, suppose you have two call centres, one in Toronto, Ontario, and one in Vancouver, British Columbia. Both have essentially the same mix of occupational groups and organizational structure. The only real difference is that the Toronto operation is significantly larger and in a location with generally higher wages and a higher cost of living. The types of jobs are almost exactly the same and it is possible, subject to employee expectations, to use a step-rate type of salary administration program. That is what I mean when I say you can have the same overall compensation plan. However, the difference would occur in the actual dollar amounts paid to the same job in the two different locations. According to one reliable survey, the job of secretary had a median market value of $31,600 per year in Vancouver and $35,300 per year in Toronto.
- Look at the strategic business units or profit centres in your organization. Each such unit will normally have a compensation strategy tailored to its special characteristics.
- Look at the relevant legislation. Private sector employers under provincial jurisdiction (for employment law) in Ontario and Quebec have to comply with pay equity legislation. Those in Alberta do not.
- Cost is also a factor. Setting up a job evaluation plan, especially with the use of external consultants, can be time consuming and expensive. It is possible to use one job evaluation plan in all parts of Canada and still have a variety of compensation plans that are based on that one job evaluation plan.

WHO SHOULD YOU COMPARE WITH?

This issue revolves around what organizations you compete with for employees. In other words, what is your labour market? These are the major ways you can look at this issue:

- occupational group;
- geography;
- industry;
- size of company.

Occupational Group

In spite of the warning issued earlier in this chapter, using the occupational group as a basis of comparison is still quite valid and is usually the starting point for any market survey. This simply means that you compare your engineering pay rates with those of other employers of engineers. You will compare your pay levels for maintenance mechanics or occupational health nurses with those of organizations that employ such staff.

Geography

It is quite common to look at pay rates on a geographical basis. The usual rule of thumb is that the lower the level of the job to be surveyed in the organization, the more local is the labour market. Conversely, the higher the level of the job, the wider the market gets.

Clerical and factory jobs are generally considered to have local markets. For example, if you have an office in Cambridge, Ontario, that employs a significant number of clerical staff, you would consider only rates paid in Cambridge to be of interest in establishing your pay package for clerical staff. On the other hand, you may also have a number of executives at your Cambridge office. Generally speaking, you would consider the market to be national for executives. This table illustrates the general relationship between geography and occupational group.

Occupational Group	Labour Market
Executive	National
Middle Management	Regional/National
Supervisory/Sales/Professional	Regional/Provincial
Clerical/Hourly	Local/Municipal

This table is a very general guideline. There are many exceptions to this rule. Here are two examples from the mining industry. The Nanisivik Mine is located at the north end of Baffin Island. Before the mine was established there was virtually no settlement. This means that there is no local labour market with which to make comparisons. The management of the company would have to set clerical pay rates based on some other criteria. There are also no local rates for the skilled miners who work underground at such an operation.

At first glance miners (who are usually paid hourly) would seem to be an obvious choice for comparisons with the local market. However, they are quite a mobile occupation. Since most mines run out eventually, a large proportion of the mining community expects to relocate several times in their career. I don't mean every year, but it is not uncommon for a skilled underground miner to make a major move every five to ten years or so. This means that the employer, in the case of the Nanisivik mine, has to look at rates for miners throughout Canada.

In the case of clerical rates for this location, since most of the workers will be females married to the male mine workers, the company will probably have to consider pay rates for clerks in the mining industry throughout Canada.

Industry

It is often necessary to compare your compensation levels with those in your specific industry. Trucking companies compare their wages with those of other trucking companies and community colleges check what other community colleges are paying their instructors. Since labour is one of the largest costs of most industries in Canada, it is obviously important that you keep your costs similar to those of your competitors. However, you also have to recognize that many of the occupational groups that you employ, such as accountants or maintenance mechanics, are employed by many other industries as well as your own.

Size of Company

It is generally accepted that, for most jobs, even those at the lowest level of the hierarchy, larger companies pay more than smaller ones. Most salary and wage surveys will report data sorted by company size. Size is usually measured by revenue (sales), number of employees or assets. In not-for-profit organizations, such as school boards, annual budget is commonly utilized.

Using the size of the company as a point of comparison is quite valid, especially at the executive level. It intuitively makes sense that the president of a company with $10 million in sales will earn less than the president of a company that is selling $1 billion worth of products per year. The same holds for other executive positions at the vice-president and director level.

However, I question this separation for clerical or hourly paid jobs. There is no question that there is a clear difference in pay between large and small organizations. Suppose you have a small company (95 employees) in a medium-sized city in Western Canada. To keep it simple, let's assume there are two other companies in town: Company A has 1,000 employees and pays its general labour $15 per hour; Company B has 100 employees and pays general labour $10 per hour. If you decide to compare yourself with just Company B, because it is similar in size, you will have to set your general labour rate at $10. The impact of this is that you will have no chance of attracting new people to your company from Company A. In fact, to attract those from Company B you will have to emphasize parts of your reward package beyond base pay, since Company B employees will only break even in terms of base pay by coming to work for you. I have gone through these comparisons many times and have come to the conclusion that, in circumstances like this, you have to ignore size of company and, instead, concentrate on the whole labour market in which your future, potential employees are to be found.

SETTING YOUR POLICY LINE

This process of "setting the policy line" really means the level (average, third quartile, etc.) in the labour market, identified in the previous section, at which you will set your target compensation. Policy line generally refers to only cash, short-term and long-term incentives. The term does not normally include benefits, working conditions or work/life conditions.

Let's take one component of the package at a time. Suppose that you only offer a salary to prospective employees. There is no bonus plan, short or long-term, and no stock plan of any sort. Employees receive a base salary (with annual adjustments for labour market conditions) and a basic benefits package. You have identified the market in which you have to compete as those companies in automotive parts manufacturing in the Greater Toronto Area.

Any survey that you may purchase, or conduct yourself, for this purpose will report various statistics for each job in the survey. I have never seen a survey that did not include averages. Most include medians and some also report first and third quartiles. The largest and most sophisticated often offer deciles as well. Setting your policy line simply means deciding which of these statistics you will use to set the "job rates" when you develop a salary structure. The process of setting job rates and a salary structure is described in much more detail in Chapter 6, "Salary Surveys", and Chapter 7, "Putting it All Together — Basic Salary Administration".

If you also decide to have a cash bonus (or profit-sharing or gainsharing) plan in addition to base salary, the setting of a policy line becomes somewhat more complicated. The issue then becomes at what levels you set base salary and total cash compensation.

You have four points of comparison here. The statistic you have decided to use as your point of comparison is the average for both base salary and total cash compensation. You also have to set your levels of base salary and total cash relative to those two lines. Here is a table that shows some of the possible combinations:

Item	Point in Survey	Point in Survey	Point in Survey
Base	Average	80% of Average	Third Quartile
Other Cash	Average	Third Quartile	Average
Total Cash	Average	Above Average	Above Average

BENEFITS STRATEGY

In the compensation literature and professional journals you will often read articles about "strategic benefits" or how your benefits strategy must be designed to support your business strategy. Generally speaking, these opinion pieces are nonsense.

The purpose of any component of the rewards package is to "attract, retain and motivate" the best qualified staff available. Benefits may play a role in attracting and retaining but they will have very little effect on motivation. Nobody will be motivated by the fact that your group life insurance pays somebody else two times the employee's annual salary if they die! Benefit packages provide a foundation that gives an employee protection in the event of illness or accident, and for retirement.

The only real decision you have to make about benefits is whether to provide an "average", "cadillac" or "basic" package. Another option, of course, is to provide no benefits at all. I have put the terms average, cadillac and basic in quotation marks because these statistical terms are not as useful in defining your policy line or assessing the labour market as they are in assessing levels of salaries or cash bonuses. This will be covered later in Chapter 8, "Benefits Basics".

There are four issues that have to be addressed in the development of your benefits strategy:

- competition in the labour market;
- total cost;
- your obligation to provide for or protect your employees;
- the demographics of your current and potential employee population.

Competition in the Labour Market

The issues in looking at the labour market regarding benefits are essentially the same as for cash compensation (salaries, wages and bonus plans). These include the industry, geography, size of company and occupational group. You also have to look at the benefits equivalent of the salary "policy line".

Obligation to Protect or Help Your Employees

This issue is unique to the benefits component of your compensation package. It is simply not part of the deliberations about salary or wage policy. It does not occur for all benefits either. The common benefits for which this issue arises are:

- life insurance;
- dental insurance;
- registered pension plans (not CPP or QPP) and other retirement plans.

Let's use life insurance to illustrate the issue. If you provide group life insurance and an employee dies, his or her family will have financial resources to, at least partially, see them through the crisis. If you do not and the employee does not purchase insurance on his own, his family will suffer. Unfortunately, most people do not purchase their own life insurance. The obligation question for you therefore comes down to whether or not you will recognize this common failing and do something about it.

ORGANIZATION OF THE COMPENSATION FUNCTION

Another part of your overall compensation or rewards strategy is the question of who will be responsible for the compensation function. Who is going to do all this work? This is essentially a function of the size of your organization. Size, in this case, is measured by the number of employees you have, the number of divisions and geographical locations of the organization and the complexity of your compensation program.

Number of Human Resources Staff

It is very difficult to generalize about the size of the human resources function since it can vary according to these factors:

- number of employees;
- number of locations;
- turnover;
- whether any employee groups are unionized;
- nature and size of the pool of potential employees;
- location of operations, *i.e.*, big city, small town, remote; and
- expectations of management regarding the human resources function.

However, a very rough rule of thumb that many human resource professionals use is that there should be about one person (professional or support) in the human resources department for each 100 employees.

You cannot take this rule too literally. Many companies with fewer than 100 employees have full-time human resource professionals on board. In my consulting practice I have worked with a company employing fewer than 50 people which has a full-time human resources administrator whose particular job involves payroll and some other administrative functions that are not considered human resources. In the absence of a "human resources department" the functions are usually assigned to the senior finance official or the most senior operations manager.

The point here is that whatever program you set up will require that somebody in your organization be given the specific responsibility for maintaining it.

General Duties of the Compensation Function

Here is a list of the major duties, relating to compensation, that have to be done by somebody. Of course, the ones that are actually assigned in your organization will depend on the programs that you decide to implement. The following have been grouped according to the major components of any compensation or rewards program.

* Base salaries:
  * job evaluation;
  * salary surveys;
  * review and approval of salary increases;
  * salary range adjustments;
  * all non-standard salary changes, such as promotions or demotions;
  * maintenance of pay equity.
* Incentive plans (profit sharing, gainsharing, teams, employee share ownership plans):
  * design of plan(s);
  * monitor effectiveness of plan(s);
  * calculate and authorize payments;
  * resolve exceptions to regulations, *e.g.*, membership.
* Benefits and working conditions:
  * participate in, and monitor, surveys;
  * recommend changes to plans;
  * negotiate with insurance carriers;
  * administer claims processing;
  * resolve exceptions.
* Communications:
  * write and maintain employee handbook for all programs;
  * issue regular communications regarding current status or changes to all programs;
  * deal with individuals (management or staff) with questions about any aspect of their compensation package;
  * conduct and analyze surveys of employee opinions;
  * maintain any intranet and/or internet communications vehicles;
  * supply and control compensation data for recruitment advertising.

Structuring the Human Resources Department

If there is only one person in the human resources department, job design is quite easy. All the compensation functions in the preceding list that you have chosen to implement will have to be done by that one person. However, when you get to more than one professional employee, there are two major approaches you can take: a functional organization; or a customer-based focus.

Suppose you have a department of two human resource professionals. One is titled Human Resources Manager and the other is the Human Resources Administrator. In both cases the manager will generally retain responsibility for policy development and monitoring.

A functional organization would have the administrator do all the compensation functions for all employee groups, while the manager would carry out all other human resources functions, such as recruiting, human resource information system, payroll, employee relations, labour relations (if there is a union), and health and safety.

The customer-based type of organization would split compensation responsibilities by employee group(s). For example, one large financial services organization split the compensation functions so that the Director of Human Resources performed those functions related to the managerial groups while the Human Resources Administrator performed all compensation functions related to non-management staff. In fact, each of them did all human resources functions with respect to those two categories of employee with the exception of training. Since the company did a large amount of in-house training there was also a training section, the head of which reported to the Director.

WORKSHEET FOR STRATEGIC COMPENSATION PLANNING

I have developed a worksheet which can be used for developing your compensation strategy. The following is a summary of the steps to be followed:

- Define the employee group, *e.g.*, all management, unionized staff in Red Deer, Alberta, clerical staff in Kingston, Ontario.
- Specify the geographical area for employees — this could result in subdividing the employee group. For example, non-management, non-union employees could be grouped by province.
- Decide between person-based pay or job-based pay.
- Select the type of job evaluation system you will use — this may be dictated by the province, *e.g.*, pay equity legislation in Ontario precludes certain types of job evaluation.
- Define the market with which you will compare your rewards package, *e.g.*, all companies in the area, all companies with less than $50 million in sales, companies with 500 to 1,000 employees.
- Specify your policy position — do you want to set your pay rates at the average, third quartile, or average less 10% of the specified companies in the area selected.
- Name the components of the rewards package.

The worksheet is included on the accompanying CD-ROM so you can print and use it. The one shown on the next page has examples which I hope will illustrate the point.

CONCLUSION

In this chapter we have reviewed the major components of your compensation strategy and laid out the decisions you need to make regarding each one. There is a worksheet which should help you go through the process in a systematic way. I have a word of caution at this point. After you have gone through this chapter and completed the worksheet do not consider your decisions as final until you have read the rest of the book. You are probably not fully aware of the impact of selecting a job evaluation plan, for instance, until you have read the next chapter. Take your time about finalizing the strategy decisions. Make sure you fully discuss them with your management group and utilize whatever type of employee involvement you have decided on.

WORKSHEET FOR STRATEGIC COMPENSATION PLANNING

Employee Group	Geography	Person or Job Based	Job Evaluation System	Definition of Market	Policy Line	Components
Executive	National	Job	Ranking	Manufacturing – sales of $10 million to $20 million	Third quartile	Base + stock options + short-term cash bonus
Middle management	Western Canada	Job	Point-factor	As above	Middle	Base + short-term cash bonus
Hourly	Calgary	Job	Point-factor	All industries	Average	Base only

3

Selecting a Job Evaluation Plan

INTRODUCTION

Job evaluation can be defined as "the process of determining the relative value of jobs within the organization". This chapter introduces job evaluation and takes you through the process of deciding what type of job evaluation plan you will use. It is an essential step in the development of a fair and effective salary administration system. The following topics are covered:

- types of job evaluation;
- advantages and disadvantages of each type;
- setting up a job evaluation committee;
- selecting a job evaluation plan; and
- market pricing — an alternative to job evaluation.

It is important to distinguish "job evaluation" from the process of "performance appraisal or evaluation". As you will see later in this chapter, the former is concerned with the value of the job while the latter process focuses on how well the job is performed by the individual. Performance appraisal systems are covered in Chapter 16, "Performance Management and Rewards".

If you examine the definition of job evaluation provided at the outset of this chapter, you should take note of three key words or phrases that are the essence of the definition. These are:

- relative value;
- jobs; and
- within the organization.

The term "relative value" means that job evaluation is only concerned with the value of a job compared to other jobs. Some people, even compensation professionals, believe that it is possible to establish an "absolute" value for a job. They are wrong. It is possible to determine the market value of a job[1] but this is simply what other organizations are paying for that job on a specific date. It is not an absolute value.

The second important concept in the definition of job evaluation is that of "job". A job can be defined as "a collection of tasks, duties and responsibilities which can be performed by one person". It is critical to note that this definition does not include, or even refer to, the performance of the individual in the job. This can be included in a compensation program but must not form part of the job evaluation process.

The third important concept embedded in the definition of job evaluation is "within the organization". This means that the process only determines the value of jobs inside the employer's organization; it has nothing to do with the value of the jobs outside the company. As noted earlier the value of jobs *outside* the company is called the market value or the market rate. This is obviously important in the overall determination of pay levels but, like the performance of the individual employee in a job, it is not part of the job evaluation process.

TYPES OF JOB EVALUATION

There are four main types of job evaluation, each with its own advantages and disadvantages. This section will describe each type, with examples, and review the strengths and weaknesses of each. The four classic types are:

- whole-job ranking;
- grade description or classification;
- factor-comparison; and
- point-factor or point-rating.

One of the criteria to be considered in selecting a job evaluation system is the degree to which it complies with applicable (or possible) legislation.[2] In this regard the legislation with the most impact and relevance to job evaluation in Canada is the Ontario *Pay Equity Act*.[3] In my opinion, grade description and factor-comparison systems do *not* comply with the Act and you can therefore readily dismiss them for purposes of designing a compensation system. However, I will describe their advantages and disadvantages so that you can make your own decision. If you do not have, and don't plan to have, any operations in Ontario, Quebec or under federal jurisdiction, they may be of

---

[1] See Chapter 6, "Salary Surveys".

[2] See Chapter 1, "Assessing Your Situation", for a discussion of labour legislation.

[3] R.S.O. 1990, c. P.7.

interest although there are other technical problems with both these types of job evaluation.

Here is an outline of the four classic types of job evaluation.

Whole-Job Ranking

In order to illustrate whole-job ranking we first need a number of jobs to work with. For this purpose we will use the following job titles:

- accountant;
- file clerk;
- senior secretary;
- clerk-typist; and
- receptionist/switchboard operator.

There are several minor variations on this method but one of the easiest is to identify the most valuable and the least valuable of the five jobs. You do this by comparing each "whole job" with each other "whole job"; hence the name. I have used these five jobs to demonstrate whole-job rankings in many situations and the usual consensus is that of these five, the job of accountant is the most valuable to the employer. Similarly, the job of file clerk is most often considered the least valuable of the group. It only remains to rank the other three jobs.

Starting with the clerk-typist, I feel that it is worth more than the file clerk and clearly less than the senior secretary. Its value relative to the receptionist (for the sake of brevity I will drop the switchboard part of the title but it should still be considered) is not as clear but I think the clerk-typist job is worth less to the employer than the receptionist. Most people think that the senior secretary is worth more than either the clerk-typist or the receptionist. Therefore the overall ranking of the five jobs, from highest to lowest is as follows:

- accountant;
- senior secretary;
- receptionist/switchboard operator;
- clerk-typist;
- file clerk.

Another variation of whole-job ranking is called "paired comparison". It is somewhat more rigorous than the method described above and therefore much more useful when dealing with a larger group of jobs. I have successfully used this method with several hundred jobs. I would not normally recommend the use of paired comparison with that many jobs but this particular assignment entailed several factors that made it appropriate. Paired comparison works as follows. First, you need a worksheet that looks like this (this worksheet is also on the accompanying CD-ROM):

EXAMPLE — PAIRED COMPARISON WORKSHEET

JOB	Senior Secretary	Accountant	File Clerk	Receptionist/ Switchboard Operator	Clerk- Typist	TOTAL
Senior Secretary						
Accountant						
File Clerk						
Receptionist/ Switchboard Operator						
Clerk-Typist						

The point is to work across the horizontal rows one job at a time and compare it with each other job in terms of its total or "whole" value to the organization. Start with the job of senior secretary and compare it with the accountant. We have already determined that it is worth less than the job of accountant; therefore no notation is necessary. Now compare senior secretary with the job of file clerk. Since it is considered to be of greater value place a tick mark or X in the box. Similarly, comparing the job of senior secretary with the clerk-typist and receptionist jobs, it is considered to be worth more so tick off the next two boxes. Add up the ticks and enter the number in the last column. The top row will now look like this:

JOB	Senior Secretary	Accountant	File Clerk	Receptionist/ Switchboard Operator	Clerk- Typist	TOTAL
Senior Secretary			✓	✓	✓	3

If you follow the same process for the other rows the whole worksheet should be the same as the one shown below:

JOB	Senior Secretary	Accountant	File Clerk	Receptionist/ Switchboard Operator	Clerk-Typist	TOTAL
Senior Secretary			✓	✓	✓	3
Accountant	✓		✓	✓	✓	4
File Clerk						0
Receptionist/ Switchboard Operator			✓		✓	2
Clerk-Typist			✓			1

The rank order, from highest to lowest, is given by the total number of tick marks. The job of accountant, with four, is considered to be of the highest value, while the poor file clerk, with zero ticks, is at the low end of the scale. I hope that you are not surprised that the results of the paired-comparison exercise are exactly the same as the basic method of whole-job ranking. This exact duplication is partly a function of the low number of jobs used in the example. It is quite possible that, with a larger number, *e.g.*, 50, there would be minor variations between the two methods. The big advantage of paired comparison over standard whole-job ranking is the higher degree of rigorous analysis. Each job is compared with each other job, not once but twice.

At this point I should mention that there are two very important elements of job evaluation that I have left out. However, many job evaluation projects have gone ahead successfully without them. These two items are job descriptions and the criteria for determining the relative value of jobs.

In the examples here I allowed you to rate jobs but the only concrete data you had about them was the job title. You were not provided with any information, written or otherwise, regarding the nature, contents or qualifications required of the job. This is an extremely dangerous practice.

In pay equity literature the use of job titles is considered a prime source of gender bias. For example, the title of secretary is almost always used for a female-dominated job[4] and using just the title automatically results in a lower

---

[4] Section 1 of the Ontario *Pay Equity Act* contains a specific definition of "female job class", but for now I will use this term to mean a job that is normally, or usually, filled by a woman.

value being placed on the job, especially by male evaluators. I cannot recommend too strongly that you use a job description questionnaire ("JDQ"). This may sound like you are overcomplicating the simplest method of job evaluation but it will result in significantly more equitable evaluations and protect you where there is pay equity legislation or the possibility thereof. The methodology of using JDQs will be described in Chapter 5, "Conducting Job Evaluation". For whole-job ranking you do not need to use the extensive JDQ that you would for a point-rating plan; a simplified form will be quite adequate. An example is provided in Chapter 4, "Obtaining Information About Jobs".

The other item that I left out was any description of the factors to use when determining the relative value of jobs. Without some direction, the evaluators will probably use a wide variety of criteria, often different from each other, and frequently in conflict or overlapping. Virtually all job evaluation plans use the following four factors to appraise the value of jobs:

- skill;
- effort;
- responsibility; and
- working conditions.

These four factors are also those used in both the Ontario and Quebec pay equity legislation, although neither law defines them. Some plans, especially point-rating plans, break these main factors into 10 to 20 components, or sub-factors. Eight to ten factors is the more common number.

The definitions of the main factors also vary frequently but the generally accepted definitions are as follows:

- *Skill* — the total of skill, abilities, knowledge, training, experience and/or education required to perform the job. This is normally understood to be the minimum required to do, or obtain, the job. It is not the qualifications of the ideal candidate; I often refer to skill as the requirements you would put in the newspaper advertisement. It is also important to distinguish between the qualifications required for the job and minimum hiring standards for the company as a whole. For example, I used to work at S.C. Johnson Wax in Brantford, Ontario, which had a policy of hiring people in the factory, warehouse and office at entry-level jobs and promoting them as jobs came open. Since the company also had a policy of no lay-offs (of permanent staff), this meant that employees would be hired in their late teens or early twenties and stay with the company until they retired. We insisted that all new hires have at least a high school diploma although the entry-level jobs (general labour in the warehouse and factory; mail clerk in the office) *did not require this level of education*. However, when we evaluated the jobs, using a point-rating system, we used the actual qualifications required by the jobs, usually less than high school. This is an important distinction but, in my experience, many job evaluation committees have found it difficult to understand. To be honest, I am not sure why, but you should be aware that this difficulty occurs quite often. You should also be prepared to spend some time discussing it since it often bogs down a committee.

- *Effort* — normally considered to be comprised of two parts: (i) mental effort; and (ii) physical effort. Physical effort includes bending, lifting, awkward work positions, standing continuously or repetitive movements. It is often measured in terms of the frequency (number of times per day) and duration (*e.g.*, 10 minutes at a time) and the amount of effort (lifting 50 lb.). This factor is also a favourite of the pay equity advocates as they claim, with some justification, that traditional job evaluation systems do not recognize the physical effort involved in female-dominated job classes which tends to be small but continuous. For example, compare the "male" job of warehouse order picker, which involves lifting cartons of about 30 lb. 20 to 30 times a day, with the small but continuous finger movements of a data entry operator, who also has to sit in the same position all day. Job evaluation plans should recognize both types of physical effort. Mental effort is the amount of mental or intellectual exertion involved in performing the job, which can result in mental fatigue, and considers the accuracy required, deadlines, concentration on detail, interruptions, and the frequency and/or duration of activity. This can be one of the most difficult factors to use but it is important to include in a job evaluation plan.
- *Responsibility* — often called accountability. According to the dictionary the two words are interchangeable. I once won a bet with a client who maintained vigorously that the two words meant different things but when he looked up responsibility the first meaning in the dictionary was accountability. An easy way to understand this factor is to think of it as the "size" of the job. For example, the sales manager who handles $1 million in sales does not have as much responsibility as the sales manager who takes care of $50 million. This is true even if the two job descriptions are identical in wording. Similarly, the vice-president of a division has more responsibility than a first-line supervisor.
- *Working conditions* — refers to the environment in which the work is performed. It includes exposure to dust, dirt, fumes, heat, cold, noise, vibration and inclement weather. It should also include any exposure to health and safety hazards. One organization, which raised Holstein bulls for breeding purposes, added exposure to dangerous animals to this factor since these bulls weighed up to 2000 lb. and often had foul tempers. This illustrates the point that any factor or sub-factor has to take into account the unique circumstances of your company.

Point-Rating Plans (Point-Factor Plans)

Point-rating plans involve the following five elements:

- factors;

- degrees;
- weightings;
- point tables; and
- point bands.

Factors are the elements which are used to measure the value of jobs relative to each other. They include such items as working conditions, physical and mental effort, responsibility, communications/contacts, supervision (number and types of staff), accountability, complexity of the work, education, experience and language skills. Most plans have eight to ten factors.

Factors are broken down into degrees. Degrees can be thought of as amounts of the factor ranging from zero to the largest amount possible in your company. Here is an example of a factor and its degree levels. The factor is called "Communications/Contacts". Note that this factor has five degrees but the number of degrees varies from factor to factor. Some factors can have 15 degrees while some others have only three.

COMMUNICATIONS/CONTACTS

Factor Definition
This factor refers to the requirements of the job for interaction with people inside and outside the organization for the purpose of exchanging information, providing explanations, reaching agreement with others or influencing their actions. It considers the nature and frequency of the contact and the level of persons contacted.

Rule(s) of Application
1. No credit is to be given for supervisory contacts recognized under the Supervision factor.

Degree Levels
1. Contacts are with immediate associates only. Contacts are for the purpose of giving, obtaining and/or exchanging information of a routine nature.
2. Some contacts outside the immediate area of work or outside the organization. Contacts are for the same purpose as Degree 1 and may require the employee to integrate work effort with that of others.
3. Many contacts outside the immediate area of work or outside the organization. Contacts require judgment, tact and diplomacy in order to obtain co-operation and/or approval of action.
4. Regular contacts outside the immediate area of work or outside the organization. Contacts are of a demanding nature and require judgment, tact and diplomacy to obtain co-operation, agreement or approval of action in many difficult situations.

5. Extensive contacts outside the immediate area of work or outside organization. Contacts involve working with or influencing others in potentially controversial or sensitive situations.

Suppose that you are evaluating a job and decide that it best fits the description in Degree 3. You would also do this for all the other factors. You then have to turn to the point table which looks like this:

EXAMPLE OF A POINT TABLE

FACTOR	DEGREE LEVELS AND POINTS						
	1	**2**	**3**	**4**	**5**	**6**	**7**
Communications/Contacts	5	10	**15**	20	25		
Complexity	10	20	30	40	50	60	
Mental Effort	5	10	15	20	25		
Physical Effort	5	10	15	20			
Accountability	15	30	45	60	75	90	
Initiative	5	10	15	20			
Working Conditions	10	20	30	40			
Supervision	10	20	30	40			
Education	15	30	45	60	75	90	105
Experience	20	40	60	80	100	120	140

If you refer to the above table you will see that Degree 3 in the Communications/Contacts factor receives 15 points. If you follow the same procedure for the other factors, the final evaluation of a sample job could look like the table below:

COMPLETE RATINGS/POINTS OF A SAMPLE JOB

FACTOR	DEGREE RATING	POINTS
Communications/Contacts	3	15
Complexity	2	20
Mental Effort	1	5
Physical Effort	4	20
Accountability	3	45
Initiative	1	5

FACTOR	DEGREE RATING	POINTS
Working Conditions	4	40
Supervision	1	10
Education	2	30
Experience	1	20
TOTAL POINTS		**210**

POINT BANDS

SALARY GRADE	POINT BAND
1	1 - 49
2	50 - 99
3	100 - 149
4	150 - 199
5	200 - 249
6	250 - 299
7	300 - 349
8	350 - 399
9	400+

You can see that the point total for this sample job comes to 210. This does not mean very much in administrative terms unless you also have a set of point bands. An example of point bands is shown above. The 210 points will place this job in the band of 200 to 249 points which is salary grade 5. Placing a job in a salary grade is the ultimate objective of job evaluation. This determines the salary/wage range or rate. This will be discussed in more detail in Chapter 7 "Putting it All Together — Basic Salary Administration".

Classification

Classification systems, which are also called grade description systems, group jobs into job families such as secretaries, engineers, accountants, lab technicians or typists. Here is an example of part of a classification system for clerical staff:

FACTOR	LEVEL A	LEVEL B	LEVEL C	LEVEL D
Summary of Responsibility	Incumbents perform routine, elementary and repetitive office duties.		Incumbents perform simple and repetitive clerical duties requiring a limited knowledge of clerical methods.	
Complexity and Judgment	Work involves the performance of specific routine tasks that are straightforward and repetitive in nature. Work is performed in accordance with detailed instructions requiring little, if any, authority to exercise independent judgment. Work is closely controlled through the structured nature of the work.		Work involves the performance of specific routine tasks that involve related steps, processes or methods. Work is performed in accordance with detailed instructions requiring very little, if any, authority to exercise independent judgment. Work is closely controlled through the structured nature of the work.	
Supervision of Others	None		None	

FACTOR	LEVEL A	LEVEL B	LEVEL C	LEVEL D
Contacts	Contacts are primarily within own work unit.		Contacts are primarily with individuals at comparable or lower levels within the company or occasionally with individuals outside the company.	
Working Conditions	Work occasionally requires minor muscular exertion and/or physical strain. Duration of sustained concentration on a single activity is greater than 15 minutes but not greater than one hour. Work environment does not involve disagreeable elements or exposure to job hazards.		Work does not require exertion or physical strain. Duration of sustained concentration is greater than 15 minutes but not greater than one hour. Work environment does not involve disagreeable elements or exposure to job hazards.	

As you can see, the descriptions are quite general. The description for the actual job to be evaluated is compared with the descriptions in vertical columns and the best fit (level) is chosen. Often the job will fit two descriptions quite well and it can be difficult to choose between them. Salary ranges are developed for each pay grade (level in the example). In the example, descriptions are not provided for Levels B and D. This is quite common in classification systems.

Factor-Comparison

The factor-comparison method of job evaluation is also one of the "quantitative" methods along with point-rating. It is unique in that it is based on current or market pay rates for benchmark jobs. Like point-rating plans it also uses factors; often the same ones. The pay rate is broken down into the parts of it that can be attributed to each of the factors. Assume that two benchmark jobs, warehouse worker and general labourer, are paid, respectively, $15 and $11 per hour. Also assume the plan will use the standard four factors: skill; effort; responsibility; and working conditions.

$/Hour	Skill	Effort	Responsibility	Working Conditions
8				
7				New Job
6			Warehouse Worker	
5	Warehouse Worker			
4	New Job	New Job		General Labourer
3		General Labourer	New Job	
2	General Labourer	Warehouse Worker	General Labourer	Warehouse Worker

Normally, a plan will have more than two benchmark jobs but the preceding table illustrates the methodology. When a job needs to be evaluated, it is compared with each of the benchmarks on each factor and placed on the scale of dollars per hour. In the table above, I have shown "New Job" as ranked between the two benchmarks on skill, just above general labourer on effort and responsibility, and considerably above both benchmarks on working conditions. The wage rate for the new job is determined by adding up the wages for each factor. Thus the new job should receive:

$4 for Skill + $4 for Effort + $3 for Responsibility + $7 for Working Conditions = $18 per hour.

ADVANTAGES AND DISADVANTAGES OF THE FOUR METHODS

Whole-Job Ranking

The primary advantage of whole-job ranking is that it is simple to set up; it can be done quickly and is quite inexpensive. There is little training required. You can basically set up a committee, take them through the example provided and start evaluating jobs. They will learn as they go. In addition, there is almost no preparation required, aside from getting job descriptions.

The major disadvantage of this method is the lack of specific measurement. Although I outlined the factors normally used in all job evaluation plans, and these can be explained to the evaluators, they tend to get mashed together. The evaluators often change the emphasis they place on the factors from job to job. This can result in a lack of consistency. There is also a lack of documentation of the reasons why one job is rated higher or lower than another. You may find that, when you revisit the evaluations years later, you can't for the life of you recall why a specific job was given the rating it received. This becomes even more of a problem when the evaluators or committee members have changed. Whole-job ranking also becomes more difficult as the number and complexity of the jobs increase. In addition, there is a tendency to let the performance of the incumbent influence the ratings, especially if you only use job titles.

Classification

The advantages of the classification (or grade description) method of job evaluation are that it is simple to use for a homogenous group of jobs, it is quite easy to understand and, like whole-job ranking, it is quickly implemented. The results are also fairly satisfactory. However, there are disadvantages which include the fact that the method is not suitable for groups of jobs, other than specialists, or job families such as secretaries, chemical technologists or analyst-programmers. It is also difficult to evaluate jobs that vary from the norm in that a job needs to meet all the descriptions for a particular grade. Sometimes jobs meet the description of part of a grade (*e.g.*, for accountability) but fit better into another grade for another factor, such as working conditions. In cases like this you essentially have to force the job rating into a grade that really doesn't fit.

The major disadvantage of the classification method is that you cannot compare jobs between or across job families. For example, the method does not provide a way to compare an engineering job with a clerical job. This alone makes it unsuitable for use where pay equity legislation is in effect, as in Ontario.

Factor-Comparison

The factor-comparison method is considered a pretty reliable method of job evaluation. It is also quite rare. I have been involved in human resource consulting for more than 20 years and I have never run across a factor-comparison plan. One American text says that "classic factor comparison plans are now essentially nonexistent".[5] They are still reported in

---

[5]   West Group, *Compensation Guide* (Eagan, Minnesota: September, 1996), p. 9-10.

some surveys but I suspect that the number is probably inaccurate because many practitioners confuse factor-comparison plans with point-rating plans, which are also referred to as "point-factor" plans. The factor-comparison method is easy to use within a small organization and the compensable factors can be tailored to your particular company.

The disadvantages of this method are formidable. It is difficult to use with a large number of jobs. There are no degree definitions. It tends to perpetuate salary inequities and it is hard to evaluate new or revised jobs. Since it is based on current salaries or wages (either actual or labour market) it is totally unsuitable for pay equity purposes as these are considered, by definition, to be gender-biased.

Point-Rating

The major advantage of point-rating plans is that they are capable of complying with pay equity legislation. They break the decision-making process down into discrete parts (equivalent to the factors) and, using a quantitative process, result in a numerical total. The whole process can be viewed as objective and mathematical.

The disadvantages of point-rating plans are that they:

- are expensive and time-consuming to set up;
- are not easily adaptable;
- require a long process to evaluate new jobs;
- need a fair amount of administrative effort; and
- can be difficult to communicate.

SETTING UP A JOB EVALUATION COMMITTEE

There are two major ways to conduct job evaluation. One is to assign this responsibility to a human resources (or other) officer who will evaluate the job and advise those concerned (normally the supervisor and the incumbent) about the results. The advantage of this approach is speed; the evaluation can be done quickly. However, a major disadvantage is that the human resources officer may not have an adequate understanding of the job and/or be able to look at it from the viewpoint of the whole organization. His inherent biases (and we all have some) might affect his judgment. Similarly other employees may feel that he is biased in favour of certain jobs and may tend to view some jobs as less valued than other people might.

The way to offset these drawbacks is to use a committee. A committee will bring a variety of viewpoints to the process and will be able to represent the total values of the corporation much better than one individual can.

The ideal size of a committee is five to ten persons, although it could be as few as three. The number will vary according to your ability to find members for the job evaluation committee with the characteristics desired. They should be:

- representative of all sections, levels, departments and divisions of the company;
- a cross-section of the demographic profile of the organization in terms of age, seniority, gender, education, ethnicity, etc.;
- considered to be "opinion leaders" by their respective constituencies, sufficiently well respected that their peers will feel comfortable being represented by them;
- willing to act as spokesperson for their group;
- reasonably articulate, able to express the concerns of the employee group that they are representing;
- objective not only in assessing the value of a job but also in separating the job from the person currently holding it; and
- capable of understanding the concepts involved.

Not all these conditions can be achieved in all organizations, but try to meet as many of them as possible. Once the committee has been formed you will have to train them in job evaluation. Many human resources associations provide seminars on this subject. A list of such associations is provided in Appendix A, at the end of this book.

SELECTING A JOB EVALUATION PLAN

The advantages and disadvantages of the four major types of job evaluation plans have been discussed above. Assuming that you have read this material, and have at least some preliminary views, I will make it even easier for you.

In my opinion, neither a classification system nor a factor-comparison plan are suitable for companies at the start of the 21st century. I have two reasons for this opinion. The first is that both plans are specific to job families (this is more true of classification systems than factor-comparison) and are therefore unsuitable for use across organizations. Companies should be designing compensation plans that apply equally across all job categories, since there is a tendency to transfer employees between different categories more frequently than in the past, and also because job families are much broader than they were before. For instance, some classification systems used to have separate scales for clerks, clerk-typists and typists.

The second reason is that neither system complies with pay equity legislation. Currently, this is only a problem for the private sector under Ontario, Quebec and federal legislation. However, Canadian labour law has a tradition of successful innovations spreading from one province to another. It is therefore quite likely that the other provinces will follow suit in the not-too-distant future. In addition, pay equity legislation in Ontario is starting to bring the earnings of "female" jobs more in line with those of "male" jobs and the traditional justification for separate systems (that there were separate labour market rates) is starting to disappear. Your new compensation system might as well recognize this reality at the start and avoid the necessity of changing if your province does bring in pay equity legislation for the private sector. Besides, it will make you look "leading edge", progressive and all those other good things.

If you accept my recommendation to reject classification and factor-comparison, that leaves you with a choice between whole-job ranking (of some sort) and point-rating plans. This decision is even easier than the previous one. If you have less than 50 (approximately) jobs and you are in a hurry, use the ranking method. Otherwise, I think it is best to go with a point-rating job evaluation plan.

BUY, BUILD OR ADAPT

If you decide that you prefer a point-rating plan, there are more choices for you to make. Essentially, there are three options:

- Adapt the Tyson-Totten[6] Job Evaluation Plan which is provided in Appendix D.
- Design a custom plan for your organization from the ground up.
- Purchase an "off-the-shelf" plan from a consulting firm.

Here are the arguments for and against each option:

- Adapting the Tyson-Totten plan has the advantages that it is readily available as part of this book and is a proven product which has been used in a variety of different organizations with 300 or fewer jobs. It is also very adaptable, as it allows for the addition or deletion of factors and degree levels. The disadvantage is that you have to do the work of adapting it to your organization by yourself (although the process is clearly provided in Appendix F) without external consulting assistance.
- Designing your own plan would result in a product that very definitely reflects the values and culture of your organization and the expectations of employees and management. The people who design and use it will have a serious commitment to the plan. The downside of building it yourself is the elapsed time and cost which is usually measured in the hours spent by a committee of managers and employees. Starting with a blank sheet of paper

---

[6] This plan was originally developed by me and my colleague, Bob Totten, President of Totten and Associates Inc. of London, Ontario, in the late 1980s. We have both installed it successfully in a wide variety of organizations. However, since these organizations differ in many ways the plan in this book is now somewhat different than the one used by Mr. Totten.

and getting to a fully documented working point-rating plan can take a considerable amount of time. Several years ago I was the consultant to the management half of a joint union-management committee involved in such a project. The joint committee met every Wednesday for 14 months and held two one-week sessions. The management team also spent at least a couple of hours each week preparing for the Wednesday meeting. Another disadvantage is that you may have to hire a consultant to help you with the process. I recommend that you do so unless you already employ somebody with direct experience in this area.

- The final option is to purchase an existing plan from a consulting firm. Virtually all of the major firms who operate in the "compensation" field have a plan that they will provide to you. Although I may be prejudiced about my competitors, I will admit that their plans all work. There are two pitfalls to be aware of if you decide to go this route. The first is that it will cost you, probably quite a bit. You can't just go to ABC Major Consulting Firm and purchase their job evaluation plan the same way you bought this book. What you have to do is engage the firm to install their plan with the help of their consultants. They charge by the hour and most consultants from major firms in Canada will cost you between $200 to $400 per hour. You pay for the time of the consultants and the plan is included in the price. Another concern with this option is the degree of flexibility the consulting firm is prepared to provide regarding its plan. Some such plans have been around, and widely used, for over 50 years. The firm is often very inflexible about adjusting its plan. Question the consultant about this and ensure their requirements meet your expectations. There are advantages to this approach as it makes inter-company comparisons of jobs quite easy.

MARKET PRICING — AN ALTERNATIVE TO JOB EVALUATION?

Strictly speaking, market pricing is not a form of job evaluation, although the end result of a market pricing exercise is the same as that produced by a "true" job evaluation and market survey process. Market pricing does not comply with pay equity legislation, in my opinion, and therefore cannot be used in those jurisdictions with such legislation. However, you should be aware of it for the following reasons:

- If you bought this book because you do not have a formal salary administration program, you are probably already doing it.
- It works reasonably well.
- A greater percentage of American companies than Canadian companies use it as their method of "job evaluation".
- You should know about it as an alternative to the usual methods.

Here is how market pricing works. Using either your own, custom-designed or published surveys you establish the market rate for as many of your jobs as possible. Some authorities insist that you do this for at least 50% of your jobs but I think that you should get market rates for as many of your jobs as possible. The more jobs that you can establish market rates for, the more likely it is that your resulting salary structure will reflect the labour market in which you compete for employees.

When you have as many market rates as possible, list the jobs in descending order according to the market data.

The next step is develop tentative salary range control points. Set the control point for the lowest Salary Grade 1 at the market rate for the lowest job. Then create control points above this by adding a standard percentage until one of them approximates the market rate for the highest jobs. You can use the spreadsheet on the CD-ROM included with this book to do this. Start with 5% differentials but try various others, such as 10% or 7%. You have to watch the number of salary grades that result, but keep trying until there is a control point which closely matches the market data for the top job in the group of jobs. As a rule of thumb you do not want this to result in more than 10 to 15 salary grades unless the organization is very large. Let's call the result of this exercise the "proposed salary structure".

The next step is to place each of the jobs for which you have market data into the appropriate salary grade. For each job, select the grade for which the proposed control point is closest to the market or survey data for that job. If you follow this procedure for all the benchmark jobs (*i.e.*, jobs for which you have reliable survey data) you will have a preliminary classification structure which will look like this:

SALARY GRADE	JOB TITLE
12	President
11	
10	
9	Financial Comptroller Operations Director
8	Systems Manager
7	Store Manager Accountant
6	
5	Head Mixer
4	Lead Hand

SALARY GRADE	JOB TITLE
3	Merchandising Assistant
	Junior Sales Associate
	Receptionist
2	Cleaner/Helper
1	Gift Maker

A classification structure is the end result of any job evaluation methodology and can be used on an ongoing basis until there are major changes in the nature or mix of jobs in the group. New or revised jobs can be slotted into this structure using whole-job ranking. With this type of system, jobs can be moved up or down in the structure if the market value for them changes significantly.

In order to finalize this preliminary classification structure, the final step in the market pricing process is to "slot" all the jobs for which you do not have market data into the classification structure. You can do this by comparing the "whole" job with the jobs already in the structure on the basis of the total value of the skill, effort, responsibility and working conditions associated with the job. Follow this procedure and place each of the remaining jobs in a salary grade. Now you have the final classification structure.

CONCLUSION

In this chapter you have learned about the different types of job evaluation and the advantages and disadvantages of each of them. You have been provided with detailed descriptions of whole-job ranking and point-rating job evaluation along with instructions on how to select and operate a job evaluation committee. You now have to obtain information about the jobs in your organization that will be included in the evaluation process. This is covered in the next chapter.

4

Obtaining Information About Jobs

INTRODUCTION

In this chapter we will review the various methods you can use to obtain the information about job content that you need to build a compensation program. This is an absolutely unavoidable step in the process. However, there is one caveat to this comment. It assumes that your overall philosophy is to "pay the job" first and then to "pay the person". One of the latest trends in the compensation field, called competency-based pay, focuses on paying the individual rather than the job. This was discussed in Chapter 2, "Strategy". However, it can be summed up by reversing an old cliché. Competency-based pay theory asserts that you pay the Ph.D. for having the Ph.D. (and possibly getting another one) instead of paying her for driving the taxi. Generally accepted compensation practices, and this book, assert that it is essential to start with the pay rate for the job, *i.e.*, driving the taxi, and then determine the actual pay of the individual.

In the normal course of events you will collect job information and then perform job evaluation, the process that was covered in the last chapter. This chapter follows the one on job evaluation because you have to choose a job evaluation plan before you can design a job description questionnaire ("JDQ").

This will become clearer as you progress through this chapter (and also Chapter 20, "Putting it All Together — The Design Process") which covers the following topics:

- whether or not to have job descriptions at all;
- methods of obtaining job information;
- different types and uses of job descriptions;

- development of a JDQ;
- distribution of JDQs and other issues.

METHODS OF OBTAINING JOB INFORMATION

There are three major methods which you can use to obtain information about the content of jobs. These are:

- the incumbent(s) writes the job description;
- the supervisor writes the job description;
- a third party prepares the documentation (this could be someone in the human resources department, an outside consultant or some other analyst).

There are various pluses and minuses of these three methods. The advantage of the incumbent doing the work is that the person who knows the job best is describing it. This is a major, major advantage. In addition, the employee is able to feel that she has had at least some input into the process and that she has been consulted about her own job. There are two exceptions to this. The first occurs when there is no incumbent or she is quite new to the job and either is not performing all the duties or is unfamiliar with them. The second exception is when the incumbent(s) is not fluent enough in the language of the workplace to adequately complete the document. In both situations, one of the other methods of obtaining job information must be used.

If you decide that the supervisor should write the job description, the plus side is that a person who is (or should be) very close to the job will be completing the document. This is not quite as good as having the incumbent do it but it does come close. There can be a problem when the supervisor has a large number of staff reporting to her and it becomes a workload issue. It is also quite common for many supervisors to not clearly understand the duties and responsibilities of some of the people who report to them. It is not uncommon for a supervisor to say, after an employee has written his own job description, "I didn't know that you did that". This is especially true when the employee is in a different profession than the supervisor, *e.g.*, a human resources manager who reports to a vice-president of finance.

The final option, having a third party complete the job description, is also viable when there is no incumbent or the incumbent is not fluent in the appropriate language. This second issue is becoming more of a problem in the multilingual major urban areas of Canada such as Montreal, Toronto and Vancouver. Using an inside staff person, such as a human resources officer, is effective but does divert the person from other duties and can stretch out the process for a much longer period. Using outside consultants has three problems. One is that they may not be familiar with the organization or its occupational mix. Secondly, the process may take longer unless you use a lot of them. Thirdly, they cost money which you may not have.

In summary, I have presented the three choices you have about obtaining job information in my order of preference. In my opinion, having the employee prepare the job description is by far the best choice but there are circumstances in which one of the other two methods should be used.

DIFFERENT TYPES AND USES OF JOB DESCRIPTIONS

There are a variety of types of job descriptions which are used for different purposes. The major difference among the types of job descriptions is the length and the nature of the information included. Here are some of the uses for job descriptions:

- job evaluation;
- advertising;
- handling of grievances;
- union certification proceedings;
- employment contracts;
- training;
- training needs analysis;
- pay equity complaints;
- internal job postings;
- organizational analysis and design;
- compensation surveys.

In most salary surveys[1] the job descriptions usually consist of the title of the job and two or three lines about the duties. Here is an example from the 1997 Metropolitan Toronto Board of Trade *Clerical Compensation Survey*:[2]

ACCOUNTS PAYABLE/RECEIVABLE CLERK
Under general supervision performs clerical duties concerning the processing of the accounts payable and/or receivable function.

Typical duties:
1. Administers the accounts payable and/or receivable sub-ledger accounts. 2. Reconciles input and output of the accounts payable and/or receivable accounts. 3. Files invoices, billings, accounts payable and/or receivable documents. 4. Answers inquiries regarding the payable and/or receivable accounts.

Job descriptions in salary surveys are typically the shortest example of the species that you are likely to see. Those used for job evaluation purposes are closer to the other extreme. Job evaluation has been defined as "the process of

---

[1] See Chapter 6, "Salary Surveys".
[2] Board of Trade of Metropolitan Toronto, *Clerical Compensation Survey* (1997), at p. 43.

determining the relative value of jobs within the organization" and was discussed in detail in the last chapter. In job evaluation you need more than the title and a list of duties in order to conduct the process adequately, especially with point-rating plans. You need information about such items as the number and types of subordinates, the education and experience required to do the job, the complexity, level of responsibility and physical and mental demands of the position. This usually entails an eight to ten-page document. In Appendix E at the end of this book you can find the JDQ which is meant to be used with the Tyson-Totten Job Evaluation Plan. You can consider this a typical example of this type of document.

In between these extremes are job descriptions that are used for internal job postings. These will typically include the job title, name and title of the supervisor, major duties, the salary grade and/or range, and the qualifications required. A job description used for external advertising would probably be a little more extensive but would not include the salary grade as this information would be meaningless to any reader outside the company. It would include additional material, such as the nature of the company, various locations, the main business, and training and advancement opportunities available. At the most detailed extreme in terms of length is the job description that is used for training purposes. These have to be quite extensive as they should include all the duties, to a high level of detail.

DEVELOPMENT OF A JOB DESCRIPTION QUESTIONNAIRE

Common Elements

All questionnaires should ask for the following:

- name of the incumbent(s);[3]
- job title;
- name and title of the immediate supervisor;
- name and telephone number of the person who completed the JDQ;
- a summary description (two or three sentences) of the job;
- a list of the major duties and responsibilities of the job and the approximate percentage of time[4] spent on each over the course of a year.

An example of a short form JDQ appears on the next page.

---

[3] See the discussion later in this chapter as to who completes the JDQ if there is more than one incumbent in a job.

[4] Asking this can be a problem; it is discussed in more detail later in this chapter.

SHORT FORM JOB DESCRIPTION QUESTIONNAIRE

NAME OF ORGANIZATION: _____

The purpose of this questionnaire is to obtain a complete, accurate description of the duties and responsibilities of your job, as well as other data necessary for the evaluation of the job. The questionnaire is not concerned with the characteristics of the person in the job or how well he/she is performing the job.

1. Please read the entire form carefully before completing any of the sections.
2. Describe the job as it currently exists.
3. Add additional sheets if extra space is required.
4. Print or write clearly (or have your answers typed).
5. Forward the completed questionnaire to your supervisor for review.

JOB TITLE: _____

DEPARTMENT:_____

SUPERVISOR (NAME/TITLE): _____

INCUMBENT(S): _____

PREPARED BY: **TELEPHONE:**

JOB SUMMARY

Please provide a two or three sentence summary of the overall purpose of the job. It is better to complete this section after the rest of the questionnaire has been filled out.

_____
_____
_____
_____
_____
_____
_____
_____

DUTIES AND RESPONSIBILITIES

List the major duties/responsibilities of your job. Indicate the approximate percentage of time that you spend on each duty over the course of a normal year.

DUTY/RESPONSIBILITY   **APPROXIMATE PERCENTAGE**
                                         OF TIME

_____
_____
_____
_____
_____
_____

Many employers use a questionnaire like this. However, I do not recommend it for two reasons. One is the existence, or probable passage in the relevant political jurisdiction, of pay equity legislation. An abbreviated JDQ like this is unlikely to be sufficient documentation to protect you in the case of a complaint or review by a government official. Secondly, without additional questions, the evaluators will probably make assumptions about such variables as the complexity of the job after reading the list of duties and responsibilities. This is very likely to result in poor, inaccurate or gender-biased evaluations.

I suggest that you have at least one question about each of the major factors used in all job evaluation plans: skill; effort; responsibility; and working conditions. These were discussed in Chapter 3, "Selecting a Job Evaluation Plan". They do not have to be complex or difficult questions. Their only purpose is to elicit information that cannot be obtained simply by reading the list of duties. Here are some examples of questions that can be used.

MAJOR FACTOR	SAMPLE QUESTIONS
SKILL	1. What education is required to do this job?
	2. How much experience is necessary for this job?
	3. What knowledge, skills and abilities are necessary to do this job?
	4. List any special qualifications required for this job.
EFFORT	1. Describe the amount of effort necessary to complete these tasks.
	2. What mental and physical effort is required by this job?
RESPONSIBILITY	1. Describe the impact of this job on the organization.
	2. What are the end results of the successful completion of these tasks?
	3. If the job is not done satisfactorily, what is the effect on the company or the department/section?
WORKING CONDITIONS	1. Describe the physical conditions under which the work is performed.
	2. List any unusual extremes of temperature, climate or noise experienced in this work.
	3. Outline any dangerous conditions in the job.

Questions in a JDQ for a Point-Rating Plan

If you have decided to use a point-rating job evaluation plan (either off-the-shelf or custom-designed) you have to have at least one question for each of the factors in the plan. In the Tyson-Totten Job Evaluation Plan provided in Appendix D there are ten factors and there is one or more question(s) for each of them. These are shown in the JDQ (Appendix E) that is part of the plan. The main problem is ensuring that the questions reflect the definition of the factor in the job evaluation plan. This is not much of an issue with whole-job ranking because the factors are not defined. Usually they are not even identified, let alone defined.

The problem with questions in the point-rating plan is ensuring that the question matches the definition of the factor. This is especially true in the case of custom-designed plans or off-the-shelf plans that have been modified for your use. Take the factor working conditions, for example. Actually, take the issue of travel by the job-holder. Travel can be part of the definition of working conditions (where it is usually included) but can also be considered in the factor of physical effort. In Chapter 3, I discussed the issue of careful definition of the factor. In this section the issue is now extended to supplementary questions in the JDQ.

Here is another example of matching the question to the factor. One very common factor in point-rating plans is supervision. The definition, rules of application and degree levels of the factor from the Tyson-Totten Job Evaluation Plan in Appendix D are shown here:

SUPERVISION

This factor measures the degree of responsibility for supervision and direction of employees (direct and indirect). It considers the level of employees supervised and the number of positions supervised.

It also measures the extent to which the employee is responsible for the supervision and guidance of the work of other employees. Supervisory functions may include: planning, organizing, scheduling and coordinating of work; assigning of work and/or personnel; maintaining quality, accuracy and quantity of work; giving instruction, direction, guidance, discipline and advice; developing work methods, procedures and standards for the work group.

Rules of Application

1. In rating a job under this factor only use directly reporting positions when considering the number of positions supervised.
2. a. "Group A" will be understood to mean jobs that require a formal education of secondary school graduation or less.
   b. "Group B" will be understood to mean jobs that require more than secondary school graduation OR "full supervision" or at least a small unit of "Group A" employees.
3. "Full Supervision" is defined as the ability to effectively recommend the hiring, firing, discipline and assessment of employees.

Degree Levels

1. Supervisory responsibility is not normally part of the job requirements, but there may be a requirement to show other employees how to perform tasks or duties.
2. The job requires the employee to periodically assume some of the normal supervisory responsibilities over other employees.
3. The job requires that the employee act as a "team leader" to other employees. This requires that the employee normally does the same work as the employees that are supervised but, in addition, performs some of the normal supervisory functions.

4. The employee is responsible for "full" supervision of a unit of 1 to 10 Group A employees.
5. The employee is responsible for "full" supervision of a "large" (11+) unit of Group A employees OR a "small" (1-10) unit of Group B employees.
6. The employee is responsible for "full" supervision of a "large" (11+) unit of Group B employees.

There are three variables in this factor: (i) the nature of the supervision; (ii) the total number of employees supervised; and (iii) the qualifications of the employees supervised. This requires at least three questions.

The first variable is addressed by the inclusion of an organization chart in the questionnaire. It can also be answered by looking at the list of duties and responsibilities. Secondly, you have to ask the total number of employees supervised by this job. It is important to distinguish between the total number of employees and the number of employees who report *directly* to this job. Both numbers are used in job evaluation plans; the only point is to make sure that the question reflects the number you are trying to obtain.

The answer with respect to the third variable can be obtained in two ways. One is by asking the question directly: What education is required for each of the jobs shown on the organization chart in the JDQ? The other is by looking at the JDQs completed by the incumbents of those jobs. The Tyson-Totten Job Evaluation Plan in Appendix D uses the latter approach simply because it makes completion of the questionnaire easier.[5]

Here is another example of the different types of questions you might ask depending on the definition of the factor. In the table below I have illustrated two definitions of the experience factor and the sort of questions you could use.

FACTOR DEFINITION SUMMARY	QUESTION(S) FOR JDQ
The factor measures the minimum amount of experience required to perform the job.	What is the minimum amount (in months or years) of experience required for an employee to perform this job?
The factor measures the minimum amount of experience in related or lesser jobs plus the amount of time required to learn the duties of the job satisfactorily.	How much experience is required, in total, to (a) obtain this job and (b) to learn the job duties satisfactorily after the person is appointed to the job?

---

[5] Please note that I say that it is easier because I am assuming that all employees are completing a JDQ at the same time and therefore current information is available. If the JDQ is a single exercise, it may be appropriate to include the second type of question.

DISTRIBUTION AND COMPLETION OF JDQ

Once you have designed the JDQ it is necessary to distribute it to the employees. In this section I have assumed that you are starting a compensation program from scratch and therefore need to have all, or most, employees complete the questionnaire. There are a number of issues that arise from this necessity. Most of them are questions that will be asked by employees when you announce the process. The issues and the recommended actions are:

- *Who completes the JDQ?* This was discussed earlier in this chapter but there is another issue: multi-incumbent jobs. If you have 20 people doing the same job you don't want each of them completing the form. The job evaluation committee will be overwhelmed. The usual practice is to have one person (or a group of two or three) complete the form and then have it reviewed and approved by all incumbents. There should be space on the form for all of them to sign. There will often be one or more individuals who are not comfortable with somebody else describing their job (even though it is generally recognized that the jobs are the same). In such a case it is best to let that individual complete a separate JDQ. It means more paper, and a little more work for the job evaluation committee, but it is well worth it in terms of "buy-in" on the part of the employee who is raising the concern.
- *The employee will say that he "can't possibly describe the percentage of time spent on each duty".* There are several possible responses to this. The first is that yes, he can do it; thousands have done so successfully. Secondly, it is very important information. For example, take a job that involves only two responsibilities (this is a silly example designed to make the point): conducting basic research in the field of nuclear physics; and typing and filing. If the first duty entails 90% of the job and the second only 10%, the rating of the job on a factor such as complexity will be very different than if the ratio is reversed. Thirdly, the answers are not supposed to be extremely precise; normally I would not expect anyone to provide anything closer than ±5%. Fourthly, remember that this exercise is supposed to cover a complete, "normal" year. Finally, here is a technique many people have found useful. Assume the job has four duties. Use a table like the one following; list the duties and assign each of them 25% of the time.

DUTY	PERCENTAGE OF TIME
A	25
B	25
C	25
D	25

In virtually all jobs this distribution of time will not be correct. However, since it is much easier to edit than it is to write on a blank page, the employee can now proceed to adjust these numbers to fit reality. Many people have found this to be an extremely useful technique.

- *"I can't describe my job in this amount of space or only eight to ten duties."* My response is usually, fine, take as much space as you like; add extra pages and list as many duties as you feel are necessary. Just remember that the job evaluation committee may have to read hundreds of these documents and may not like to have to look at a 20-page document for your job when most of the others are only 10 pages.

- *"What if my supervisor and I don't agree?"* Handling this is usually just a matter of telling the parties to discuss and resolve the problem. One of the major side benefits of conducting this process is that it forces employees and their supervisors to talk to each other. I have often found that it is the first time they have ever discussed their understanding of the job, even though they may have worked together for years. This usually works, but in the rare case where it does not, you may have to resort to having someone from outside the department complete the JDQ. This could be someone in higher management, the human resources department, or even an outside consultant.

- *"I can't write very well (for reasons such as language, education, talent, etc.) and won't be able to describe my job so that it is given a fair rating by the committee."* My answer assumes that you have taken my advice in Chapter 3 and carefully selected a job evaluation committee. Since the committee is a cross-section of the company's employees, they will all have at least some knowledge of the job. Some will be very knowledgeable about it. This concern arises frequently and intuitively makes sense but I have found that it very seldom becomes a problem.

- *Who is going to complete the JDQ for the 20 employees in this job? Do you want 20 separate documents?* It is normally not necessary for all 20 incumbents of one job to complete a JDQ, assuming that: there is general agreement that there is one job and 20 positions (see the glossary in Appendix C for definitions of "job" and "position"); all individuals agree on who will complete the questionnaire; and they all sign the completed document.

OTHER JOB DESCRIPTION FORMATS AND USES

Many organizations require their human resources or compensation department to take the information in the JDQ and rewrite it into a formal "job description". Most clients for whom I have developed basic job evaluation systems ask me how I usually arrange for a job description to be written after I have explained the use of JDQs. My quick answer is that I don't do that. Let me explain.

The information in the JDQ is sufficient for the purposes of job evaluation. Obviously, it has to be since the document was specifically designed for just that purpose. There is no need to refine the information any further before doing the job evaluation. However, many employers do just that. They have a compensation specialist, either on staff or a temporary or contract employee, do the job. The person is required to take the JDQ and rewrite it using "standard" or common language. In my opinion this is a waste of time and money. In fact, it can be quite counter-productive in several ways:

- The act of rewriting may change the information in the original JDQ since the compensation specialist is probably not familiar with any technical terms related to the job.
- Verbs and adjectives can be extremely value laden. Rewriting the data in a common format may make use of terms that imply different values than the original author.
- One of the virtues of using the JDQ is that the incumbent(s) in the job gets to describe their own job in their own words. Having someone else rewrite the job description to make it "better" negates this advantage.
- It can extend the process of getting a complete set of "proper" job descriptions to unacceptable lengths. As a rule of thumb you should allow about two days' working time for the writer to take the original JDQ, read and understand it, perhaps interview the incumbent and then draft the new document. He should then send it to the incumbent and supervisor for their review and approval. Further revisions will result from this process and add to the time involved.
- Finally, it is not necessary. Such "proper" job descriptions are almost never used. They are put in a binder and forgotten.

CONCLUSION

In this chapter we have looked at the different methods you can use to obtain the information about jobs that you need to develop a compensation program. Once you have selected a methodology, you can design a JDQ which will be compatible with the job evaluation plan you chose in Chapter 3. You have also covered the dominant issues involved in getting the JDQ distributed and completed. When the JDQs have been completed you can go to Chapter 5 and proceed to actually evaluate jobs.

5

Conducting Job Evaluation

INTRODUCTION

Now that you have selected or modified your job evaluation plan and obtained information about the jobs in your organization, you are able to start actually doing job evaluation. This chapter will take you through:

- setting up a job evaluation committee;
- rules for the job evaluation committee;
- rules for conducting job evaluation;
- selecting benchmark jobs;
- weighting the factors;
- setting up a point table; and
- establishing point bands.

SELECTING A PLAN AND SETTING UP A COMMITTEE

In the following discussion I assume that you have decided to use the Tyson-Totten Job Evaluation Plan and have modified it to suit your particular needs and organization's culture. I also assume that you have set up a job evaluation committee according to the guidelines provided in Chapter 3, "Selecting a Job Evaluation Plan".

RULES FOR THE JOB EVALUATION COMMITTEE

Before you start evaluating jobs, you will need to establish some rules or guidelines that will govern the operations of the committee. It is very important that you establish these rules *before* starting the actual evaluation of jobs. If you do not, your committee will be continually bogged down in procedural arguments and disputes. Subjects that should be included are:

- *Voting or consensus* — When you need to make a decision, such as whether the job being evaluated is Degree 3 or 4 on the working conditions factor, will the committee vote formally or try to reach a consensus? If the committee opts for voting, is a simple majority enough or will you require something larger, such as two-thirds?

- *Selection of the chair* — If the company has a human resources officer who will be responsible for the ongoing administration of the job evaluation plan, it is quite common to have this person chair the job evaluation committee. However, if this person is neither knowledgeable nor senior enough for this role, there are other alternatives. These include having the most senior (in rank, not longevity) person on the committee or, if you have engaged a consultant to help in the process, have her become chair.

- *Role of the chair* — This essentially means whether or not you will allow the chair to vote on all issues or only when there is a deadlock or tie (see the first point). It is also possible to prohibit the chair from voting at all. This is quite common when you are using an outside consultant as chair. Since he will not be nearly as knowledgeable about the jobs or the company, it is considered unfair to give him a vote.

- *Confidentiality* — Committee discussions are not supposed to be about the personality, characteristics or performance of an individual in a job that is before the committee. This is a laudable objective and one that you should certainly try for. It is also quite unrealistic. Discussions about the individual are virtually guaranteed simply because of human nature. You will be amazed at what you will learn from these discussions. The only way I know to ensure that this information does not get spread beyond the committee is to swear everyone to secrecy. Any and all matters discussed, including any decisions taken, should not go out of the committee room unless senior management has agreed to such disclosure.

- *Quorum* — You will need to decide on a quorum for your meetings. Some committees have decided that everybody should be there before it can start work or make any decisions. This has several advantages. One is that the resources available for the process, *i.e.*, the knowledge and analytical skills of the committee members, are always there. Another is that the members are always up-to-date. I have seen committees bog down because a member was not there when critical decisions (such as the rating of a benchmark job[1] on a particular factor) were made and the absent member did not accept the decision. Another advantage is credibility with the other employees; they will be more comfortable with the evaluation of their jobs if they can be told

---

[1]   See the definition of benchmark job later in this chapter.

that all jobs were consistently evaluated by the same people. The most obvious disadvantage of a quorum of 100% is that it makes it more difficult to schedule and hold meetings. Committee members have their own full-time jobs and their bosses may not always be understanding about time needed to attend meetings. Other committees have decided on smaller quorums but I have never seen one that went lower than two-thirds of full attendance.

- *Committee members and the evaluation of their own jobs* — You must decide what role a committee member will play when it comes time for the committee to evaluate their job. In this regard I will be totally clear. They should not be in the room during this process. Furthermore, they can be shown the results of the rating of their job but there should not be any discussion in the committee. People are seldom capable of being truly objective about their own job. Prohibiting discussion limits the possibility of committee members arguing about ratings of their job, at least during the meetings. I have experienced only one instance where I was not able to convince a committee to go along with this recommendation. Usually, it is quite easy. This particular time I was the advisor to the management half of a six-person committee. The other members of the committee were union representatives who also had a consultant advising them. The client was a very large museum with a history of bad labour relations. The union people were totally aghast when my client suggested that they might not be able to be objective about their own jobs. As a compromise position we even suggested that they be present but not allowed to vote. For several reasons, the management side was essentially forced to agree to let the union committee members be involved in the evaluation of their own jobs. The result was absolutely awful; the tension in the room was almost tangible. This is the only time I have ever seen this done so I cannot claim a lot of empirical evidence. However, on the basis of this experience, I have no hesitation in advising you to avoid such a situation at virtually all costs.

- *Schedule of meetings* — It is quite productive, during the first meeting of the committee, to develop a schedule of meetings. As a rule of thumb you can figure on two to four days of orientation, training and/or modifications to any "off-the-shelf" job evaluation plan or job description questionnaire ("JDQ") that you may have acquired. Another useful guideline is that most committees can do about 10 jobs per day once they are up and running. It is also more productive if you schedule two or more days at a time. If you set up one-day meetings weeks apart, you will be astounded at how long the committee takes to get back up to speed.

RULES FOR CONDUCTING JOB EVALUATION

Here are the rules of job evaluation:

- *Evaluate one job at a time* — Some committees prefer to look at all jobs but just evaluate one factor. For instance, they will rate all jobs on the initiative factor and then proceed to the supervision factor. In my experience, it is easier and more comprehensive to rate a single job on all factors and then proceed to the next job.
- *Do the jobs in random order* — This will ensure that all jobs are evaluated more consistently across the organization than if you do them by job family or department. It will also prevent "tunnel vision" with regard to any particular type of job.
- *Rate the job, not the person* — This rule should be in upper case, 30-point type. It is the most important rule of all. Job evaluation is about the value of the job – not the value of the person in the job. It is also *not* about the performance of the incumbent. You will probably find it useful and productive to keep repeating this. Job evaluation committees seem naturally inclined to rate the person and not the job.
- *Use the documentation you have in front of you* — There are two parts to this. The first is that all the committee members will have an opinion about the job to a greater or lesser extent. These opinions may be based on factual knowledge but frequently are not. The only factual information you have is in the JDQ. Use it. The other aspect of this rule is that jobs frequently change. Duties are added or deleted, authority levels are decreased or increased, and qualifications are changed. You cannot rate the job on what it used to be and you should not rate the job on what it might or might not be in the future. The only concrete information that you have is the job as it exists today. Evaluate it with this data. Anything else is speculation.

SELECTING BENCHMARK JOBS

Benchmark jobs, in a point-rating plan, serve two functions. First, they become the test jobs on which you will determine whether the factors and degree levels that you have tentatively chosen will work. Secondly, they form an integral part of the job evaluation plan as they are considered excellent examples of each degree definition. When you are finished setting up the plan, a page in the plan for any factor will look like this:

[*FACTOR NAME*]

Definition

Degree Level	Benchmark Job
1. Degree Definition	Benchmark Job A Title
2. Degree Definition[2]	Benchmark Job B Title
	Benchmark Job C Title
3. Degree Definition	Benchmark Job D Title
4. Degree Definition	Benchmark Job E Title

Benchmark jobs are not included in the prototype plan in Appendix D because the plan is generic. It is designed to be used for a wide variety of jobs, organizations and employee groups. Benchmark jobs can only be selected in a specific group of jobs; generic benchmark jobs do not work.

In selecting benchmark jobs look for the following characteristics:

- multi-incumbent jobs rather than single incumbent ones;
- well-understood jobs which do not involve obscure technology or require very unusual skills;
- visible jobs, in the sense that most employees will have seen them — a receptionist or sales representative is a good example of a highly visible job;
- non-contentious jobs which have not been subject to disputes regarding content (duties), required skill and knowledge and/or grading;
- well-established jobs, not newly created ones that few people understand well;
- cover the whole range of jobs;
- good examples of degree levels (this is difficult to determine ahead of time and is usually finalized during the initial evaluation proceedings);
- good data about the job being readily available (do not select a job for which the incumbent and/or supervisor is unlikely to co-operate or pick a job in which none of the incumbents speak the official language(s) of the organization).

---

[2] Note that there are two benchmark jobs in Degree 2 — it is possible, and often desirable, to have more than one benchmark job in each degree.

WEIGHTING THE FACTORS

Once you have rated all the benchmark jobs, you have to weight (not weigh, you don't care how heavy they are) the factors. You can do this after you have rated all the jobs but I prefer to do it after the benchmarks have been evaluated.

Weighting the factors is necessary unless you consider them all to be of equal significance. Some plans make all the factors equal but this is very rare. Hardly anybody considers the working conditions factor to have the same impact on the value of a job as a factor such as accountability. You can do this exercise before you start evaluating but I have found that the evaluation process helps the committee members to clarify and refine the definitions of the factors. Therefore, weighting the factors after doing the evaluations results in a better product. To do the weighting requires a worksheet like this:

FACTOR WEIGHTING WORKSHEET

FACTOR	FIRST WEIGHT	SECOND WEIGHT	THIRD WEIGHT	FINAL
Communications/Contacts				
Complexity				
Mental Effort				
Physical Effort				
Accountability				
Independent Action/Initiative				
Working Conditions				
Supervision				
Education				
Experience				
TOTAL	100	100	100	100

Have each committee member work separately. In the first column, they should place the percentage of the total weight that they think should be allocated to each factor. They can be as precise as they like but it is easier and more realistic to use multiples of 5%. Obviously, the total should come to 100. Two other columns are provided as they often need several tries at this. Once each individual has done this on his own, have the group post their results on a flipchart or blackboard. You can then use your facilitation skills to reach a consensus. This is much easier than most people think when this process is first described to them. I have never failed to have a committee agree on an acceptable weighting of the factors. The following table shows the typical range of weightings used in organizations in North America:

FACTOR	TYPICAL RANGE (%)
Communications/Contacts	5 - 15
Complexity	10 - 20
Mental Effort	5 - 10
Physical Effort	5 - 10
Accountability	10 - 20
Independent Action/Initiative	5 - 15
Working Conditions	5 - 10
Supervision	5 - 15
Education	10 - 20
Experience	10 - 20

DEVELOPING A POINT TABLE

Once you have weighted the factors you are now in a position to develop a point table based on these weightings. There are three major ways to develop a point table but for all of them you need a worksheet that looks like the one below:

WORKSHEET FOR DEVELOPING A POINT TABLE

FACTOR/ DEGREE	1	2	3	4	5	6	7	8
Communications/Contacts	10							
Complexity	10							
Mental Effort	5							
Physical Effort	5							
Accountability	15							
Independent Action/Initiative	5							
Working Conditions	5							
Supervision	10							
Education	15							
Experience	20							
Other factors								

Place the weightings developed in the previous step in column 1 which also represents Degree 1 or the first degree in each factor. Use this same method for setting the value of the first degree in all three methods of building a point table. As a quality control check make sure the values in that first column add to 100. Following that, there are three ways to proceed. (Each of the following methods has a corresponding spreadsheet on the CD-ROM that comes with this book. You can record the results of your evaluations in the spreadsheet you choose to use, then try different variations of the same method to see how the point totals turn out.)

Method A

Pick a multiple (usually 5 or 10) which will be the maximum number of points that a job can obtain. Since the minimum number of points that any job could be given is 100 (if the job is evaluated at Degree 1 in every factor but this is very unlikely), if you select 5 as a multiple the maximum number will be 500. If you select 10 the maximum will be 1,000. As a rough rule of thumb any company with fewer than 200 jobs should be able to make do with 500 maximum points. Over 200 jobs you should consider using 1,000 points. You may have to experiment with both options to determine which is best.

For the rest of this example, I will assume that you have chosen a multiple of 5 and therefore a maximum of 500 points. Allocate this 500 points to each of the factors in the same proportion as the weights. Here is a table showing the calculation:

CALCULATING POINTS FOR THE HIGHEST DEGREE LEVEL

FACTOR	WEIGHT	WEIGHT x 5
Communications/Contacts	10	50
Complexity	10	50
Mental Effort	5	25
Physical Effort	5	25
Accountability	15	75
Independent Action/Initiative	5	25
Working Conditions	5	25
Supervision	10	50
Education	15	75
Experience	20	100
TOTAL	**100**	**500**

The value in the right-hand column becomes the number of points for the highest degree of the factor. Since the number of degrees usually varies from factor to factor this means that the highest number of points in the factor does not always go to the same degree number. Here are two examples.

Factor	Number of Degrees	First Degree Value	Highest Degree Value
Working Conditions	4	5	25
Mental Effort	5	5	25

You now have to calculate the point values for each degree level within each factor. Actually you have to calculate the increment between degree levels and then determine each degree level. Here is the formula for this procedure:

$$\text{Increment} = \frac{\text{Highest degree level} - \text{lowest degree level}}{\text{Number of degrees} - 1}$$

Here are the calculations for both factors:

Factor	Number of Degrees	Calculation	Result = increment
Working Conditions	4	$\dfrac{25 - 5}{4 - 1}$	6.7
Mental Effort	5	$\dfrac{25 - 5}{5 - 1}$	5

This would make the point values for all degrees in each factor as follows:

Factor	Degree 1	Degree 2	Degree 3	Degree 4	Degree 5
Working Conditions	5	11.7 **(11)**	18.4 **(18)**	25.1 **(25)**	
Mental Effort	5	10	15	20	25

You can see that in the working conditions factor this formula results in a decimal number. Using fractions for the increment implies a level of precision to a point-rating plan that in fact does not exist. Therefore when the calculation result is a decimal like 6.7, I take this to mean the increment should be either 6 or 7 and adjust the calculation of the degree point values so that the increment increases as you go up the scale. The boldface numbers for working conditions in the table illustrate this. The increment (that I will use) between Degrees 1 and 2 is 6 points and the two other increments are 7 points. In contrast, with the mental effort factor, the formula resulted in an increment of an even 5 points. You do not have to smooth it out as I have shown with the working conditions factor but I find that doing so makes the point table less cluttered.

Method B

The second method of building a point table is to arbitrarily pick a number to be the increment for all factors. Let's use 7 to illustrate this. Use the same weights for Degree 1 as in the previous method and simply add 7 until there is a value for each degree. Here is the calculation for two other factors using this method:

Factor	1	2	3	4	5	6	7	8
Communications/Contacts	10	17	24	31	38			
Education	15	22	29	36	43	50	57	64

Method C

The third method is to use the weight, or the value of Degree 1, as the increment for that factor. Let's use the factors in the table above to illustrate this method. You can see that, in the communications factor, Degree 2 becomes 20 points, Degree 3 is 30 points and so on.

Factor	1	2	3	4	5	6	7	8
Communications/Contacts	10	20	30	40	50			
Education	15	30	45	60	75	90	105	120

Choosing a Method of Building a Point Table

All of the methods shown above work satisfactorily. There are two factors that you should consider in choosing a methodology:

1. How much do you like the logic of the method? The logic for each method is slightly different. Technical staff, like engineers and accountants, tend to like the first method but the other two are used frequently.
2. How easy is it going to be to communicate? Consider the audience (*i.e.*, the occupational groups covered by the plan), their degree of sophistication and the amount of interest they are likely to show. To be honest, most employees couldn't care less how you build the point table.

ESTABLISHING POINT BANDS

Once you have evaluated all the jobs and calculated the point total, the remaining step is to establish your point bands. To do this, list all the jobs in descending order of point totals, *i.e.*, from highest to lowest. You can use any of the spreadsheets for Chapter 5 from the CD-ROM that comes with this book — just sort by the column with the point totals. Here is a partial example of such a list taken from a client which manufactures and distributes personal care products in their own and franchised retail outlets:

JOB TITLE	POINT TOTAL
Director, Retail Operations	472
Financial Comptroller	468
Operations Director	446
Franchising Director	438
Systems Manager	400
Corporate Business Manager	389
Manager, Store Support	385
Human Resources Manager	363
Maintenance Manager	357
Production and Quality Control Manager	349
Warehouse Manager	348
Store Manager	341
Customer Service Manager	335
Accountant	332
Payroll Supervisor	315
Training Coordinator	314
Machine Operator	302
Office Manager	298
Warehouse Supervisor	287
Communications Assistant	285
Production Scheduler	282
Franchise Coordinator	281
Shipper/Receiver	279
Head Mixer	267
Accounting Clerk	258
Customer Service Representative	238
Consumer Help Desk	227
Accounts Payable Clerk	223
Merchandising Assistant	215
Compounder	214
Payroll Clerk	212
Junior Sales Associate	203
Packer	196
Training Coordinator	189
Receptionist	189
Picker	187
Shrink Wrap Operator	171
Cleaner/Helper	148
Gift Maker	130
Assistant Customer Service Representative	125

You can see from the description of Method A that no job can have less than 100 points and no more than 500 points. This means that there are 400 points available for distribution. With Methods B and C the minimum remains the same while the maximum varies slightly. The objective of this exercise is to determine how to "group" those 400 points in Method A. Similarly, with the other methods, it is to group the difference in points between the minimum of 100 and the maximum points available.

First, obtain several coloured pens or pencils. Then scan the list and, using one colour, draw lines between the jobs that you feel should be separated in pay (always assume that the job is being performed satisfactorily and that there is no difference in length of service of the incumbents). There are several possible reasons why jobs should have separate pay rates. One is that a particular job is the manager or supervisor of the other. For example, the accounting supervisor is normally paid more than an accounting clerk who reports to her. Another reason is that there is a hierarchy of jobs, such as master carpenter and apprentice carpenter, and the master is always paid more. The most common reason is that there is a "perceived" difference in value between two jobs. Once you have done this, count the number of groupings you have established. Divide this into the number of points available.

Suppose, for example, that you have roughly determined there should be 10 groupings. We have already established that there are 400 points available. Divide the points by the number of groups and you have the "point band width". In this example $400 \div 10 = 40$. You can then establish your point bands and salary grades as follows:

SALARY GRADE	POINT BAND
10	460+
9	420-459
8	380-419
7	340-379
6	300-339
5	260-299
4	220-259
3	180-219
2	140-179
1	100-139

If, on the other hand, you had determined that there should be 12 groupings of jobs, you would divide 400 by 12 with the result being 33.3. Since point tables almost never use fractions of points you can round this to 30 or 35. In the table below you can see the point bands that would result for each of these alternatives for the first 5 grades.

SALARY GRADE	BAND WIDTH = 30	BAND WIDTH = 35
5	220-249	240-274
4	190-219	205-239
3	160-189	170-204
2	130-159	135-169
1	100-129	100-134

It is usually necessary to experiment with several band widths. To see the effect, take each set of point bands and, using a different colour each time, draw lines where the point bands will fall. For example, if you want to try out a 35-point band with the set of job ratings shown here, you will draw a line between the Payroll Clerk and the Junior Sales Associate to establish the top of the band at 204 points. The bottom line (170 points) will be between the jobs of Shrink Wrap Operator and Cleaner/Helper.

Try several different options and pick the one that appears to be the "most reasonable" or the best fit with the values of your organization. There is no scientific way to make this decision. It is strictly a judgment call. The effect of selecting your point bands is that jobs are now grouped into these bands. These groupings can be numbered and they are called salary grades. In Chapter 7, "Putting it All Together—Basic Salary Administration", I will show you how to establish actual dollar amounts to go with these salary grades.

CONCLUSION

The final result of this exercise is a "classification structure". An abbreviated version of the previous list of jobs is shown on the next page as a classification structure (this particular client used 40-point bands).

EXAMPLE OF CLASSIFICATION STRUCTURE
ABC COMPANY — JANUARY 1, 2003

SALARY GRADE	JOB TITLE
9	Director, Retail Operations Financial Comptroller Operations Director
8	Systems Manager Manager, Store Support Human Resources Manager Maintenance Manager Production & Quality Control Manager
7	Store Manager Warehouse Manager Customer Service Manager Accountant Payroll Supervisor Training Coordinator Machine Operator
6	Office Manager Warehouse Supervisor Communications Assistant Production Scheduler Franchise Coordinator
5	Shipper/Receiver Head Mixer
4	Accounting Clerk Customer Service Representative Consumer Help Desk Accounts Payable Clerk
3	Merchandising Assistant Compounder Payroll Clerk Junior Sales Associate Packer Training Coordinator Receptionist Picker
2	Shrink Wrap Operator Cleaner/Helper
1	Gift Maker

What does it mean to say that two particular jobs are in the same salary grade? Essentially, it means that the jobs (not the incumbents) are considered to be equal in value. Everyone in the jobs in a salary grade will be paid the same, unless you have a salary administration system which differentiates on the basis of employee performance or seniority. For pay equity purposes, the jobs will have the same job rate. This will become clearer in Chapter 7.

6

Salary Surveys

INTRODUCTION

At this stage you need to obtain some information about what the labour market is paying for the kinds of jobs that you have in your company. This means using one or more published (also known as "off-the-shelf") surveys or conducting a survey yourself. This chapter will start by briefly discussing why you need to use surveys at all. It will then describe the major types of surveys and outline the advantages and disadvantages of each of them. After that we will look at the mechanics of using published surveys (including ageing the data) and/or conducting your own. The final section in this chapter will show you how to take the information obtained and build a set of salary range control points that can be used to build a salary structure (discussed in the next chapter).

WHY DO SALARY SURVEYS?

The end result of the processes described in Chapter 4, "Obtaining Information About Jobs", and Chapter 5, "Conducting Job Evaluation", is a classification structure, which is a list of jobs ranked according to their relative value to you, the employer, and grouped into a series of salary grades.[1] The problem here is that the classification structure does not have any dollar or monetary values attached to it. It tells you that job A is two salary grades higher than job B but not how many dollars each of them should be paid. You could just arbitrarily assign monetary values to the grades but you would not have any

---

[1] See the example at the end of Chapter 5.

assurance that the resulting numbers will bear any resemblance to what other companies are paying. Since you need to pay enough in order to attract new employees to your company and to ensure that your current employees do not go elsewhere for more money, it is necessary to find out what the labour market is paying. To do this you have to acquire (buy or borrow) and/or conduct salary surveys. The major types of surveys are discussed below.

TYPES OF SALARY SURVEYS

Published Surveys

The first are called published, canned or off-the-shelf surveys and are conducted by Boards of Trade, Chambers of Commerce, industry associations, magazines, management consulting firms and various government bodies. A list of some of the publicly available surveys in Canada is provided in Appendix B. They are listed by the organization conducting the survey with information about the occupational groups and geographical areas covered, and the type of data (salaries, bonuses, benefits, working conditions, etc.). Contact data is also provided.

Published salary surveys can be an extremely useful source of information but they do require a certain amount of interpretation. The important thing to remember is that they are done for the purposes of other organizations, not yours, and you therefore have to work at extracting the information that is relevant to you. The information is there but you usually have to dig for it.

The advantage of canned surveys is that the work is already completed and the data is quickly available. I have listed below the disadvantages of such surveys. The list seems extensive but in practice is usually overwhelmed by the fact that you can quickly obtain the data. Here is the list:

- They are expensive. For example, the 1997 Metropolitan Toronto Board of Trade *Clerical Compensation Survey*[2] for the Greater Toronto Area is available to non-members (of the Board) for $419, to members for $335.20, and to companies who participate in the survey for $80.[3] Obviously, participating in the survey can save you a lot of money but this means that you have to know that you will require the data about six months in advance.
- They often don't include the jobs, geography or industries about which you need information. Take the *Clerical Compensation Survey* just mentioned: it is an excellent survey in terms of the number of companies and number of jobs that are included but it is restricted to the Greater Toronto Area ("GTA"). If your company is located in Yellowknife this survey is of no use whatsoever. It does include a large number of industries but only breaks

---

[2]   Board of Trade of Metropolitan Toronto, *Clerical Compensation Survey* (1997).
[3]   Add GST to all these prices.

them down into major groupings, such as durable goods manufacturing, government or finance. If your company is one of the five to ten in a small industry such as great lakes shipping, it can be difficult to get the data you need. If you want data about your own industry in a particular part of the country it can be even more difficult to utilize such a survey.

* They are out of date before they are published. The larger the survey, either in number of jobs or participating companies, the more truth there is to this statement. For example, there is one national survey of executive positions which collects data as of January 1st but is usually not available until the following June. In many cases this is not a problem; major changes in salary levels or programs take many years to become common practice, especially in larger companies. However, in smaller companies, or in job categories in which change is frequent and significant, such as information technology ("IT"), this can be problematic.

Executive Compensation Data

In both Canada and the United States, securities regulators have decreed that companies have to report various aspects of the compensation packages of their senior executives. The timing, specific executives and particulars of their compensation vary between the jurisdictions. However, this does mean that data on executive compensation, in public companies, is readily available. Unfortunately, since it is put in annual reports, it can be quite old when it is actually available. Here is a very brief summary of the rules for Canada which were set by the Ontario Securities Commission in 1993.

Companies are required to report in their information circulars or proxies the following information:[4]

* Compensation for these executives:
    * Chief Executive Officer ("CEO"), regardless of pay;
    * the four highest paid executives, other than the CEO, who are employed at the end of the fiscal year and earned more than $100,000 in salary and bonus during the last fiscal year;
    * any executive who left the company during the last fiscal year who otherwise would have been reported as one of the four highest paid executives.
* A summary table for all officers of the company for the past three years showing:
    * salary;
    * bonus;
    * other compensation, such as perquisites, interest or dividends on securities, options and stock appreciation rights ("SARs");

---

[4] This data can be obtained from the annual reports of the companies and/or at the website www.sedar.com.

- long-term compensation, including number of options, restricted stock and restricted stock unit awards, and long-term incentive plan payments in dollars.
- A summary table showing the number and terms of options and SARs granted. These must also be shown as a percentage of those granted to all employees during the last fiscal year. Grants must be shown separately.
- A summary table showing the aggregate number of option SARs exercised in the last fiscal year.
- An option/SAR repricing table for all officers whose options/SARs are priced downward.
- Performance-based long-term incentive plans or awards in the last fiscal year.
- Defined benefit or actuarial plan disclosure including supplementary or excess pension award plans.
- Employment contracts, termination, severance and change-of-control arrangements.
- Director compensation, including the name of each director and the amount paid. Non-standard arrangements must also be provided.
- Compensation committee interlocks and insider participation.
- Directors, executive officers and senior officers who are indebted to the company for purchase of company stock or other reasons.
- A report by the compensation committee.
- A performance graph which provides five years of company performance relative to a broad market index, such as the Toronto Stock Exchange 300. Performance is measured by cumulative total return to shareholders.

Third-Party Surveys

If you are a major, or even a minor, player in your area or industry you will often be asked to participate in surveys done by third parties. These are usually other human resource managers who are conducting their own custom survey. These can often be time-consuming and of little use to you if not done well. It therefore behooves you to examine carefully how the survey will be done before agreeing to participate. You may be contacted prior to the survey questionnaire being issued. This is a good sign; it means that the person conducting the survey is ensuring that there will be a respectable number of qualified participants before actually sending out the document. If you receive an unsolicited survey in the mail (regular or electronic) take a careful look before spending the time to complete it. The items to look for are really the same items you should consider in designing your own custom survey:

- Are the survey jobs ones that exist in your organization?
- Does it cover the geographical area in which you operate?
- Will it provide data that you don't have or can't obtain by more effective means?

- Are you confident that the survey sponsor will actually produce a participants' report in a timely manner? If they don't, you receive no benefit from participating. This is quite a serious problem. (One major cultural institution in Toronto did a large survey of non-management staff in the late 1980s. As usual, it promised all the other major institutions a participants' report but, for a variety of reasons, was unable to do so.)
- Does the timing of the final report meet your needs?
- Does it include employers about which you would like data or, putting it another way, are they organizations with whom you compete for staff?

SELECTING AND INTERPRETING PUBLISHED SURVEYS

Which surveys should you use? Cost is an obvious criterion. However, in addition to cost, you should look at both the jobs in the survey and the geographical area covered. You will often have to use more than one survey to obtain enough data to build a salary structure. In order to illustrate the decisions involved, I have shown the relevance of two surveys for two types of companies in different cities in Canada. One company is located in Calgary and is an IT consulting company. The other sample company is located in Toronto and is an auto-parts manufacturer. The Calgary company is Tundra Consulting Associates and the Toronto organization is Cheap Parts Inc. The two surveys I compare are the Compensation and Benefits Survey for Hourly Employees conducted by the Alliance of Exporters and Manufacturers of Canada[5] and the Executive Compensation Survey produced by the Board of Trade of Metropolitan Toronto. Here is the comparison:

COMPANY/ EMPLOYEES	ALLIANCE HOURLY	BOARD OF TRADE EXECUTIVE
Tundra/Clerical	Not relevant	Not relevant
Tundra/Executive	Not relevant	Not relevant
Cheap Parts/Clerical	Somewhat relevant	Not relevant
Cheap Parts/Hourly	Relevant	Not relevant
Cheap Parts/Executive	Not relevant	Very relevant
Tundra/Middle Management	Not relevant	Somewhat relevant

Surveys have to be interpreted carefully. It is not inaccurate to say that I can prove practically anything you want me to prove using several published surveys. This is one of the less obvious reasons why most human resource

---

[5] Formerly the Canadian Manufacturers' Association.

departments keep the surveys that they purchase under lock and key. Employees who are not trained in using salary surveys tend to "see what they want to see" when they are looking at these surveys.

Once you have selected the survey, the first step is to identify the jobs included in it that will match jobs in your company. This is the opposite of the process used in doing your own survey, where you pick the jobs you want to survey and then venture forth and get information about them. I have already discussed the need to try and find at least one job, for survey purposes, in each of the grades in the classification structure. This is not always possible. This is one of the reasons why you do job evaluation. A classification structure allows you to set salary range control points for jobs for which there is no market data, since it establishes the value of such jobs relative to those that you are able to price in the labour marketplace.

With published surveys, you are often able to find market data for several jobs in one salary grade and no data at all for jobs in other grades. Obtain the market data from a survey for as many jobs in the classification structure as you can. It is very difficult, and unusual, to get too much market data. Once you have identified the jobs in the survey that are a close match with those at your company, you have to look at the salary data.[6]

Surveys vary widely in the amount of data that they provide but this is one of the items that affects your choice of survey. Many surveys, especially those for jobs that appear in the lower levels of an organization (*e.g.*, clerical, hourly or non-supervisory), often just report base salary and then only the median or average. The type of jobs is not the possible problem. It is the data reported. If your policy position[7] is to pay at the middle of the market, then averages and/or medians are fine. However, if your policy is to set base salaries at the third quartile and the survey only provides averages, you have a problem. In fact, the survey is virtually useless to you.

However, since most employers say that their policy position is to be at the middle of the market, any survey that reports averages or median will be useful as long as it includes jobs that can also be found in your company. Reproduced below are several lines from a widely used survey in a major Canadian city. Let's look at the data. (Some of the headings have been shortened further than in the actual survey for space reasons.)

---

[6] Using benefits surveys is covered in Chapter 8, "Benefits Basics".
[7] See Chapter 2, "Strategy", for a discussion of compensation policy.

JOB	Mail Clerk	Travel Administrator	Customer Service Representative
Total # of Organizations	201	12	167
Total # of Incumbents	452	31	1897
First Quartile	$22,652	$27,983	$28,700
Median	$24,600	$31,365	$32,288
Third Quartile	$27,367	$37,105	$35,465
Avg. Range Minimum	$21,320	$26,958	$27,983
Avg. Range Maximum	$29,213	$36,900	$38,950
Avg. Actual Salary	$25,112	$32,288	$32,390
No Bonus — Avg. Actual Salary	$24,702	$30,750	$32,185
% of Organizations with Bonus Plans	33	19	29
% of Incumbents Receiving Bonus	86	X	79
Avg. Actual Base Salary	$25,933	$37,925	$32,697
Avg. Bonus Paid Last Fiscal Year	$1,127	X	$1,742
Avg. Target Bonus as % of Base Salary	5.1	X	4.9
Avg. Total Compensation	$27,163	X	$34,645

Let's look at several of the more critical categories, starting with the number of organizations and number of incumbents. These are two of the most critical variables; they affect the credibility of the data. Basically, for these two variables, more is almost always better. The larger the sample, both of incumbents and organizations, the more likely the data is to be valid and useful. Of the three jobs shown in the table above, mail clerk and customer service representative report very large numbers and can be considered representative of the labour market. On the other hand, the third job, travel administrator, shows a relatively smaller number of observations in both categories. Although this makes the data less reliable, it does not mean you should reject it. It will often be the only data obtainable. I have often used survey data which contained only three observations. (Most surveys do not report any data if there are fewer than three observations.) Selecting the data to use is very much a balancing act between the reliability of the data available and your need for some numbers. It can also be very important if you have to present the data to a body, such as the

Board of Directors and the Vice-President of Human Resources of your parent company.

Looking at the numbers of organizations reporting and incumbents will enable you to narrow down the possible number of job matches. Once you have done this, you can then look at the salary data you want to use for each job. Before you can do this you have to review your policy position; that is, at what point in the spectrum of values in the marketplace do you want your salary position to be? The survey results shown here report the upper and lower quartiles and the median. It also shows the average actual salary, although this piece of data is three rows further on. Remember that these results are for base salary only, not total cash compensation. If your policy position is that you want to pay at the middle of the market then the median and average numbers are the only ones you need. (If I have to choose between the median and the average, I will take the median, but both are perfectly acceptable.) If, on the other hand, you want to pay base salaries that are above or below the market, the upper and lower quartiles are the ones you need. This assumes, of course, that you want to pay at one of the quartile positions. Some employers develop a policy position that they will pay base salaries that are, for example, 10% below the middle of the market and total cash compensation that is above the market. The difference between base and total is made up by bonus, profit-sharing or productivity gainsharing plans of some sort. This exercise is relatively straightforward. The use of the next pieces of data is more complex.

This particular survey (like many others) reports the average minimum and maximum of the salary ranges for each job. Personally, I don't find this very useful data. This is because you normally construct your salary ranges around your policy position (*e.g.*, upper quartile) regarding the labour market and the salary range width you have selected. The survey does not report policy position or average range widths (some surveys do report range widths) and therefore it is impossible to compare your practices with the companies in the survey. The average range minimum is somewhat useful in that you can compare your minimum with it to show how low you can go when determining starting salaries. This is much more important when using a step-rate salary range than with a 3M system.[8]

The next item in this survey is the average actual salary of the incumbents. This is really only a substitute for the median as you can see that the averages provided in the table are virtually identical to the medians for the same job. It is sometimes useful to compare the average to give you an idea of the distribution of the data. The next item is the average actual salary of those incumbents who are not eligible for a bonus. You can contrast this with the average actual salary of those who are eligible for bonuses (three rows down). This is often very useful data especially when you are researching pay for jobs where bonuses are

---

[8]   Step-rate and 3M systems of salary administration are defined in the next chapter.

a large part of the total cash compensation package. This is not usually the case with lower-level jobs, such as the ones in this particular survey.

All of the following data relates to companies and/or employees who have, or participate in, bonus plans. If you have decided that these types of jobs will not be part of any bonus plan(s), you cannot just ignore this data, since it is all part of the labour market in which you are competing for staff. Companies with bonuses for these types of jobs form a significant proportion of the market. For example, 29% of the companies reporting on the messenger jobs have bonus plans, while 34% of those with customer service representatives have such plans.

The next item in the table is the percentage of incumbents who actually receive a bonus. Ninety per cent of the mail clerks and 84% of the customer service representatives receive a bonus. One of the things these numbers indicate to me is that these companies have what I call "token" bonus plans. In other words, if such a high percentage of employees are receiving a bonus, is it really contingent on performance or is it just like salary except that it is paid in a different format and at a different time of year? Perhaps I am just a cynic. The next item is the target bonus as a percentage of the base salary. This is not particularly useful information, except to tell you that the companies in the survey have set "normal" or realistic targets for their bonus programs.

The final number is the average total compensation. This is particularly useful if you have decided, in your policy deliberations, that you wish your base salary to be competitive with the total cash compensation of other companies. There are several caveats that you need to be aware of with this particular piece of data. First, strictly speaking, it is not total compensation, since compensation includes benefits, perquisites and other items. It is probably more accurate to describe this item as total cash compensation as opposed to a total of *all* compensation, which usually includes many non-cash items, such as life insurance or a pension plan. Secondly, it is the average total only for those employees of companies in the survey which have bonus plans. Thirdly, it is not clear from the survey report whether or not this number includes cash payments, such as those from a team incentive or productivity gainsharing plan. Some surveys separate bonus plans from other types of variable pay, which are still paid in cash, such as cash profit sharing, lump sum, merit awards or commission plans for sales representatives.

Suppose that your policy is to pay at the middle of the labour market for clerical employees. This survey presents you with four choices about which piece of data to use. These are shown in the next table with the actual data for the three jobs:

SURVEY ITEM	Mail Clerk	Travel Administrator	Customer Service Representative
Average Actual Salary	$25,112	$32,288	$32,390
No Bonus – Average Actual Salary	$24,702	$30,750	$32,185
Average Actual Base Salary (with bonus)	$25,933	$37,925	$32,697
Average Total Compensation	$27,163	N/A	$34,645

This is a dilemma. Your policy position is quite clear but you have a choice of four numbers with two of the jobs and three for the travel administrator. In the following table, I have shown four variations on your policy position along with the four choices of "middle" market data numbers that can be used. In the body of the table, I have indicated my opinion as to the usability of each number with each policy position. As you can see, there are at least two survey numbers that could be used validly with each variation of "the middle of the market". There is really no scientific way to decide this issue. It is very much a judgment call. Use the number that you feel most comfortable with. If you have an employee advisory committee, or even an executive committee at your company, consult with them. Remember that your decision will be tested quite rigorously when you go to the market and try to hire people. Also, don't be fooled by the particular numbers in the sample data I have presented here. Some of the options are quite close in this example, but in other surveys or other job matches there can be significant differences.

POLICY RE: BASE SALARY	AVERAGE BASE SALARY ALL COMPANIES	AVERAGE BASE SALARY NO BONUS	AVERAGE BASE SALARY WITH BONUS	AVERAGE TOTAL WITH BONUS
MIDDLE	Yes	Yes	No	No
MIDDLE NO BONUS	Yes	Yes	No	No
MIDDLE WITH BONUS	No	No	Yes	Yes
MIDDLE TOTAL	No	No	Yes	Yes

AGEING THE SURVEY DATA

Once you have selected the statistic(s) from the survey that you want to use, you have to age the data. This means adjusting it so that all the numbers you use are current as of the date that you want your salary structure to be effective. To illustrate, let's assume that you have used one survey which collected data effective April 1, 2002. You are now in November of the same year and want to have your new salary program effective January 1, 2003.

If you use the data from the survey without adjustments, it will be nine months old on the effective date of your new salary structure. Compensation is a moving target and, in order to keep your salary program current, you need to update this data. There are two sources of statistics that you can use for this purpose — reports of salary movements in the past year and/or changes in the Consumer Price Index ("CPI") issued by Statistics Canada. However, the most important item that compensation practitioners are interested in is the price of labour.

A word of warning here about the CPI. Most people, when they talk about how their compensation package has increased or decreased during a specific period of time, will quote changes in the CPI. This has a great deal of validity, since the CPI represents the purchasing power of their compensation package. However, you have to recognize that it measures changes in the cost of a basket of goods consumed by a "typical" family as defined by Statistics Canada. This "basket" contains virtually all the items that will be purchased by this family except for labour. The CPI does not measure the cost of labour in any way. In spite of this warning, survey change data and CPI numbers are usually so close that many compensation professionals use them interchangeably. However, if you insist on being a purist when you age your survey data, you have to use salary survey increase data. I prefer to use salary survey data.

The methodology used to age your data is the same with both statistics. Assume that the surveys indicate that, over the past 12 months, salaries increased by 4% and that the same surveys forecast an increase of 4% for the next 12 months. Therefore the data indicates that salaries are increasing by 0.33% per month. In the example given here you need to age the survey data by nine months. If you had a benchmark (survey) job which had a median salary as of April 1, 2002, of $60,000 the calculation will look like this:

Salary Jan. 1/03 = Salary April 1, 2002 + (number of months × average % increase per month)
= $60,000 + (9 × 0.33%)
= $60,000 + 2.97%
= $60,000 × 1.0297
= $61,782

This means that you will use $61,782 as the piece of survey data in the development of your salary range control points, discussed further on in this chapter.

CONSOLIDATING SEVERAL SURVEYS

It is quite common to be in a position where you have several surveys available to you. If you wish to use all of them it becomes necessary to consolidate the results. As part of this chapter, I have provided a spreadsheet (on the accompanying CD-ROM) which you can use to record the data from a variety of surveys that you think you might need and then assess it later. This is useful because you are often limited in the amount of time you have to look at a survey that is borrowed or may be in a library. The various headings are shown here. Simply fill in the data; age it according to the instructions in the previous section; then, in Column Q, you can pick the numbers that really matter to you.

Here is a table with the column titles from the worksheet and a brief explanation of the data to be input or the formula that is already in the spreadsheet. (It is in three parts simply for space reasons.)

Name of the employee	Your job title	Current salary	Name of survey	Job title in the survey	Geography	Specifications	Number of organizations	Number of incumbents
A	B	C	D	E	F	G	H	I
Optional (It is not strictly necessary for survey purposes)	Use the official job title from your organization	Put in the current salaries	Name of the survey you are using	Title of job in survey matched to your job in column B	Area for survey data to be used	Sales volume/ number of employees/ assets/type of industry	Number of organizations that provided data for this job	Number of incumbents reported in this job

Average	Median	Third Quartile	Ageing factor	Adjusted average	Adjusted median	Adjusted Q3	Select Yes/No	Selected number
J	K	L	M	N	O	P	Q	R
Average salary	Median salary	Third quartile salary	Put in a factor to age the data	Column M × Column J	Column M × Column K	Column M × Column L	Put "Yes" if you decide to use this particular piece of data	Copy the selected number here

Survey # as % of actual salary		
S		
Column R as a percentage of Column C		

CONDUCTING YOUR OWN SALARY SURVEY

Although it is easier and faster to use published surveys, it is sometimes necessary to conduct your own, since published surveys may not:

- include or separate out your industry;
- contain the types of jobs you need to identify;
- report the data you want, such as top decile numbers for base salary, salary ranges, a particular geographical region, or bonuses;
- be available when needed (for example, the *Clerical Compensation Survey* reports data as of the spring and is usually available in late summer or early fall — if you are developing a new salary program in February, you can either use data that is almost one year old or conduct your own survey).

There are a number of issues that you need to resolve before you start your research. These include (in the approximate order in which you should consider them):

- the jobs to be included;
- the cash[9] compensation information to be requested;
- the area in which to conduct the survey;
- the companies which will be invited to participate;
- whether to conduct the survey by mail, telephone or in person; and
- whether to provide a participants' report.

Jobs to Include

Custom surveys are usually a second choice when the published ones do not provide the data that you need. This usually means that you do not have data about certain jobs. Normally, you are able to obtain market data for a range of jobs in your classification structure. The lack of data for certain jobs is the normal motivation to conduct your own survey. These jobs are often in the middle half of the classification structure.[10] This is because the jobs at both ends of the structure are easy to locate in surveys. At the lower end, jobs such as general labour, junior clerk and messenger/mail clerk are quite common in surveys, since virtually all companies have them. The same situation exists at the other end of the spectrum. All companies have a president, CEO or general manager and vice-presidents or directors. Such jobs are always included in managerial or executive surveys.

---

[9]   For the purposes of this chapter, I will restrict my comments to surveys about cash compensation. Benefits surveys are covered in Chapter 8. However, you should note that custom surveys often combine cash compensation and benefits.

[10]   See the sample structure at the end of Chapter 5.

As I said, the problem lies in the middle and/or with jobs that are unique to your company. They are not only harder to find in published surveys, though not impossible, they are harder to match with your own jobs when you do find them. Examples of such middle jobs include those in human resources, such as the manager of the department or the person responsible for all recruiting. Other examples are the manager of accounting (reports to the vice-president of finance), chief engineer and customer service supervisor. The problem with these jobs in surveys is that the pay is often more dependent on the qualifications for the job, the industry or such variables as the number of subordinates. Take the human resources manager — in some labour intensive, leading-edge industries, this is often a high-profile position requiring a university degree, professional accreditation (such as Certified Human Resources Professional ("CHRP"))[11] and a significant amount of experience. The human resources manager will often have a staff of four or five and report to the CEO. In other less labour intensive companies, the human resources manager may be the whole department, report to the chief financial officer and require little formal qualifications. If you look in a survey and match only by job title and overall size of company, you will miss these significant variables. Contrast this with matching jobs such as president and mail clerk; the job titles and size of company provide more than adequate matches and pay data you can rely on.

Information to be Surveyed

The comments in this section will be restricted to cash compensation. You have to decide what components of the pay package you need information on. Notice that I said "need" not "want". It is important to remember that one of the most difficult parts of conducting custom surveys is getting co-operation and participation. The best way to do this is to keep your survey questionnaire as short as possible so that the person completing it can do so quickly and easily.

The primary factor affecting your choices will be, once again, your policy position. Remember that all data will be requested on a job-by-job basis. Given that, you can either ask for the salary of each incumbent *or* the average/median salaries of all incumbents (and the number of incumbents) in that job. I prefer to obtain the data for each individual in a job, rather than a composite number of a group of incumbents, for two reasons. First, this makes it easier for the person filling in the survey. Secondly, it ensures that you have the raw data you need to compile the survey summary and prevents the use of complicated arithmetic wherein you have to calculate an average of the averages at each participating company. Here is the data you should ask for *by job*.

---

[11] Granted by the Human Resources Professionals Association of Ontario. See Appendix A for contact information.

Survey Data to be Requested

- *Number of incumbents.*
- *Actual salary of each incumbent* — You must specify a date. Most published surveys use January 1st, but this is up to you. You may want data as of the first or last day of your fiscal year as it will be more relevant to you. Remember, it is your survey so you can control this. Another important item is the pay period for the data. Is the respondent providing data by the week, month, year or possibly a bi-weekly pay period? If you don't specify this in the questionnaire you will spend a lot of time on the telephone clarifying it.
- *Comments on the quality of the job match* — In the survey document you will have provided brief job descriptions. The person completing the survey is the one who determines whether her company has a job that matches the description you have provided. You have two choices here. First, you can just leave it up to this person to simply indicate (yes or no) whether or not the job at her company matches the description. The other option is to provide a rating scale and/or space for comments about the quality of the job match. This section of the survey questionnaire could look like this:

> Indicate how well the job at your company matches the job description in this survey.
>
> 1. Our job is much less   3. Excellent match   5. Our job is greater
>
> | 1 | 2 | 3 | 4 | 5 |
>
> Please describe the differences between the survey job description and the job for which you are providing data.
>
> _____
> _____
> _____

If you do provide a section like this example, you can then decide whether you wish to include this data in your analysis and reporting. This gives some more control over the quality of the survey data, but also requires more effort both on your part and those completing the questionnaire.

- *Other cash compensation* — This could be a general question such as: "Report any other cash compensation provided to this job." On the other hand, you may wish to find out how this extra cash is generated. For example, it could be from cash profit sharing, productivity gainsharing, small group incentives or individual bonuses. Unless you are interested in the incidence of these types of plans, you do not need to ask for this information. It is normal to ask for the amount paid in the last fiscal period, usually the year, although you might ask for the month.

- *Salary range points* — Surveys often ask for the minimums, midpoints and maximums of the salary range for each job. Personally, I do not find such information very useful. However, some compensation practitioners find it helpful to compare their range points with those of other companies. If you think it will be useful, go ahead and ask for it. Be sure to request the effective date of the range being reported and the pay period.

The Area in which to Conduct the Survey

In determining the geographical area in which to conduct your survey, you have to look at the type of jobs you have decided to include, not the specific jobs. As a general rule it is true to say that the higher the survey job is in your organization, the bigger the area that you have to cover. Let's look at two jobs at opposite ends of the job-worth hierarchy (*i.e.*, the classification structure): the CEO or president; and the mail clerk. You can pretty well count on the fact that these two jobs will be in the highest and lowest salary grades in all companies. The type of job determines the area of the labour market. In other words, how big an area would you cover if you were advertising for someone to fill either of these two jobs? Usually candidates for the job of president for any reasonably sized company can be found almost anywhere in the country. In contrast, candidates for the mail clerk job will only be found locally. Very few of them will be willing, or financially able, to relocate across Canada. Candidates for president will often be found scattered across the country. Another way to look at the problem is where, in geographical terms, are you likely to find job matches. Since most companies have a job that at least resembles the mail clerk job, you don't have to go very far. You could argue that this also applies to presidential jobs and you would be right, but with the higher level jobs you also have to match by company size (sales, number of employees or assets), industry (*e.g.*, pharmaceuticals) or broad industry sector (manufacturing — non-durable goods). This brings us to the next issue in conducting custom surveys.

Which Companies do you Invite to Participate?

Ideally, a survey which includes the job of president will be directed towards companies of the same size and in exactly the same industry. This is not always possible. Remember when IBM had 90% of the mainframe computer market, Honeywell had 5% and the rest was divided among a myriad of smaller companies. If you were conducting a survey for IBM which included the job of president, you would not be able to find even one other company of the same size, in the same industry, in Canada or even in the world. Therefore, in order to get some survey data, you have to expand the criteria. The industry category, computer manufacturing, can be enlarged to that of high-tech manufacturing or even further to durable goods manufacturing. Size measured by annual sales (the most common way to look at company size) could be $50 to $100 million instead of $106 million, or it could be just $100 million or more. The other major size categories of assets and number of employees can also be expanded.

If, on the other hand, your survey includes a job like that of mail clerk you can look at local companies. One useful way to do this is to just draw a circle with a radius equal to the commuting distance of an average employee. Alternatively, check the addresses of your current employees, in similar level jobs, to see how far they are commuting.

No matter what type of job you are including in your survey, you should try to get at least ten companies to agree to participate. This should ensure that any particular job will have enough matches to provide you with sufficient data for the statistics to be useful.

Conduct of the Survey

There are four ways to actually conduct the survey once you have identified the companies you want included and obtained their agreement to participate. These are: (i) telephone; (ii) mail; (iii) e-mail; and (iv) in person.

The choice of methodology will be influenced by: the number of survey jobs; the time-lines; the location of participating companies; and the accuracy required, especially regarding job matches. If there are a large number of jobs it will not be practical to conduct the survey by telephone or in person, since the amount of time to complete the survey is significantly increased using either of these methods. Conducting the survey by telephone is normally only practical when there is a small number of jobs; it is also the best way when you are in a hurry. You will be faced with the usual difficulties of playing telephone tag, etc., but when your president is screaming at you for some survey data, telephone is the quickest method. Conducting the survey in person is useful when there is likely to be wide variation in the possible job matches. You are able to thoroughly discuss the matches and even review job descriptions or other documentation while you are there. It is also politically useful at the executive level, where the person providing the data is a senior executive who would neither fill out a questionnaire nor spend a lot of time on the telephone with you. Since he may be providing very personal compensation data (like his own), I have found that such executives like to look you in the eye when they are disclosing their bonus (or lack of) for last year. Here is a table summarizing the major advantages and disadvantages of the four survey methods:

SURVEY METHOD	ADVANTAGES	DISADVANTAGES
Mail	• good data • more jobs • more companies • low cost	• can't control job matches • need follow-up with many participants
Telephone	• fast • better control of job matches	• fewer jobs • fewer companies • long distance costs • difficult to contact people
E-mail	• low cost • very fast • no paper • electronic data	• same as regular mail
Personal visit	• best job matches • higher comfort level for participants • high level of accuracy	• fewer jobs • fewer companies • slower • time-consuming • travel costs • not suitable for lower-level jobs

Report to Participants

Only one type of survey does not normally entail a report of the survey results to the participating companies. This is the telephone survey with very few participants and a small number of survey jobs. For example, your company may have decided to hire an IT person who specializes in object-oriented programming. Your first foray into the market indicates that the salary range you were hoping to use may not be adequate.[12] You have therefore decided to conduct a quick telephone survey of two jobs in this very specialized field with five companies that you know employ them. In a survey like this, it will be very unusual to get more than three matches for each job you are seeking. In fact, you will be doing well to get even that many of them. Three is the usual minimum number of observations needed to include the data in a written report. Even with three, you can only report central tendency numbers like medians and means; quartiles and deciles are totally meaningless.

On the other hand, with mail and in-person surveys, it is almost a rule that you produce a report for the participants. You basically make a deal with them. They meet with you and/or complete a questionnaire and, in return for their time and effort, you provide them with the survey results. It is extremely difficult to get co-operation without offering a report. I have had clients who

---

[12] Be careful not to take the word of employment agencies paid on commission for this. They have a vested interest in obtaining the highest possible starting salary for candidates they place with an employer.

have conducted a survey, promised a report and then failed to deliver. In the short term, there is little the offended party can do, but the offender has no hope of ever being able to conduct such a survey again. The lesson here is that, if you or one of your employees conducts a survey, make it a very high priority to ensure that the participants' report is completed. It should also be done as soon as reasonably possible after the completion of the project. Delay will affect the usefulness of the report as well as your reputation.

What do you include in a participants' survey report? Before proceeding to the general issue of what to include for each job, it is necessary to consider which companies will be included in the report. The first issue is whether you will include your own data. You have the choice of putting data from all companies in the survey or all companies without your company. Including yourself is the more common practice and with a large number of companies this is not an issue. However, with a smaller number of participants it can be a problem. Most of my clients who have asked me to do a survey have done so because they suspected, for various reasons, that their pay scales were behind the market. They were usually right. This meant that their data would distort the market survey down; especially since they almost always raised their pay levels after doing such a survey. Therefore, including their data would be misleading. As I said, this is especially true when there is a small number of companies in the survey.

Another variation on the question of which companies to include is whether or not you provide each participant with a report which includes all the other companies except his own. The report for Company A (for one job) could look like this:

ITEM	COMPANY A	ALL OTHERS
Average base salary	$xx,xxx	$yy,yyy
Median base salary	$xx,xxx	$yy,yyy
First quartile base salary	$xx,xxx	$yy,yyy
Third quartile base salary	$xx,xxx	$yy,yyy
Average bonus	$xx,xxx	$yy,yyy

This makes the report more useful for the participant but more work for you. It is a judgment call on your part. As a general rule this sort of detail is more useful and relevant in a smaller survey, say ten companies, than in a very large survey, such as the Toronto Board of Trade surveys which often have several hundred companies included.

If you decide not to tailor each report to the individual participating company the report will basically contain the same information in the left and right columns in the preceding table. In very large surveys you may wish to add the decile statistics for base salary. Remember that there is a separate section for each survey job. There should also be a general (*i.e.*, not related to a specific job) section which could include the following:

- names of participating companies;
- job descriptions; and
- salary increase information (average overall salary increase, average adjustment to salary ranges and average pay equity adjustment).

USING SURVEY DATA TO BUILD SALARY RANGE CONTROL POINTS

General

You now have some market data for most, if not all, of the levels in your classification structure. If you place this data on a graph, with the X axis being the salary grade and the Y axis being market data in annual dollars, the graph will look something like this.

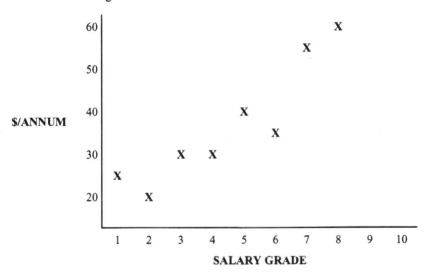

As you can see, if you joined these survey values together with a line it would be quite erratic. What needs to be done now is to smooth out the line so that the control point for each salary grade is both a consistent amount above the control point below it and as close as possible to the market value. What do I mean by this? Take the survey data for Salary Grades 3, 4, 5 and 6 from the preceding table. Here are the actual numbers comparing each one with the one in the salary grade below:

SALARY GRADE	MARKET VALUE $/YEAR	% ABOVE RATE BELOW
6	$33,000	(10.8)
5	$37,000	32.1
4	$28,000	0
3	$28,000	N/A

Some of you are probably saying "the market could never be that erratic; it's illogical". Exactly! The market is frequently erratic; it is often worse than this example. There is a very large number of variables that affect what a market is paying a particular job at any given time and it frequently does not reflect the logic and consistency of an employer's job evaluation system. This fact is one of the main reasons why companies have job evaluation systems. It allows them to make sure that they establish relative pay rates for jobs based on their own internal values and those of their employees, and not those of that amorphous concept called "the market".

What you have to do now is use this data to develop a set of "salary range control points". These are also known as "job rates". These can be defined as: "The amount that a person, in a job in that salary grade, should be paid, if he or she is performing at a satisfactory level, after a reasonable period of time on the job."

There are several important concepts buried in this definition. One is that the control point applies to the salary grade first. Then, since all jobs are placed in a salary grade, each job will have a salary range control point. Reasonable period of time means that the person in the job will not be paid the control point amount right away, but only after they have spent some time on the job. As a rule of thumb, think of this period as three to five years. This assumes, of course, that you have decided not to utilize a single-rate system.

Increments Between Control Points

Before you start to build your salary range control points it is necessary to select the way in which the points will increase from one to the next higher point. There are two choices — percentage increases and fixed increments. Percentage increase means that each control point is expressed as a percentage increase of the point below it. Here is an example with the lowest control point at $10 per hour and the increment equal to 12%:

SALARY GRADE	CONTROL POINT $/HOUR	INCREASE
3	12.54	12%
2	11.20	12%
1	10.00	

Contrast that table with the following example of a fixed increment system with the same starting point ($10) and an increment of $1.20:

SALARY GRADE	CONTROL POINT $/HOUR	INCREASE
4	13.60	9.7%
3	12.40	10.7%
2	11.20	12%
1	10.00	

In the second table, the dollar and percentage increases from Salary Grade 1 to Salary Grade 2 are the same as in the first table. Thereafter the dollar increments remain constant at $1.20. You can see that the percentage increases from one grade to the one above it become smaller as you go up. Of course, if you have enough salary grades the percentage increase will become infinitesimal although the dollar increment remains the same.

The disadvantages of the fixed increment system are pretty obvious. The fact that the percentage increments decrease as you go up are a major flaw, in my opinion. It is also contrary to common practice in most organizations. The difference between the top two levels in any organization, president and vice-president are typically in the order of 30% to 50%. On the other end of the scale, the difference between the two lowest salary grades is usually in the 5% to 10% range. Therefore, to use flat dollar increments from the top to the bottom of the organization will put your salary administration program out of step with the rest of the world.

However, there are situations in which a fixed increment will be suitable. They are often found in union situations. It is not the presence of the union that makes them acceptable. It is the fact that there is a relatively homogeneous group of employees with a limited differential between the pay rates of the highest and lowest levels. For example, there might be a unit of maintenance workers in a factory who are treated separately for compensation purposes. There are many possible reasons for this but the most common is that they have been certified as a separate bargaining unit by a provincial labour board. Fixed increment plans will generally not work with a salary structure that includes all, or most, employees (*e.g.*, president to general labourer). You will simply not be able to develop a set of control points that approximates the labour market you have chosen to compare with.

Another possible advantage to the fixed increment method is that some employees may see it as more equitable than the percentage increase method. The fact that the increment between job levels is a constant $1 will simply strike some as fairer than the alternative of a constant 10% increment.

VARIATIONS ON PERCENTAGE INCREMENTS

In the preceding section I presented the percentage increment version using a constant number. In the example, I used 12% as the differential between salary range control points. This was largely for the purpose of illustrating the difference between fixed and percentage increments. In reality, and common practice, the percentages often vary as well. However, there are several guidelines that you should observe if you decide to go this way. Here is an example of a typical set of control points with differing percentage increments:

SALARY GRADE	TYPICAL JOB	ANNUAL $	INCREASE %
12	President	xxx,xxx	40
11	Director of Operations	xx,xxx	25
10	Accounting Manager	xx,xxx	20
9	xxxxxxxxxxxxxxxx	xx,xxx	20
8	xxxxxxxxxxxxxxxx	xx,xxx	15
7	xxxxxxxxxxxxxxx	xx,xxx	15
6	xxxxxxxxxxxxx	xx,xxx	15
5	xxxxxxxxxxxxxxxx	xx,xxx	10
4	xxxxxxxxxxxxx	xx,xxx	10
3	xxxxxxxxxxxx	xx,xxx	10
2	xxxxxxxxxx	xx,xxx	10
1	General Labourer	xx,xxx	

Note that, if the percentage increment is not a constant, it increases as you go up the scale from the lowest to the highest salary grade. The acid test is whether you can get the control point for the top grade to be comfortably close to the market rate you have established from the surveys.

Sometimes, you will find that even this will not work. Even with a low but constant percentage, the top control point does not come close to the market rate. This is usually due to an unusual distribution of jobs in the organization whereby there are few jobs in the middle of the hierarchy. Unlike very large companies, where there are a large number of jobs in most salary grades, smaller companies often have a gap. Essentially, there is no "middle management" layer. There is the management group, consisting of the president or general manager, and several directors. Below that there are first line supervisors or lead hands and then the workers. In this case, you can create a gap in the scale and either have a percentage increase that is larger or smaller than the increment below it. For example, if you use the last table with the same group of jobs it would not be uncommon if there were a noticeable gap between Salary Grades 6 and 7. In other words, all the jobs in Salary Grades 7 to 12 are clearly senior management, while all those in Salary Grades 1 to 6 are either non-management or first line supervisors:

SALARY GRADE	TYPICAL JOB	ANNUAL $	INCREASE %
12	President	xxx,xxx	40
11	Director of Operations	xx,xxx	25
10	Accounting Manager	xx,xxx	15
9	xxxxxxxxxxxxxxx	xx,xxx	15
8	xxxxxxxxxxxxxxxxx	xx,xxx	15
7	xxxxxxxxxxxxxxx	xx,xxx	35
6	xxxxxxxxxxxxx	xx,xxx	15
5	xxxxxxxxxxxxxxxx	xx,xxx	10
4	xxxxxxxxxxxxx	xx,xxx	10
3	xxxxxxxxxxxx	xx,xxx	10
2	xxxxxxxxx	xx,xxx	10
1	General Labour	xx,xxx	

CONCLUSION

It is important to recognize that building a set of salary range control points is very much an exercise in judgment. Although there are a lot of pseudo-scientific terms used, and various mathematical techniques along with modern spreadsheets, the use of common sense and good judgment is highly recommended. In fact, it is absolutely essential. In the final analysis, you have to determine whether these control points are a reasonable blend of external competitiveness and internal equity. There is a spreadsheet on the CD-ROM accompanying this book that may help you to build a set of control points.

7

Putting it All Together — Basic Salary Administration

INTRODUCTION

You have now done virtually all the preliminary work required to put together a basic salary administration program. You will have developed and/or acquired the following:

- a classification structure;[1]
- labour market values for most, if not all, of the levels in the classification structure;[2]
- a company policy position regarding base salaries;[3] and
- salary range control points.[4]

With these four items you can now make the decisions necessary to construct a salary administration program which will enable you to:

- determine the starting salary of a new hire;
- determine the amount of salary increases for each new and current employee;
- select the date(s) for salary increases;
- identify the basis for determining the size of salary increases;
- select the width of the salary range;

---

[1] See Chapter 5, "Conducting Job Evaluation".
[2] See Chapter 6, "Salary Surveys".
[3] See Chapter 2, "Strategy". In this chapter, I will use the term salary as synonymous with wages or hourly rate.
[4] See Chapter 6.

- deal with inflation; and
- deal with changes in jobs.

SALARY RANGES

The first item of business is to determine whether or not you wish to have salary ranges. The only alternative is to treat the salary range control points as the only rate for the job. This is known as the "single rate" system of salary administration. If you look at the following table you will see that Salary Grade 4 has a control point of $32,000 per year:

SALARY RANGE CONTROL POINTS

SALARY GRADE	$/YEAR – JANUARY 1, 2003
9	$51,536
8	$46,851
7	$42,592
6	$38,780
5	$35,200
4	$32,000
3	$28,800
2	$25,920
1	$23,328

Using the single-rate method means that all employees in all the jobs in Salary Grade 4 will be paid $32,000 per year or $15.38 per hour.[5] New hires will start at this rate and stay at it until it changes because of inflation or because labour market conditions have changed. There is no provision for paying any employee beyond this rate for either seniority or performance.

The great advantage of the single-rate method is simplicity. It is extremely easy to administer and explain. The disadvantages are obvious. You cannot recognize seniority or merit in any form with this method. When I point this out to clients they, as employers, are quick to recognize this. When I meet with employee groups, they will also usually point out the same disadvantages. Most employees will feel that it is not fair that a brand new employee is paid the same amount as an employee in the very same job (let alone the same salary grade) with several years experience with the company. Fewer employees, but still a significant number, also believe that the company should be able to recognize

---

[5] Assuming 2080 hours (40 hours per week).

different levels of performance with different base salaries. I should warn you here that, in my experience, virtually all management believes in the efficacy of "merit" pay. This belief is much less common among non-management staff, usually because they have had bad experiences with it or they just don't trust management to do it right. You as the owner/manager will probably have trouble believing this but they have a point. I will elaborate on this later, particularly in Chapter 16, "Performance Management and Rewards".

However, if you decide that you want the ability to recognize merit and/or seniority in the base salary, you have to go beyond the single "job rate" and develop a "salary range". This simply means that you develop a "range" of salary below the job rate which allows you to hire or appoint staff to a job at a salary below that of experienced staff and then progress them to the job rate in some sort of systematic manner. Similarly, you can extend the "range" above the job rate and use this to recognize seniority or performance beyond that required for the employee to reach the job rate. Using the job rate of $32,000 from Salary Grade 4, as in the preceding example, a range will often look like this:

MINIMUM	MID-POINT	MAXIMUM
$25,600	$32,000	$38,400

In this example the job rate has been set at the middle of the range. New hires, or employees promoted to a job with this salary range, would start between $25,600 and $32,000. Ideally, they would start at exactly $25,600 but this is usually not realistic. They would then progress systematically to the job rate of $32,000. Employees with extra-long service or superior performance can be paid between $32,000 and $38,400.

This is a very simple example but it does raise a number of issues, such as: the width of the range; the location of the job rate in the range; the determination of the exact starting rate; and the method by which the employee progresses through the range. In order to discuss such issues further it is necessary to identify the two major types of "salary range systems", since the options regarding all the issues are different in each case. The two types are the "step-rate" system and the "3M" system. One convention that I will use from here on is to express all other points, in either type of salary range, as a percentage of the job rate. You will see what I mean.

STEP-RATE SYSTEM

General

In most versions of the step-rate system, the job rate or control point is set as the maximum of the range and a series of "steps" are established below this rate. For example:

STEP	A	B	C	D	MAXIMUM
Percentage	80	85	90	95	100
$/Year	$25,600	$27,200	$28,800	$30,400	$32,000

In this case, I have established five steps including the maximum. The first row shows each step as a percentage of the job rate or maximum. The last row shows the actual dollar amounts that would result if the job rate is $32,000. The usual way such a range is used is that an employee is hired at Step A and then progresses to the following steps, again "usually" at one year intervals. In almost all versions of this system the only merit component is a requirement that the employee exhibit "satisfactory" performance in order to advance to the next step. Once the employee reaches the maximum, there is no further progression unless the range itself is adjusted for inflation or labour market conditions.

Adjusting for Inflation

Such adjustments are carried out as follows. The maximum is increased by the amount determined to be necessary to keep up with the market. Suppose, for example, that you have conducted a survey and calculated that your ranges should be increased by 4%. The maximum would therefore become $32,000 × 1.04 = $33,280. Steps A to D are calculated in the same manner as the originals, as a percentage of the maximum. They will be:

A	B	C	D	MAXIMUM
$26,624	$28,288	$29,952	$31,616	$33,280

An employee who was at the previous Step C of $28,800 will automatically be moved to the new Step C of $29,952 on the effective date of the new ranges. I have never seen any provision in a step-rate system for a merit review before an employee moves to a new step in a new range. It is completely automatic.

Setting the Steps

The following issues have to be addressed in the design of a step-rate system:

- number of steps;
- the percentage of the maximum for each step;
- time between steps;
- reasons for advancing (or not advancing) a step; and
- whether or not to have steps above the maximum.

The first three items on this list are very closely interrelated so I will discuss them collectively. All three are a function of the amount of time you feel is reasonable for an employee to work in a job before being paid at the job rate. This typically runs between three and five years. If you provide that an employee can progress from one step to the next after one year, the example shown above would require that the employee take four years to move from Step A to the maximum. If you wish it to take longer you can add more steps or increase the time an employee spends at each step. Alternatively, if you wish the employee to progress more quickly, you can decrease the time between steps or the number of steps or both. Here are some examples.

TO INCREASE THE TIME TO REACH MAXIMUM

STEP	A	B	C	D	E	MAXIMUM
Percentage	75	80	85	90	95	100
Time	18 months	18 months	18 months	18 months	18 months	

In this example it will take the employee seven and one-half years to progress through the entire range. I have seen step-rate systems that require as much as 12 years. In my opinion this is ridiculous. Anything much beyond five years exaggerates the idea that the time to progress through the range roughly reflects the amount of time required to learn the job and reach a satisfactory level of performance.

TO DECREASE THE TIME TO REACH MAXIMUM

STEP	A	B	C	MAXIMUM
Percentage	85	90	95	100
Time	6 months	6 months	6 months	

You may also determine that you would like a wider range which will give you more steps and therefore more choice, but are reluctant to increase the time to reach maximum beyond five years. If so, you could set up a system like this:

WIDER RANGE/MORE STEPS

STEP	A	B	C	D	E	MAXIMUM
Percentage	75	80	85	90	95	100
Time	6 months	6 months	12 months	12 months	12 months	

Having shorter time periods for the first two steps has the additional advantage that it is consistent with the general theory that learning is faster when the employee is first appointed to the job. Therefore it is appropriate to reward the person sooner rather than later.

In all the examples so far, I have used five percentage points as the standard increase. As I mentioned in a previous chapter, the psychologists tell us that any increase or bonus payment should be 3% to 5% of base pay in order for it to be meaningful to the employee. Steps of five percentage points are quite common and lend themselves to easy communication and administration. However, there is nothing sacred about five percentage points; you could just as easily use three, four, six or seven percentage points.

You can see that there are endless numbers of combinations of the three variables: number of steps; time required at each step; and size of the step increase. The four major criteria you should use to decide on the right combination are:

- Is the step big enough that the employee will notice and appreciate the increase?
- Are there enough steps that you can hire employees at steps other than Step A but still have a reasonably significant difference between that step and the maximum?
- Is the total time to progress through the range reasonable, and does it correspond roughly with the length of service you, the employer, believe should be served before an employee is paid at the job rate?
- Is Step A high enough to enable you to hire qualified employees so that you are not regularly starting new staff above Step A?

Reasons for Advancing a Step

The fourth issue that is involved in the design of a step-rate system is what, if any, justification is required for an employee to move from any step to the next one. Most step-rate systems do not require anything other than the passage of time (some cynics say that the body just has to be warm). If you are using the last example and the employee started at Step B, after six months her salary would be increased to Step C and after another 12 months it would be placed at Step D and so on. Some programs require that the immediate supervisor of the employee affirm that she is performing at least satisfactorily. This would ensure that employees whose work needs improvement do not get rewarded for unsatisfactory performance.

Step-rate systems are not suitable for "merit-type" ratings beyond a requirement for minimum satisfactory performance since the size of the available increases are fixed amounts and cannot be varied to suit different levels of performance. I recommend a system which requires that at least one level of management recommends an employee for the step increase.

Steps Above the Job Rate

The final issue about step-rate systems is whether or not to have steps beyond the "maximum" or job rate. Of course, if you do decide to have such steps, the term "maximum" becomes meaningless. It is then more appropriate to use the term "job rate". The reason for having steps above the job rate is that it enables you to recognize performance and/or length of service above that required to be paid at the job rate. Such systems usually have one or two steps above the job rate. The difference between the steps is usually the same as that below the job rate. Using the first example, with five steps and five percentage points between them, the range will now look like this:

STEPS ABOVE THE JOB RATE

STEP	A	B	C	D	JOB RATE	MERIT STEP 1	MERIT STEP 2
Percentage	80	85	90	95	100	105	110

This now raises the question of how, why and when an employee can move to either of these two merit steps. The first question is the time. Usually the time at the job rate or first merit step is at least as great as that at the last step below the job rate; in the example this is Step D. Often the time period is longer. If the time required at Step D is 12 months, it would not be unusual for the time spent at the job rate to be 18 months. Remember, if you are using merit steps properly, a very small percentage of your employees should be at these steps; probably no more than 5% to 10%.

The next question is why an employee would be moved to either merit step. It could be simply the passage of time, as described in the last paragraph, but usually employers insist that the performance of the employee be rated higher than "satisfactory" before he or she is moved to either merit step. For example, if you have a performance appraisal system with a scale of 1 to 5, such as shown in the following table, the employee would only progress to a merit step if he received a rating of either 4 or 5 and the required amount of time had elapsed.

PERFORMANCE RATING SCALE

RATING	DESCRIPTION
5	Exceptional
4	Exceeds standards
3	Satisfactory *or*[6] meets job requirements
2	Needs Improvement
1	Unsatisfactory

You can vary these requirements in a number of ways. You could, for example, require that an employee be rated either 4 or 5 on the scale to move from the job rate to the first merit step, and that she receive a rating of 5 to move to the second merit step.

The downside of adding merit steps to a step-rate system is that it increases the complexity of administration and communication of the system. This disadvantage is considerable, since one of the major pluses of the basic type of step-rate system is its simplicity and ease of administration. The use of merit steps also requires the installation of a performance appraisal system which in itself can be very complicated and time-consuming. The plus side is that it allows you to recognize seniority and/or performance in the base salary. However, if you really want to do this, it is better to use the 3M type of salary range described in the next section of this chapter.

Two other points should be made. First, if you do have merit steps there will always be a great deal of pressure exerted by employees and, frequently, their supervisors, to move them to the merit steps. Not having such steps neatly avoids this problem. Secondly, step-rate systems are extremely common in union situations. In fact, it is very unusual to see any other form of salary ranges in a collective agreement.

3M SALARY RANGES

General

The "M"s in 3M systems are simply: minimum; midpoint; and maximum. In these types of ranges the job rate is established as the mid-point of the range and the minimum and maximum are determined as a percentage of this amount. A typical 3M range looks like this:

---

[6] Please note that I use the term satisfactory (or meets job requirements) which refers to the performance of the individual compared with the demands of the job. I deliberately *do not* use a term such as "average" which compares the individual with others in a group. I will explain this in more detail in Chapter 16 on performance appraisal systems.

EXAMPLE — 3M SALARY RANGE

	MINIMUM	MIDPOINT	MAXIMUM
Percentage	80	100	120
$/Year	25,600	32,000	38,400

This is referred to as a ± (plus/minus) 20% range since the minimum and maximum are both 20% off the midpoint. Just to confuse you, it is also referred to as a range with a 50% spread because the maximum is 50% more than the minimum (120/80). This example is probably the most common form of a 3M range. However, it is also quite common for ranges to be narrower (±15%) for jobs lower in the organization; for example, below the level of first-line supervisor. It is also quite conventional for ranges to be wider (±30% or more) for higher level jobs, such as vice-president and above.

Establishing the width of a 3M range is the easy part. The more difficult part is developing a system to have an employee attain his or her proper placement in the range. Some employers simply use the range as a guideline and arbitrarily set the employee's salary at what they consider to be the appropriate point in the range. This certainly meets the test of simplicity but fails to meet the requirement of expectancy theory outlined in Chapter 1, "Assessing Your Situation". The "failures" of such a non-system are detailed in the following table:

EXPECTANCY THEORY REQUIREMENT	FAILURE
1. Employees must value the offered reward.	1. All they know is a vague promise of "more money".
2. Employees must believe they can achieve the expected results.	2. They have not been told what these expected results are.
3. Employees must believe that they will actually receive the rewards promised.	3. They have no evidence that management will produce, since they are not told what others have received for similar levels of performance.

If that is as far as you are prepared to go, I recommend that you stick with a step-rate system.

Number of Salary Range Segments

In order to administer salaries using a 3M system, it is necessary to divide the range into sections, usually thirds, quarters or fifths. The next table shows this, using an 80 to 100 to 120 spread:

SALARY RANGE SEGMENTS

SECTIONS	PERCENTAGE OF MIDPOINT OF RANGE					
Thirds	80	93	107	120		
Quarters	80	90	100	110	120	
Fifths	80	88	96	104	112	120

When the range is divided into thirds, the sections are referred to as the lower third (80% to 93% of the midpoint), the middle third (93% to 107%), and the upper third (107% to120%). When the range is split into quarters, the sections are called the first quarter (80% to 90%), second quarter (90% to 100%), third quarter (100% to 110%) and the fourth quarter (110% to 120%). Although some practitioners use the term "quartile", this is technically incorrect; the statistical term "quartile" is not the same as a quarter. All these systems are based on the same assumption — that your major objective in administering salaries is to have employees who are performing satisfactorily, and have been on the job three to five years, paid at the midpoint of their respective range. Paying them exactly at the midpoint is an ideal situation but a more realistic objective is to pay them *around* the midpoint. Employees who are newly hired or placed in a job should be in the lower section and your better performers should be in the upper section of the range. You will also want to keep employees at roughly the same spot in the range when you adjust it for either inflationary or labour-market reasons.

Increases in Salaries

How do you determine a starting rate, move employees through the range, and keep their salaries "whole" when the range is adjusted? For the purpose of discussing these issues, I will assume you have divided the range into thirds as shown in the last table. The three main reasons employers use to move employees through the range are performance, length of time since the last increase, and position of current salary in the salary range (lower, middle or upper third). If we assume that the range will be moved X% (because the labour market has changed by that amount), and that you have a five-point performance measurement system as shown in the performance rating scale table above, you could set up a salary increase table like this:

SALARY INCREASE TABLE — JANUARY 1, 2003

POSITION IN RANGE	RATING 1	RATING 2	RATING 3	RATING 4	RATING 5
Below Minimum	X	X + 2	X + 4	X + 6	X + 8
Lower Third	X - 2	X	X + 2	X + 4	X + 6
Middle Third	0	X - 2	X 12 months	X + 2	X + 4
Upper Third	0	0	0	X	X + 2
Above Maximum	0	0	0	0	0

With a table like this, the salary of the satisfactory employee (performance rating of 3) who is already in the middle of the range will stay in the same position, since the salary is increased by the same amount as the range increase. All the other increase amounts are built around this fundamental premise which is shown in the middle box on the above table. Now take the horizontal row in which that box appears and you will see that the size of the merit increase goes up as the performance rating does. Similarly, as the performance rating declines, the merit increase does the same. In the sample table, I have shown the increase for Level 2 performance as X% minus 2 points. For example, if X is 6%, the amount will be 4%.

Many employers would argue that such a rating does not deserve an increase and the amount in the box should be zero. However, there is a good argument that such employees are only one rating step away from satisfactory and should not fall behind as much as those with a performance rating of 1. I have never heard anyone (except the employee in question) argue that a performance rating of 1 should get an increase.

Now look at the vertical column under the performance rating of 3. Here you can see that, as the position in the range of the current salary decreases, the size of the merit raise increases even though the performance level is a constant. This means that the employee's salary will move through the range and eventually end up in the middle third, which is where you want it to be.

Some examples might make this clearer. Using the 80 to 100 to 120 range with a midpoint or job rate of $32,000 divided into thirds, here are the calculations for different employees at different points in the range and at different performance levels. Assume that X is 4%.

EXAMPLES OF SALARY INCREASE CALCULATIONS

Example	Initial Position in Range	Actual Current Salary	Performance Rating	Percentage Increase	Salary	Final Position in Range
A	Below Minimum	$25,000	4	X + 6 = 10	$27,750	Lower Third
B	Below Minimum	$24,000	3	X + 4 = 8	$25,920	Lower Third
C	Lower Third	$26,000	3	X + 2 = 6	$27,560	Lower Third
D	Middle Third	$33,000	5	X + 4 = 8	$35,640	Upper Third

On the next date for salary increases you can simply repeat this process; except that there is a new salary, in some cases a different position in the salary range, and possibly a different performance rating. In the examples A and B above, you can see that the employee is now in a different position in the range, having moved from below minimum to the lower third. In example C, the employee has stayed in the lower third. In example D, the employee performing at level 5 has moved into the upper third of the range, which is where you want employees of this calibre.

You may be wondering why an employee would be below the minimum of the range. This could happen if the employee was hired at the exact minimum of the range and shortly thereafter you, the employer, increased the range. In most 3M systems, individual salary increases are *not* automatic when the range changes and therefore the employee will end up below the minimum. Occasionally, you will hire a new employee in, or promote a current employee to, a job for which they are not completely qualified and you cannot justify paying them at the minimum. The first scenario is the more common situation. The second does happen but should be relatively rare.

Timing of Salary Increases

The next issue in the selection of a salary increase table is the question of timing. There are two parts to this: the exact date of the increases; and the amount of time between increases. I will deal with the date of increases first.

There are two choices about when you process salary increases with a 3M system. The first is to use a common date for all employees, such as the first day of the fiscal year or some other arbitrarily selected day. The other option is to determine the increase date by the amount of elapsed time since the date of the employee's last salary increase or appointment to the job. Using the same date for all employees, usually January 1st, is by far the most common approach. However, common as it may be, I am highly opposed to the use of this method for the following reasons:

- Although it is meant to be a common date for all employees, the reality is that you will have to treat a large number of them as exceptions. If your turnover rate is 25% then this proportion of your staff will have to be exceptions to the rule unless they happened to start the job on January 1st. This largely negates the supposed advantage of being able to calculate all salary increases at the same time.
- The common date has no relationship to the employee's length of time on the job and therefore does not reflect her performance. If your common date is January 1st, what relationship does this have to the performance or learning curve of somebody who started December 1st, or November 15th or July 12th? The answer is nothing; it is a completely meaningless date to the employee.
- Performance appraisals will be rushed since they all have to be done at once. The unavoidable fact is that managers do not like doing performance appraisals and will avoid them for as long as possible. The common date then forces them to do them virtually all at once; this means that they are done hastily and also poorly. I once worked at a large management consulting firm which used a common date. The last working day before this date was both chaotic and comical. The partners would sally forth from their offices and summon one of their staff. The door would close, the players would take their seats and an intense discussion would take place (the partners had glass interior walls so we were able to observe). Actually, it usually seemed to be more of a monologue; guess who talked and who listened. After about 10 minutes the door would open, the staff member would emerge, often with a puzzled look on his face, and the next victim would be summoned. The process would then be repeated. The bottom line is that these appraisals served no useful purpose at all except to enrich forms and paper manufacturers. The common date was not the only cause of this lack of effectiveness but it certainly was a major contributor.
- If you use January 1st as the date, you also place a large administrative burden on a number of functions, particularly management and payroll. If a manager has 12 people reporting directly to her, she will have to spend a considerable amount of time preparing for, and conducting, the appraisal interviews. Actually, the preparation can take a lot more time, if done properly, than the actual interview. Similarly, the start of the year is a very busy time for payroll departments with tax changes and new Employment Insurance (formerly Unemployment Insurance) and Canada Pension Plan/Quebec Pension Plan rates to install. Using anniversary dates spreads the work for such departments throughout the year, making the process easier and more effective.

Variable Dates for Salary Increases

If you are now convinced that the use of a common date is counter-productive, it is necessary to look at the use of different dates. To be more precise, this means different amounts of elapsed time since the last salary increase. You simply decide what period of time will elapse between increases. The most common approach is to use 12 months. For example, if you had an employee who started in the lower third of the range at $26,000 on March 1, 1999, she would be eligible for an increase on March 1, 2000. If her performance rating is 3, she will get an increase of X + 2% which, if X is 4%, equals 6% (see the preceding salary increase table). Her new salary will be $27,560, which will still be in the lower third of the range. Therefore, she will be eligible for another 6% increase on March 1, 2001. Following the chart this would continue until the employee's salary is in the middle third of the range.

The other major variable is the amount of time. As I said, most employers see reviewing salaries annually as appropriate. However, as with step-rate systems, it is possible to have more frequent increases when the person is lower in the salary range or is performing beyond the norm. You could, for example, grant raises for satisfactory employees every six months while their salary is in the lower third of the range. Our sample employee, who started at $26,000 on March 1, 1999, could be eligible for the same size increase as above but on September 1, 1999. Since her new salary of $27,560 will still be in the lower third she will again be eligible for review on March 1, 2000.

If you decide to use different periods of time depending on the position in the salary range and the performance of the individual, your salary increase table will need to include time periods along with the size of the increase. Here is the salary increase table from earlier with example time periods added:

EXAMPLE – TABLE OF SALARY INCREASES AND TIMING

POSITION IN RANGE	RATING 1	RATING 2	RATING 3	RATING 4	RATING 5
Below Minimum	X	X + 2 8 months	X + 4 6 months	X + 6 4 months	X + 8 2 months
Lower Third	X - 2	X 12 months	X + 2 8 months	X + 4 6 months	X + 6 4 months
Middle Third	0	X - 2 16 months	X 12 months	X + 2 8 months	X + 4 6 months
Upper Third	0	0	0	X 12 months	X + 2 8 months
Above Maximum	0	0	0	0	0

You can see from this example table that the amount of time between increases declines as the performance of the individual rises, assuming the same position of her salary in the range. Similarly, with the same performance rating, the time between increases also goes down as the position in the range does. The employee whose salary is in the lower third will not only get a bigger increase than the employee in the middle third but will also get it sooner. Keeping position in the range constant, the higher performing employee will also receive larger raises sooner. The advantage of using these different time frames means that employees will progress to their appropriate place in the salary range more quickly and in a more reasonable time frame. This advantage is particularly noticeable when inflation is relatively low. In such circumstances, an employee could take an extremely long time to reach the middle of the range. This also would mean that the amount of time would be unrelated to her learning curve. Suppose that an employee started at the minimum of the range (80% of the midpoint), that X is 2 and that she consistently receives a performance rating of 3. Using the salary increase table her progress would be as follows:

Position in Range as Percentage of Midpoint	Salary in $/Year	Increase Percentage	New Salary	Elapsed Time in Months
80	25,600	4	26,624	12
83.2	26,624	4	27,689	24
86.5	27,689	4	28,797	36
89.99	28,797	4	29,949	48
93.6	29,949	2	30,548	60

As you can see, it would take this employee five years to get (barely) into the middle third of her salary range and she is still almost 7% short of the midpoint.

There are two other ways of affecting the time to progress to the middle of the range. The first is to increase the difference in the size of the increase between staff in the lower third and the middle third of their respective salary ranges. Instead of giving satisfactory employees in the lower third X + 2%, increase their salaries by X + 4% or even X + 6%. The second way is to increase the number of segments in the range. All the examples which I have used so far assume that the range is divided into thirds. There are other options, as discussed in the next section.

Changing the Number of Salary Range Segments

In the earlier table, "Salary Range Segments", I showed an 80 to 100 to 120 range divided into thirds, quarters and fifths. These are the most common approaches. Theoretically you could divide a salary range into tenths or fifteenths but this only takes a good idea to an illogical extreme. The limiting factor on the number of segments is the size of the X amount in the middle of the

Salary Increase Table which represents the size of the increase to be granted to satisfactory performers in the middle part of the range. If you assume that X is 15% and the range is divided into thirds and you add 2 percentage points for each segment below the middle third, the increases would look like Option A in the following table. If, on the other hand, X is only 3% the increases would be as they are shown in Column B:

OPTION	A	B
POSITION IN RANGE	RATING = 3	RATING = 3
Below Minimum	19	7
Lower Third	17	5
Middle Third	15	3

The issues raised here are: whether you are prepared to grant 19% increases to anybody and whether it is acceptable for an employee at the minimum of the range to vault into the middle third after only one increase (80 + 17% = 93.6). If you divide the range into fifths the problem becomes worse; see the next table.

OPTION	A	B
POSITION IN RANGE	RATING = 3	RATING = 3
Below Minimum	21	9
First Fifth	19	7
Second Fifth	17	5
Middle (3rd) Fifth	15	3

On the CD-ROM included with this book there is a formula that you can use to try out the various options. The file is titled "3M Salary Increase Table Design". The file combines the variables of:

- number of segments in the range;
- width of the range;
- number of performance categories; and
- the difference between increase amounts.

Administration of Salary Increases with a 3M System

What process should you use to administer salary increases so that all employees get the increase warranted by their performance, time on the job and current salary with a minimum of effort? When you are designing an administrative process, it is very important to keep the "KISS"[7] principle in

---

[7]   "Keep It Short and Simple" or "Keep it Simple, Stupid!"

mind; simplicity is a major virtue. It will ensure that everything goes smoothly and there is a minimum of disruption. In my opinion, salary administration systems should impose the minimum amount of work on line managers, consistent with giving them the tools they need to manage their people.

One of the fundamental issues that you have to face at this point is how much autonomy you will give your line managers to grant salary increases. This involves deciding:

- Who will initiate the increase?
- Who will do the performance appraisal?
- Which form(s) will be used?
- How many levels of line management need to approve the increase?
- How many persons in human resources/payroll have to approve the increase?

Let's start with the premise that you believe that the line manager should be given as much control over salary increases as possible. Therefore you will provide them with these items:

- a classification structure;[8]
- a current salary increase chart (all such charts should have an effective date);
- a salary increase authorization form;
- a performance appraisal form; and
- the procedures manual regarding these items.

The procedure should be something like this. The immediate supervisor of an employee, at any level, should be continually monitoring the performance of her staff. If you have fixed time periods for the elapsed time since the last increase at various performance levels and range position, she will be able to note in her diary when the employee will be eligible for an increase. You, the employer, should make it perfectly clear to managers and supervisors that it is a major part of their responsibility to continually assess the performance of their staff. This is vital; I cannot emphasize this too much. If you really believe that part of your overall policy of "motivating" employees is through the size of their salary increases, you must be constantly reminding anyone with responsibility for staff of their ongoing obligation to assess performance.

Let's assume that a manager has an employee in an 80 to 100 to 120 range who started his current job on March 1, 2002, at 83% ($26,560) of the midpoint. This puts him in the lower third. Your policy is to review salaries annually, *i.e.*, 12 months after the start date. This employee is eligible for an increase on March 1, 2003. Your manager has been monitoring the performance of the employee and it appears that he is performing at a 3.1 level (scale is 1 to 5) and

---

[8]   See Chapter 5, "Conducting Job Evaluation".

is eligible for an increase of X + 2%. Assume that X is 4%. The first thing your manager should do is a formal performance appraisal. The procedure is discussed in more detail in Chapter 16. She should not discuss the results of the performance appraisal with the employee until all the necessary approvals have been obtained.

The required performance appraisal form will have been completed and the necessary approvals obtained. The rest is almost automatic. The manager will need a "Salary Increase Authorization Form" such as the example below. The sample form has been completed with the information for this employee and his first increase since being hired. (This form is also available on the CD-ROM).

SALARY INCREASE AUTHORIZATION FORM — XYZ COMPANY

EMPLOYEE NAME_____

JOB TITLE _____

DEPARTMENT _____

IMMEDIATE SUPERVISOR — NAME _____

IMMEDIATE SUPERVISOR — TITLE _____

NEXT LEVEL OF MANAGEMENT — NAME _____

NEXT LEVEL OF MANAGEMENT — TITLE_____

	SECOND-LAST SALARY ACTION	LAST SALARY ACTION	PROPOSED
ACTION		Hire	Merit Increase
PREVIOUS SALARY		25,650	28,154
POSITION IN SALARY RANGE		Lower Third	Lower Third
PERCENTAGE INCREASE			6
EFFECTIVE DATE		March 1, 1999	March 1, 2000

APPROVALS

SUPERVISOR/MANAGER_____

NEXT LEVEL _____

NEXT LEVEL _____

HUMAN RESOURCES DEPARTMENT _____

Initiating the Increase

The question now is: "Who will initiate the increase?" There are two choices. A staff function, such as the Human Resources Department ("HRD") if you have one, could be assigned the responsibility of advising any person who is responsible for other people that one of their employees is eligible for an increase. If you do not have a full-time human resources function, other departments such as finance or payroll could be assigned this duty. Once the initial prompt (and any reminders) has been sent, the procedure is the same.

On the other hand, if you really believe that the first level of supervision should have the responsibility and authority to administer salaries, you can have a process whereby they are made accountable for initiating the salary increase. This option has two advantages over the one I just outlined. First of all, it puts the onus where it should be: on the supervisor or manager of the employee. Secondly, it removes the responsibility from the staff function. If it is left there, it is basically an administrative or clerical function. On the other hand, if the manager is accountable for starting the salary increase procedure, it becomes *part of the management process*. This means that it will be considered much more important than it would if it is just some form initiated by a clerk in the payroll or HRD. In a way, this question is a small thing, but it is part of a bigger picture which reinforces the idea that managers have an important part to play in salary administration. Consistently reinforcing this point should mean that you will get a "bigger bang for your buck" than the traditional approach that considers salary increases an administrative function best performed by the drones in HRD.

Levels of Approval Needed for a Salary Increase

On the sample salary increase form shown here, three levels of supervisory approval are required plus one in HRD. Actually, two approvals plus the HRD are probably sufficient in most cases, but I put three in the sample form just to illustrate the point.

However, you should know that many companies require many more signatures. I once worked for the Canadian subsidiary of an American company as Director of Personnel. Raises for my fellow directors required two approvals in Canada (mine and the General Manager) and five more in New York. This is ridiculous. It completely removed any sense of line management responsibility and/or local autonomy from the process. The result was that the employee did not have the faintest idea of why he got a raise, since he usually had never met five of the seven people who had authorized it. Generally, though, you can set up a system whereby the number of approvals are established by:

- the type of increase (merit, promotional);
- level of the employee or job;
- size of the increase; and
- position of the salary (after the increase) in the salary range.

You could use a table like the following to determine how many levels are required:

APPROVALS REQUIRED FOR SALARY CHANGES

SALARY ACTION	APPROVALS
Merit Increase – Salary Grade 1-7	1st Level + 1 level
Merit Increase – Salary Grade 8+	1st Level + 2 levels
Promotional[9] Increase	President
Salary Decrease	Vice-President

If you put this in a flow chart it will look like this:

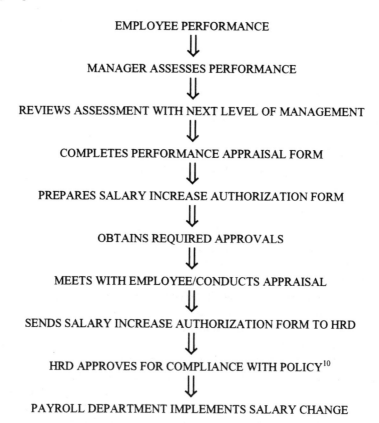

EMPLOYEE PERFORMANCE

⇓

MANAGER ASSESSES PERFORMANCE

⇓

REVIEWS ASSESSMENT WITH NEXT LEVEL OF MANAGEMENT

⇓

COMPLETES PERFORMANCE APPRAISAL FORM

⇓

PREPARES SALARY INCREASE AUTHORIZATION FORM

⇓

OBTAINS REQUIRED APPROVALS

⇓

MEETS WITH EMPLOYEE/CONDUCTS APPRAISAL

⇓

SENDS SALARY INCREASE AUTHORIZATION FORM TO HRD

⇓

HRD APPROVES FOR COMPLIANCE WITH POLICY[10]

⇓

PAYROLL DEPARTMENT IMPLEMENTS SALARY CHANGE

---

[9] This obviously assumes that the decision about which employee to promote has already been made.

[10] If you have made the policy decision that I recommended earlier (that the immediate supervisor is responsible for starting the process) the role of the HRD is restricted to ensuring that the proposed salary action is consistent with policy.

UPDATING YOUR SALARY STRUCTURE

In Chapter 6, I discussed conducting customized salary surveys and using off-the-shelf surveys prepared by other organizations such as boards of trade, management consulting firms, and professional or industry associations. You should be monitoring the labour markets fairly continuously and, if you do so, you will find that they have moved a certain percentage since you first established the salary structure or last updated it. Always use percentages when discussing movement in the labour market. This will ensure that your data reflects all the levels in your company. It is sometimes useful to observe that the market rate for a specific job, *e.g.*, programmer-analyst, has moved from $35,000 to $38,000 from the year before; an increase of $3,000. However, it is not much use to say that all jobs in the company have moved $3,000 when the range of base salaries could be from $15,000 to over $100,000.

Once you have established the labour market movement in one overall percentage you have to adjust the salary structure by the same amount. This is essentially an arithmetic exercise. On the CD-ROM accompanying this book there is a spreadsheet designed to let you do this quickly and painlessly. It allows you to input your previous set of control points and the percentage adjustment you feel is required. The spreadsheet will calculate your new ranges allowing for range spread, number of range segments and differentials between control points.

CHANGES IN JOBS

Organizations are organic in that they are continually changing. They grow, they contract, they flatten out or add layers, divisions are created, bought and sold. In some organizations, like General Electric under Jack Welch, this was continuous and often large in magnitude. This is at the macro level. At the micro level, that of the job, change is also continuous and varies in magnitude. Some jobs evolve slowly; others seem to spring up overnight, become highly valued and disappear just as quickly. Thirty years ago the job of keypunch operator was just appearing. For a time, it was almost impossible to hire them. Today, the job is virtually extinct. The job of human resources executive, which used to be called the personnel manager, is virtually unrecognizable.

The point is that your salary program is built on the foundation of paying for the job which, you may recall, is defined as "a collection of duties which can be performed by one human being". You therefore need the capability to deal with changes in job content and/or design. Jobs can change for many reasons such as:

- new reporting relationships;
- addition or deletion of duties;

- new technology; and
- new company procedures.

This process can be dramatic or it can be slow and subtle. The latter situation is the one that requires more vigilance. Employees often take on duties, one at a time. Sometimes they do so without their supervisor even knowing about it. A conscientious employee will see something that needs doing and just do it. They won't ask permission or wait for it to be assigned to them. This is the type of behaviour that employers must encourage.

Therefore, you must set up your procedures so that employees, and their supervisors, have the right to ask for a job to be re-evaluated if it has changed in some way. Since you have already established the job description questionnaire ("JDQ") as the instrument to be used for collecting information about jobs, you can continue this process. Simply have the employee complete the JDQ and obtain the usual approvals. Even if it is the supervisor who initiated the request for re-evaluation, it is appropriate to have the employee complete the JDQ. The job can then be evaluated by the job evaluation committee.

One observation about this process. It is often useful to have the supervisor obtain an additional level of approval for a re-evaluation request. In other words, you should not make it too easy for a supervisor or an employee to request a review of their job grade. Since, in all likelihood, you have a policy saying nobody will have their salary decreased because of a change in salary grade, neither the supervisor nor the employee have anything to lose by asking for a review. The supervisor will almost never oppose such a request, even if he doesn't believe it is appropriate. If he opposes it, he is the bad guy. If he nominally supports it, the employee likes him and your compensation or human resource manager ends up being the bad guy if the job is not moved up one or more salary grades. If the supervisor's budget goes up his manager will generally not hold him responsible. The manager will also assign the blame to the HRD.

NEW JOBS

When a totally new job is created, the process of establishing the salary grade is essentially the same. The only major difference is that there is usually no incumbent to complete the JDQ. There are some exceptions to this, such as when a contract job is changed to a full-time job, or even when a person who had been working as a consultant is put on the payroll.

However, in most cases of new jobs, there will not be an incumbent. Therefore, have the supervisor or manager of the section complete the JDQ. Any document describing a job that has not previously existed in an organization is at least partly speculation. This is natural. The only caution I would give is to be conservative when you first evaluate the job. It is much easier to move jobs, and therefore employees, up in the salary schedule rather than the other way around. Evaluate the job in the usual manner.

PROMOTIONS AND DEMOTIONS

Promotions and demotions can happen in one of two ways. The only difference between the two actions is the direction of the move. One is up; the other down.

A promotion occurs when an employee moves from one job to another job in a higher salary grade *or* her current job is re-evaluated, as described above, and this results in a higher salary grade. Obviously, a demotion is the opposite. Some of my compensation professional colleagues would not call a re-evaluation to a higher grade a promotion. They usually call this a reclassification and treat it differently for salary increase purposes. I disagree. The job is now in a higher grade. If you had to hire a new employee off the street to fill the job, you would place them in the higher salary range; therefore why not do the same for the current employee. The same arguments apply to demotions.

What salary action do you take when an employee is either promoted or demoted? This largely depends on whether you have chosen the step-rate or 3M method of salary administration. In both cases, it is also significantly affected by the size of the differentials between control points or job rates. As a general rule of thumb, I like to try to give an employee an increase of between 5% and 10% of his base salary when he is promoted. This is not always possible as you will see.

Given those general comments, I will deal with the step-rate system first. Let's look at two adjacent ranges with all the steps expressed as a percentage of the control point of the lower range, Salary Grade 5. The differential between the control points of Salary Grades 5 and 6 is 10%. There is not enough space to cover all the possibilities but I will try to illustrate the general principles involved.

GRADE	STEP A	STEP B	STEP C	STEP D	MAXIMUM
6	88	93.5	99	104.5	110
5	80	85	90	95	100

Suppose the employee is currently at the maximum for Grade 5. You cannot start him at Step A of Salary Grade 6. There are only two possibilities: Step D, which would be an increase of 4.5%, or the maximum, which would be an increase of 10%. Moving him to the maximum gives him a nice promotional increase but might be considered unfair to other employees in the same grade (or even the same job) who had to work their way up the steps.

One of the most significant influences on the possible size of the increase you can grant is the differential between control points. We talked about this at the end of the last chapter. Differentials between control points are typically between 5% and 15%, except for the top two or three levels, in most organizations. Look at what happens if the differential in the above example is reduced to 5%.

GRADE	STEP A	STEP B	STEP C	STEP D	MAXIMUM
6	84	89.25	94.5	99.75	105
5	80	85	90	95	100

In this example, you only have one choice. You have to move the employee to the maximum of the new salary grade. This is a somewhat extreme example in that two variables have reduced the options to a minimum. If the employee is not at the maximum of Salary Grade 5, you obviously have more flexibility. Similarly, the larger the differential between control points, the more flexibility you will have. This is something to keep in mind when you are building salary schedules, and even when you are establishing point bands. Remember that the smaller your point bands are, the more grades you will have and the smaller the differentials must necessarily be.

Demotions in a step-rate system are a little awkward. If your policy (and most companies do this) is to not decrease the actual pay of the employee, you just have to hold any increases until his current rate is at or below step in the new, but lower, salary grade. This usually means that the employee will not actually be at one of the steps. He will be "off-step". This is called "red-circling".

With 3M ranges the issues are actually easier. Since an employee does not have to be "on step" you have considerably more flexibility. Try for two objectives — put the employee in the lower segment of the range and give him a 5% to 10% increase in salary. Do not raise the employee above the control point of the new range. Certainly, if it takes more than 10% to bring him to the minimum of the new range, do so.

CONCLUSION

This chapter has provided you with the tools and theory to make the following determinations:

- Will you use a single-rate system *or* salary ranges?
- Will you use step-rate or 3M ranges?

- What are the features of the type of ranges chosen (timing of increases, number of steps/increases, width of ranges, reasons for increases, authority levels for approval of increases)?

8

Benefits Basics

INTRODUCTION

This chapter will take you through the steps of finalizing your benefits strategy, identifying what the labour market is doing, and setting up your own benefits administration program. Specifically, the following topics will be discussed:

- defining your benefits policy;
- what benefits are and are not;
- using benefits surveys;
- deciding which benefits to include in the area;
- distinguishing between "statutory" obligations and optional ones;
- costing benefits packages; and
- communicating benefits.

BENEFITS POLICY

Developing a benefits policy is quite easy compared to developing a policy for cash compensation as we discussed in Chapter 2, "Strategy". There are several components to your benefits policy. You will need to determine:

- if you have an obligation to provide for or protect your employees;
- whether or not to provide benefits;
- whether to provide a different benefit plan for each group of employees or one plan that covers all your staff;
- what the cost-sharing arrangement will be between you as the employer and your employees; and

- how your package compares with those of your competitors for labour, *i.e.*, the benefits equivalent of your policy line for base salary.

Obligation to Your Employees

Benefits are different from base salary in that it is possible to have a "compensation package" that does not include any benefits. There are companies that do not provide any benefits to their employees other than those required by legislation. It is obviously not possible to do the same with base salary. Employees will not work for a salary of zero; they will work for a reasonable salary and zero benefits.

Employers who do not provide benefits take the approach that it is not their obligation to see that their employees have health or disability insurance, retirement income or life insurance. They say that they provide a salary and the employee can choose to purchase such items in amounts and at a time of their choosing. They do not accept the idea that they have any obligation to take care of their employees. The entire onus is put on the employee. They choose to ignore, or not take advantage of, the fact that the employer has significant purchasing power which can be used to the advantage of the employees.

It is not my intention here to criticize employers who take this approach, but simply to describe it, since it is a significant characteristic of benefits that does not apply to the other major component of compensation packages — base salaries. It is a choice that you have and should consciously consider during the design of your compensation package.

The choice goes beyond just all or nothing; it also affects other aspects of your benefits strategy, such as the components and the cost-sharing arrangements.

Why Provide Benefits?

Here are the major reasons that employers provide a benefits package:

- Other companies do so and we have to be competitive.
- Employees need items like life insurance and major medical but are unlikely to provide it themselves.
- The group purchasing power of the employer means that these benefits can be provided at lower cost than employees acting as individuals.
- Having benefits means the employee will not have to worry about the financial impact of illness or other events and will therefore be more productive.

To look at the other side of the coin, here are some of the reasons employers do not provide any benefits or just provide a very basic package:

- They are expensive.
- Costs are growing faster than any other component of the compensation package, largely for demographic reasons.

- Costs are difficult to control.
- Benefits are very difficult to communicate effectively.
- Employees' appreciation of the benefits package bears no resemblance to the cost. It is almost inversely proportional.
- Employees can always purchase the benefits themselves if they choose to do so.

Sharing the Costs of Benefits

There are two extreme approaches to sharing, or not sharing, the costs of benefits between the employer and the employees.

The first is to simply provide a package of benefits which meets the general needs and requirements of the employee population and have the employees pay the full cost through payroll deduction. The employees still receive the following advantages:

- lower cost because of the group purchasing power;
- assurance of coverage they may not otherwise receive; and
- the convenience of not having to purchase all these items themselves.

The other extreme is for the employer to pay the full cost of the benefits package. Certain elements of it will result in taxable benefits for the employee, but these are not a significant concern.

Of course, there is always the option of somewhere between these two extremes, which is where most Canadian employers finally settle. If you are going to have employees pay any part of the cost, it is important to remember that it is coming out of their base salary and you have to examine your policy position regarding salaries in view of your decision about paying for benefits.

COSTING BENEFITS

When you are costing a new or revised benefit package, you can divide the benefits into three major groups. The method of costing is different for each. These groups are:

- paid time off;
- insured benefits, such as group life or dental; and
- retirement benefits.

There are also two different ways to express these costs: in terms of hours actually worked; or as an annual cost. Most people are very casual when they talk about the cost of benefits. It is almost axiomatic to say that the cost of benefits is 30% to 35% of base annual salary. This can be quite misleading as I will show you below.

WHAT ARE BENEFITS?

Exactly what are benefits? The term is used very loosely and can mean many things to employees and prospective employees. While doing the research for this chapter, I checked two major glossaries of compensation terms. Neither one included the term "benefits" by itself. Here is a list of the items that are generally considered to be "benefits":

- pensions and other retirement income plans;
- life insurance;
- accidental death and dismemberment insurance;
- primary medical/health insurance;
- long-term disability insurance;
- short-term disability insurance;
- dental insurance;
- holidays;
- vacations; and
- major medical insurance.

Pensions and Other Retirement Income Plans

Legislative Framework

The federal government provides two major components of employees' retirement income — Old Age Security ("OAS") and the Canada Pension Plan/Quebec Pension Plan ("CPP/QPP").

The *Old Age Security Act*[1] provides that all Canadians, subject to a residency requirement, and regardless of means, receive a monthly pension. If a person has lived in Canada for 40 years after the age of 18, they receive the full amount. As of January 1, 2001, this was $431.36. These are adjusted quarterly to reflect changes in the cost of living. Pensioners with net income in excess of $55,300 must repay 15% of the excess up to the maximum OAS payment. This program is funded by general tax revenues; neither the employee nor the employer is required to make contributions or deductions specifically for OAS.

The CPP/QPP provides a pension for Canadians who have worked and paid contributions for at least one year. Employees are required to pay 4.3% of their eligible earnings and the employer is required to match this amount. Self-employed persons pay 8.6% of their eligible earnings. Eligible earnings are those between the year's basic exemption ("YBE"), which was $3,500 in 2001, and the year's maximum pensionable earnings ("YMPE"), which was $38,300 in 2001. The QPP is very similar to the CPP but has some minor variations that need not concern us here.

---

[1] R.S.C. 1985, c. O-9.

Company-provided Retirement Plans

Any employer in Canada can provide one of two types of registered pension plans ("RPPs") (registered according to the *Income Tax Act*).[2] These are the defined benefit plan ("DBP") and the defined contribution plan ("DCP").

DBPs provide for a specified benefit to be paid when the employee retires. Here are two examples of how the benefit can be provided:

- The amount received during retirement is calculated as follows: X% times years of service times the average final salary. The Toronto District School Board provides a pension for its management staff that is 2% times years of service (maximum 35 years) times the average salary for the final five years of service. Suppose the employee had worked for 31 years and the salary for each of her last five years was: $80,000; $78,000; $76,000; $70,000; and $60,000. (She received a significant promotion in the fourth-last year.) Her average salary for the five years in question is $72,800. Her pension benefit will be: $0.02 \times 31 \times 72,800 = \$45,136$ per year. This type of DBP is most often used with salaried type employees.
- Another way to express DBP benefits is: X dollars will be paid each month for each year of service. This type of plan is more common with unionized and/or hourly employees. If the benefit is $100 per month per year of service, the same employee as in the previous example will receive: $100 \times 31 = \$3,100$ per month.

Note that the benefit, in the second type of DBP, is not related to the income of the individual. This is often viewed as a negative feature.

The advantages of a DBP are that retirement income is easily determined and quite easy to communicate. On the other hand, a major disadvantage is that the employer is guaranteeing a future benefit. This means that the employer has to invest the funds (supplied by the employer or the employee, or both) in such a way that they will be sufficient to provide that retirement income at some point in the future. If they are not sufficient, the employer has to make up the difference.

DCPs are the exact opposite of DBPs in this regard. Employer and/or employee contributions are invested and the funds that result when retirement occurs are used to purchase a retirement fund. This means that the employer only has to invest the funds prudently. Obviously, this type of plan is generally not as acceptable to employees as a DBP because they do not know what their retirement income will be until shortly before their actual retirement date. This makes it much harder to plan any possible supplementary investments for the purpose of augmenting the employer-provided pension.

---

[2] R.S.C. 1985, c. 1 (5th Supp.).

Other Retirement Plans

Registered retirement savings plans ("RRSPs") are very familiar to most Canadians. All Canadians who work are allowed to set up one or more plans (in trust) to which they are allowed to contribute moneys. Up to limits, which are discussed below, these amounts can be deducted from their taxable income. The moneys placed in trust are exempt from any tax (income and/or capital gains) until they are withdrawn from the RRSP. Such plans have to be closed by the year in which the taxpayer turns 69 years of age.

Most RRSPs are established by individuals, who can have as many as they want or think they need. However, some employers are now setting up group RRSPs. These are really just individual plans which have in common that they are provided by one trust company and are for employees of one company. Like pension plans, they can be set up so that either or both the employer and the employee make contributions to the plan. The contribution limits are not affected by whether an RRSP is a group or individual plan.

Deferred profit-sharing plans ("DPSPs") are a form of profit sharing (covered in more detail in Chapter 13, "Profit Sharing"). This plan is one of the four types of profit-sharing plans in Canada. They are covered by s. 147 of the *Income Tax Act* and are frequently used as a pension or retirement plan.

Like RPPs and RRSPs, companies setting up a DPSP establish a trust fund and register it with Canada Customs and Revenue Agency. Moneys are placed in the trust in the name of individual employees. These moneys are deductible to the employer but not taxable to the employee, again subject to specified limits which are discussed in the next section.

Limits on Contributions to Retirement Plans

The *Income Tax Act* specifies the maximum amounts that employers and employees can contribute to the four types of retirement plans. The following table shows the status of these contributions:

TYPE OF PLAN	MAXIMUM PERCENTAGE	MAXIMUM DOLLARS	NOTES
RPP – defined contribution	18%	$13,500	
RPP – defined benefit	No limit – subject to approval	No limit – subject to approval	
Group RRSP	18%	$13,500	
DPSP	18%	$6,750	Dollar maximum is specified as one-half amount allowed for other plans

When calculating the maximums, it is important to remember that the maximum is always the lesser of the percentage or the dollar amount. For example, if the employee is earning an annual salary of $30,000, she would be allowed to deduct a maximum of $5,400. However, an employee earning $100,000 would only be able to deduct $13,500 rather than the $18,000 determined using the percentage.

Another point is that these maximums apply to the total of both employer and employee contributions to all types of plans. Note that employees cannot contribute to DPSPs; only to RPPs and RRSPs, both group and individual.

In my opinion, and that of others concerned about this issue, linking contributions to a profit-sharing plan and a pure retirement plan is dysfunctional. If an employer decides to supplement a retirement plan by setting up a DPSP, it puts him at a disadvantage with other employers, since any contributions to his RPP detract from his ability to contribute tax-deductible amounts to the profit-sharing plan. It is also grossly unfair to establish the limit on contributions to a DPSP as a proportion of the limits for contributions to an RPP. There is no connection between the two types of plan. If an employer decides that he has an obligation to provide some sort of retirement plan but feels that he is not capable (for whatever reason) of making the regular contributions required by an RPP, he will set up a DPSP. However, this means that he can only deduct one-half of the amounts he could deduct with an RPP. There is no logic in this. Many companies, individuals and associations are advocating that the federal government change this particular aspect of the *Income Tax Act*.

Life Insurance

Most Canadian employers provide insurance on the life of the employee, usually referred to as group life insurance. It can be expressed as a multiple of the employee's annual salary (*e.g.*, two times annual earnings — if the employee receives a salary of $50,000, she would be insured for $100,000) or a flat dollar amount, such as $20,000. Multiples of salary are more common with salaried or professional employees as this approach is considered more reflective of the insurance needs of the insured employee. The flat dollar approach is more common with unionized or hourly employee groups where there are not big variations in annual income.

The employee chooses the beneficiary or, if there is none, it is paid to the estate. A variation on group life on the employee is dependent insurance, wherein the purchasing power of the group (your employees) is used to purchase low cost insurance for dependents of the employee.

The premiums paid by the company on behalf of the employee are not taxable except for those on the first $25,000 of coverage. Some employers have the employee pay the premiums for this amount. This is a dubious strategy since they have to pay the full premium instead of the tax on the premium for a benefit that most of them will never use.

Accidental Death and Dismemberment Insurance

This type of insurance is commonly referred to as "AD and D" and provides for payments to the employee, or beneficiary, of specified amounts for various horrible combinations of removal of parts of your body. The coverage actually details these combinations. For example, one company provided a package that paid $10,000 for the loss of one hand and one leg. The same policy paid $15,000 for the loss of both legs and $5,000 for the dismemberment of one arm.

The more important part of AD and D insurance is that it pays a multiple of the basic group life insurance in the case of accidental death, typically two or three times the amount. This is considered prudent insurance practice, since accidental death usually happens to those in need of more insurance coverage, such as the 30-year-old mother with two dependent children.

Primary Medical/Health Insurance

This is the basic "health insurance" that all Canadian citizens receive under the *Canada Health Act*.[3] It is provided through the provinces and paid for by employers in one of two ways. In some provinces, there is a direct payroll tax for health insurance. In others the employers pay a premium, which can vary by family status. The employer may pass this cost on to the employees. This insurance provides basic medical and hospital insurance.

Long-term Disability Insurance

The short form for long-term disability insurance is "LTDI" or simply "LTD". This provides for payments to the employee who has been off work for a specified period of time (*e.g.*, three or six months) and who has been designated, by a medical practitioner, to be off indefinitely. LTD pays a specified percentage of the employee's salary (*e.g.*, two-thirds) until one of three events: recovery and return to work; death; or the achievement of normal retirement age.

The income tax features of LTD are significant in designing your benefits package. If the employer pays any portion of the premiums for LTD, the moneys received by the employee are fully taxable to the employee. If, however, the employee pays the premiums, the benefits received are not taxable to the employee when they are received.

This means that when you decide on the amount of coverage you want for your employees, you have to consider whether it will be taxable or not. Obviously, you can purchase less insurance if it will not be taxable. The

---

[3] R.S.C. 1985, c. C-6.

downside is that the employee will have to pay for it through payroll deduction and this will reduce his or her take-home pay. In practical terms, having the employer pay the premiums and purchase more coverage benefits more employees (those who will not be using the LTD), at least in the short term. This probably means more mileage, for you the employer, from your benefit package.

Short-term Disability Insurance or Sick Leave

These plans are designed to provide protection for the employee for short-term illness, usually the period between the onset of the problem and when LTD kicks in. Short-term disability ("STD") insurance is often called "weekly indemnity", especially when it is provided in a union situation.

Sick leave works like this. Employees accumulate "sick days" according to the amount of time they have worked. For example, a not-for-profit agency in Toronto gives an employee 1.5 sick days for each month they have worked. An employee who has worked for six months and gets ill would therefore be able to be off for nine days. Some plans put a maximum on the number of days that can be accumulated. Sick leave plans like this are most common with salaried and/or non-union groups.

Weekly indemnity plans are more common than sick leave plans for unionized or hourly employees. These are usually provided through an insurance company. Here are the major aspects of a weekly indemnity plan:

- share of premium cost;
- percentage of salary replaced, usually between one-half and two-thirds;
- maximum dollar benefit to be paid per week, *e.g.*, $500;
- maximum duration of payments (unlike sick leave this is not normally related to length of service);
- waiting period before payment starts. Most plans differentiate between time off due to illness and that due to accidents not work-related (on-the-job accidents are always covered by provincial workers' compensation legislation). A typical plan would start payments after three days if the employee is off ill, and after one day if she was in a car accident.

Dental Insurance

Dental insurance comes in the basic form which provides for routine dental care, annual checkups, fillings, cleaning, etc. It can also escalate to more expensive packages to include orthodontics, restorative work and other major procedures, even cosmetic dentistry.

The amount paid for any particular procedure, such as a filling, is determined by the fee schedule issued by the provincial dental association.

Your contract with the insurance company will specify what year's schedule is to be used. It could be the current year, last year or even two years ago. This can be a source of confusion for employees and requires extra attention in your communications program.

Dental plans also usually have a deductible. If it is $100, this means that the employee pays the first $100 of the cost of the dentist's work. They also often have a co-insurance feature. This means that if the co-insurance is 20%, the employee will be reimbursed 80% of the cost, after the deductible is applied.

If the plan includes major restorative or orthodontic work, there is usually a maximum annual amount and sometimes a maximum lifetime amount that will be paid to the employee.

Holidays

Although many Canadians use the terms holidays and vacation virtually interchangeably, there is an important distinction between them for compensation specialists. A holiday is a specific day on which all employees (except critical or specified staff) are given the day off with pay. Christmas Day is an example. Vacations, on the other hand, are time off given to specific employees, usually taken at a time of their choosing, in blocks of time, such as one or two weeks.

Some holidays are required by legislation. This legislation varies according to whichever government has jurisdiction over employment standards. For example, the Ontario *Employment Standards Act, 2000*[4] requires that all employers provide eight holidays. Such holidays required by legislation are called "statutory" holidays. In contrast, Nova Scotia only requires that provincially regulated employers provide five statutory or public holidays. However, most companies of any size provide more holidays than the statutory minimum. In contrast with the Ontario *Employment Standards Act, 2000*, the majority of companies in Ontario provide an average of 11 holidays per year.

Vacations

All jurisdictions in Canada require that employers provide employees vacation with pay. The minimum is two weeks after one year of service, except in Saskatchewan where it is three weeks. After that there is considerable variety. Generally, the amount of vacation is expressed in weeks of paid time off, after specified numbers of years of service with the employer. Here is a typical vacation entitlement schedule:

---

[4]   S.O. 2000, c. 41.

LENGTH OF SERVICE	VACATION ENTITLEMENT
1 year	2 weeks
5 years	3 weeks
10 years	4 weeks
15 years	5 weeks

Often this type of schedule varies with the employee group or groups. The preceding table would be a typical one for non-management employees. It is quite common to have just one vacation entitlement for a senior executive group, such as four weeks after one year of service for all members of the group. The reasoning for this is that you can't ask an executive vice-president to receive a two-week vacation after one year just like the junior file clerks do. There is also recognition that the higher-level jobs are more stressful and require longer periods of vacation for maintenance of the individual's health.

Major Medical Insurance

This provides for medical or hospital expenses over and above those covered by the basic provincial insurance plans. These can include semi-private and private hospital rooms, orthopaedic devices such as wheelchairs or crutches, ambulance transportation or private nursing care. Some of these may require a doctor's authorization (*e.g.*, a private room) while others, such as semi-private rooms, will only be provided if they are available in the particular institution. Prescription drugs are usually included in such plans. Vision care is often included as well. Like dental insurance, major medical plans often have a deductible and a co-insurance feature.

OPTIONAL AND STATUTORY BENEFITS

Every government in Canada that has responsibility for labour and employment law specifies certain benefits that must be provided to employees, such as vacation and overtime pay. For example, in Saskatchewan employees must be given three weeks' vacation after one year of service. The employer has no choice; this is required by law. The difference between "statutory" and other holidays has been discussed. It is important to distinguish between these "statutory" and optional benefits in several situations, including:

- costing a new or revised benefits package;
- assessing the cost of hiring new employees;
- negotiating union contracts; and
- comparing your benefits package with that of other employers.

Here is a table which shows the benefits and/or working conditions which are legislated in all Canadian jurisdictions. A very brief summary of each item is also provided. However, since all of them vary depending on the government involved, there is not enough space in this book to show all the variations. Readers are advised to consult various reference works which provide the detail you may require.

BENEFIT/WORKING CONDITION	MANDATORY (for some employees)	JURISDICTION
Overtime pay	Yes	All jurisdictions
RPPs	No	Federal for income tax; otherwise provincial
Group RRSPs	No	Federal
DPSPs	No	Federal
Vacations	Yes	All jurisdictions
Minimum wages	Yes	All jurisdictions
Holidays	Yes	All jurisdictions
Health Insurance	Yes	All jurisdictions

BENEFITS SURVEYS

There is a wide variety of surveys of benefits and working conditions, although generally not as many as there are surveys of cash compensation (salaries, wages and bonuses). There are two primary reasons for this.

First, benefits surveys are more difficult and time-consuming to conduct than salary surveys. Secondly, there is much less volatility in the benefits field than in the areas of salaries, bonuses or even stock options. Although it is common practice for compensation managers to review salary levels at least once a year, a thorough review of the benefits package is more likely to be done every five years.

Nevertheless, benefits provided in the general labour market do change and you have to utilize published surveys or conduct your own survey in order to stay on top of the situation. Appendix B provides a list of published surveys which you can purchase from various management consulting firms, professional associations, boards of trade and chambers of commerce.

Benefits surveys are somewhat more difficult to use than surveys of salaries or other cash compensation. This is because they are less amenable to statistical reporting. It is more difficult to express the level of benefits offered than it is to cite the average salary paid for a specific job.

Benefits surveys differ from salary surveys in that:

- They apply to groups of employees rather than specific jobs.
- Each benefit has different characteristics (*e.g.*, life insurance can be expressed as a multiple of annual salary or a flat dollar amount).
- It is not possible to determine the average benefit in the way that you can calculate an average salary for a job.

Here is an example that will illustrate what I mean. It is from a survey of hourly employees and reports on group life insurance from four points of view:

1. Does the company provide group life insurance?

Number of Companies	Percentage of Companies	Number of Employees	Percentage of Employees
306	83.8	43,373	88.6

2. Percent of cost of group life insurance paid by employee.

Percentage Paid by Employee	Number of Companies	Percentage of Companies	Number of Employees	Percentage of Employees
0	124	34.0	21,452	43.8
1 to 49 %	15	4.1	1,935	4.0
50 %	15	4.1	1,038	2.1
More than 50 %	12	3.3	717	1.5

3. The amount of life insurance:

a. as a percentage of annual base salary;

Percentage of Base Salary	Number of Companies	Percentage of Companies	Number of Employees	Percentage of Employees
Up to 100 %	82	22.5	10,292	21.0
101 to 200 %	68	18.6	7,691	15.7
201 to 300 %	11	3.0	3,711	7.6
More than 300 %	0	0.0	0	0.0

b. flat dollar amount.

Dollar Amount	Number of Companies	Percentage of Companies	Number of Employees	Percentage of Employees
Up to $10,000	40	11.0	4,395	9.0
$10,000 to $25,000	57	15.6	9,162	18.7
$25,000 to $30,000	14	3.8	2,089	4.3
More than $30,000	22	6.0	4,948	10.1

4. Can employees purchase additional insurance at group rates through this plan?

	Number of Companies	Percentage of Companies	Number of Employees	Percentage of Employees
Yes	147	40.3	20,313	41.5
No	152	41.6	19,922	39.3

Suppose that your benefits policy is to provide a "middle" level package of benefits relative to the labour market for hourly employees — sort of the benefits equivalent of an "average" salary. Given the above data, here are the questions you would need to ask and the answers I would draw from this survey, along with some of the rationale that I would use:

QUESTION	ANSWER
Should I provide group life insurance?	Yes, the vast majority of companies do so.
What proportion of the premiums should the employees pay?	Probably zero but the survey data is not conclusive. The largest group of companies do this, but not a majority. Also, apparently a large proportion of survey participants did not answer this question.
What amount of insurance? How should it be expressed?	If there is a wide range of salaries in your employee group a multiple of base salary is better. If so, a plurality of companies provide one or two times base salary.
Should I arrange for employees to be able to purchase additional insurance?	The survey data is about evenly split. I would go beyond the survey and look at the administrative cost of doing so.

CONTROLLING YOUR BENEFITS COSTS

Benefits costs are increasing faster than any other part of the compensation package for Canadian employers. Many employers are seriously reviewing their benefits programs to try and bring their costs under control. Here are some approaches to doing this:

- Transfer at least some of the cost to the employees:
  - increase employee contributions;
  - increase deductibles;
  - increase co-insurance features.
- Impose limits on expenditures:
  - introduce dollar limits or caps for specific benefits;
  - use dental fee guide from previous year;
  - tighten definition of eligible expenses.
- Change the type of coverage provided:
  - reduce or eliminate spouse/dependant coverage;
  - reduce or eliminate retiree coverage;
  - remove hospital upgrades from plan;
  - reduce out-of-country coverage;
  - provide "catastrophic" coverage only.
- Change the prescription drugs coverage:
  - use a formulary drug plan;
  - switch to generic drugs;
  - use mail-order pharmacy;
  - limit reimbursement of dispensing fees for drugs;
  - reduce over-the-counter drug coverage;
  - introduce a drug card.
- Look at other approaches:
  - install a spending account program;
  - go to flexible benefits;
  - establish a wellness/health program.

CONCLUSION

In this chapter we have reviewed the major components of a benefits policy and discussed the nature and characteristics of the major types of benefits. We have also looked at how to use benefits surveys to establish what the "market" is providing and listed a number of ways to control your benefits costs.

9

Working Conditions

INTRODUCTION

Working conditions are features of the rewards package, in the relationship between the employer and the employee, that are paid for but are neither insured benefits nor any form of base pay or incentive program. They are virtually all related to hours worked, or not worked, as the case may be. This chapter will take you through the steps of finalizing your approach to working conditions, identifying the most common practice in the labour market, and setting up your own policies and procedures. Specifically, the following topics will be discussed:

- setting your policy regarding working conditions;
- defining working conditions;
- distinguishing between "statutory" obligations and optional ones;
- using surveys of working conditions; and
- costing changes to working conditions.

SETTING YOUR POLICY

Setting your policy about working conditions is sort of a cross between doing so for cash compensation and for benefits. For some of them (*e.g.*, shift premiums) you can determine various statistical points of reference, like averages and third quartiles. Others, like vacation, have to be looked at in the same manner as benefits and the predominant practice determined.

In the final analysis, the policy choices are between minimum standards (as determined by legislation), a middle-of-the-road package and a "cadillac" program. The issues of which companies or industries to look at, in which area, for which employees are essentially the same as setting your cash compensation policy. Review Chapter 2, "Strategy", if you need to refresh your memory.

WHAT ARE WORKING CONDITIONS?

Here is a list of the most common subjects that come under the term working conditions that affect the pay of employees:

- hours of work;
- shift schedules;
- lunch periods;
- overtime rates;
- call-in pay;
- shift premiums;
- weekend premiums;
- rest periods;
- standby pay;
- lead-hand premiums;
- bereavement leave;
- jury duty; and
- report-to-work provisions.

Here is a brief description of each of these items.

Hours of Work

There are several aspects to the subject of working hours that can affect compensation. Salaried employees often work a different work week than hourly employees. The most common work week in factories or warehouses for hourly employees is 40 hours per week. The most common work week for office staff, who are often in the same building as the hourly employees, is either 35 or 37.5 hours per week.

There used to be a significant difference in status between being hourly and salaried. In fact, in the early 1970s, it was considered quite progressive to convert your workforce to "all-salaried" status. However, the difference was more imagined than real, since salaried (non-management) employees have to be paid overtime under normal employment standards legislation. Note that the legal definition of overtime can be different than that used in your organization. In Ontario, overtime has to be paid after 44 hours worked (it does not matter whether the employee is classified as hourly or salaried for this purpose). However, the most common work week for salaried employees is 35 hours per week, seven hours per day. It is quite common for employers to have a policy that these salaried (office) employees will be paid overtime rates after seven hours in the day or 35 for the week but they are not legally required to do so in Ontario.

Overtime rates are the multiple of base hourly rate used to calculate the overtime payment. The most common rate is one and one-half times the base rate. An employee making $14 per hour normally will get $21 per hour for working overtime. Many companies have a higher overtime rate for overtime hours over a certain specified number. They will pay the usual one and one-half times for the first eight hours of overtime and two times the base rate for overtime hours in excess of eight.

Shift Schedules

Shift schedules have the following components:

- number of days per week;
- hours per day;
- which days of the week;
- flexible or fixed hours;
- cycle time for calculating weekly hours; and
- start and finish time for shifts.

Here are examples of several different shift schedules:

ITEM	OPTION A	OPTION B	OPTION C	OPTION D
Hours per day	7	8	10	12
Hours per week	35	40	40	Average 40
Days per week	5	5	4	3 or 4
Start time first shift	9:00 a.m.	8:00 a.m.	7:00 a.m.	6:00 a.m.
Start time second shift	NA	4:00 p.m.	5:00 p.m.	6:00 p.m.
Days of the week	Monday to Friday	Monday to Friday	Monday to Thursday	Monday to Wednesday/ Thursday to Saturday

Summer hours are a variation on the compressed work week which companies usually implement during the months of July and August. The usual practice is to shorten Friday and add the hours to the other days of the week.

Lunch Periods

Lunch periods can vary in duration and can be paid time or unpaid time. An employer might offer employees a 40-hour work week (five days of eight hours each). Some employers will include a one-half hour lunch break in those eight hours which is paid time. The employee will only have to actually work seven and one-half hours. Other employers will offer the same 40-hour work week but the lunch break is not paid time so that the employee will be on the job for eight and one-half hours. This can be quite significant.

Call-in Pay

Call-in pay applies when an employee is called to work, usually in an emergency, outside his regular hours. Most policies specify that the employee will be paid a minimum number of hours at a certain rate, usually his base pay. An employee whose base is $15 per hour will be guaranteed a minimum payment of three hours at that rate even if he only works 10 minutes.

Shift Premiums

Shift premiums are paid for normally scheduled hours worked on a shift other than the normal day shift. For example, one automotive parts manufacturer in southwestern Ontario pays a shift premium of 45¢ per hour for the second shift and 55¢ per hour for the third shift. These premiums are most commonly expressed in cents per hour but are also expressed as a percentage of the base hourly rate of the employee. However expressed, such premiums are not paid on overtime hours worked by an employee on another shift. The employee who works the day shift and then spends two hours during the second shift does not receive the shift premium that his fellow workers, who normally work the second shift, receive.

Weekend Premiums

Weekend premiums are for work that is regularly scheduled for Saturday or Sunday. They do not apply to employees who normally work Monday to Friday (any shift) and then have to work overtime on the weekend. They are paid overtime rates for such work. Those employees who work at ABC Drug Company have one schedule that involves working Friday, Saturday and Sunday. This is their normal schedule. For the hours they work on each day there is a premium paid. It is usually expressed in cents per hour, as with the other premiums, although it may also be expressed as a percentage of the base rate. Sometimes there are different rates for Saturdays and Sundays.

Rest Periods

Rest periods are simply those blocks of time during the working day (or shift) for which the employee may be paid but is not working. These usually include coffee and other breaks and a lunch period. There are three components to this item: length of breaks; number of breaks; and whether or not they are paid (*i.e.*, the employee is considered to be working and is therefore paid at the normal rate).

Suppose the normal work day in your factory is eight hours. If you specify that lunch will be one-half hour your schedule could be:

TIME	OPTION A	OPTION B
Start time	8:00 a.m.	8:00 a.m.
First coffee break	10:00 to 10:15 a.m.	10:00 to 10:15 a.m.
Lunch	12:00 to 12:30 p.m.	12:00 to 12:30 p.m.
Second coffee break	3:00 to 3:15 p.m.	3:00 to 3:15 p.m.
Finish	4:30 p.m.	4:00 p.m.

With Option A, you can see that in order to get eight hours of actual work from the employees, you need a later quitting time. With Option B, you pay for the lunch period but only get seven and one-half hours of work from the staff. This is obviously an additional, and substantial, cost to you, the employer.

So-called "coffee breaks" are another feature of the rest period issue. Most employment standards Acts specify that employees have to be given a break after a specified number of hours of work. Most employers usually exceed these minimums. It is difficult to get hard statistics on the number of breaks and their duration from most of the more widely used surveys of benefits and working conditions. The most common practice in Canada is to provide two breaks per day of 15 minutes each. If you have shifts that are longer than eight hours (*e.g.*, 12 hours), however, you will have to consider providing more, although perhaps shorter, breaks.

Standby Pay

Standby pay is also called on-call pay or premium. It is most commonly used for maintenance employees in operations that are very sensitive and need to be kept running virtually all of the time. When the employee is "on call", he is usually required to carry a beeper or pager or to be immediately available at a specified telephone number. A major Canadian bank has a computer facility in Toronto which runs all of its operations around the world. This facility is only allowed to be out of service 12 hours per year. The maintenance electricians and mechanics who keep the place running are required to be available and, during the period they carry a pager, they are paid the standby premium. A common arrangement is to pay a flat amount for each eight hours on standby. One company in the Northwest Territories pays $18 for this period. Another common practice is to pay the employee his standard overtime rate for the hours on standby.

Lead-hand Premiums

Lead hands are those employees who perform some supervisory functions but are not full-fledged supervisors. They are not considered members of management or supervision as most of their work is the same as the other employees. Lead-hand mechanics mostly do the same work as the other mechanics but have some responsibility to allocate assignments.

The work of lead-hands can be rewarded in one of two ways. You can pay them a premium of X cents per hour or X% of their base rate. The other approach is to build recognition of lead-hand responsibilities into your job evaluation plan and make sure, when you are building your point bands, that the lead-hand jobs end up in higher salary grades than the other jobs they are directing. If you look at the supervision factor in the Tyson-Totten Job Evaluation Plan,[1] you can see that Degree 3 recognizes lead-hand responsibilities. Be sure that you do not use both methods or you will be rewarding them twice for their lead-hand responsibilities.

Bereavement Leave

Bereavement leave is granted to an employee when a person with a specified relationship to the employee passes away. There are two parts to a bereavement leave policy — the number of days an employee is allowed off with pay, and who has to die in order for the employee to qualify for this time off with pay.

Most policies provide for three days off with pay for members of the "immediate family" which are usually specified. Here is an example from a manufacturing company in Ontario with about 100 employees of which 75 are in a union group. An article in the collective agreement says that three days' bereavement leave will be granted for the death of "father, mother, son, daughter, spouse, sister, brother, father-in-law, mother-in-law, son-in-law, daughter-in-law, sister-in-law, brother-in-law and grandparent". The same collective agreement also specifies one day for the funeral of an aunt, uncle, stepmother, stepfather, stepson, stepdaughter, stepsister or stepbrother.

Jury Duty

When an employee is required to report for jury duty (they have very little choice as anyone who has been called will tell you), you have to decide whether you will pay them for the time they are off work. Remember that they do get

---

[1]   See Appendix D.

paid by the courts for jury duty but not very much. (In Ontario they get no pay for the first 10 days and then $40 per day for days 11 to 49.) Over 45% of employers in Ontario pay full salary while about another 25% make up the difference. However, in setting such a policy, it is important to recognize that this can be a major cost for a small employer. Trials can go on for months and a temporary employee can cost more than the regular employee. In effect, you are paying for two employees for one job.

Report-to-work Provisions

When an employee reports to work fully expecting to work his or her normal shift and has to be sent home because of unforeseen circumstances (such as a power failure), many employers have a policy stating that the employee will be paid a minimum number of hours at the normal rate even though no work was done.

STATUTORY MINIMUMS FOR WORKING CONDITIONS

A number of the items included in the earlier list of working conditions is affected by labour or employment standards legislation in most of the political jurisdictions with responsibility for such legislation. Some are not covered by legislation but are so common that they seem to be.

Here is a list of the working conditions that are usually covered by some form of legislation (most commonly an employment standards Act):[2]

- hours of work;
- overtime;
- shift schedule;
- rest periods;
- jury duty;
- report-to-work provision;
- vacations; and
- holidays.

It is important to remember that the particular level of a working condition that is specified in employment standards legislation is a minimum. It is quite common for employers to exceed at least some of these minimums but you are not required to do so.

---

[2] You are advised to consult periodicals such as Carswell's *Compensation Guide* (Toronto: Carswell, 1996), and *Canadian Labour Law Reporter* (Toronto: CCH Canadian Ltd.), or the appropriate legislation in your jurisdiction, as these items are frequently changed.

SURVEYS OF WORKING CONDITIONS

As in the benefits area, there is a wide variety of surveys of working conditions although generally not as many as there are surveys of cash compensation (salaries, wages and bonuses). The reasons for this are the same as those for the low numbers of benefits surveys. First, working conditions surveys are more difficult and time-consuming to conduct. Secondly, working conditions are also slower to change than cash compensation. You should probably do a thorough review of your policies on working conditions every five years, rather than annually. Nevertheless, working conditions provided by other employers do change and you have to utilize published surveys or conduct your own survey in order to keep on top of the situation. Appendix B provides a list of published surveys which you can use for this purpose. Thirdly, the items generally included in "working conditions" often only apply to non-management groups of employees, such as the hourly paid or the clerical group.

CONCLUSION

Your policies and practices regarding working conditions, particularly vacations, holidays and overtime, can constitute a significant part of your compensation package. It is important to remember that there are minimum standards specified by legislation for most of these working conditions, although many employers exceed these minimums.

10

Implementing and Costing Your New Salary Program

INTRODUCTION

Before you can start using your new salary program, whether step-rate or 3M, you have to determine how you are going to make the transition from your existing program to the new one. Obviously, any choice will have cost implications.

This chapter will take you through the process of establishing the cost of your compensation program from various perspectives. There is considerably more to the cost of your rewards system than just saying: "We'll increase salaries by 4% this year and our costs will be 0.04 times total base salaries." I do not intend to show you the basic arithmetic involved in calculating your compensation costs. Rather, I hope to show you some different ways of looking at these expenses that are not readily apparent to someone who is not a specialist in compensation.

In this chapter we will look at:

- annual versus hourly costs;
- effect of salary increases on wage-related benefits;
- effect of salary increases on wage-related working conditions;
- costing the transition to a new salary program;
- step-rate system; and
- 3M system.

ANNUAL OR HOURLY COSTS

You can look at your compensation costs in two ways. One is total annual compensation costs. These will include:

- base pay;
- benefits;
- overtime and shift premiums;
- incentive pay;
- work/life rewards; and
- other non-recurring payments.

These can be added up for all employees or calculated for each individual employee. There are some technical problems establishing the cost of benefits and work/life rewards on a per-employee basis, although it is sometimes useful to look at per-employee costs in this way. Of course, these can vary significantly according to the type of employee or occupation involved.

The other way to look at compensation costs is to do it on a per hour of actual work performed. Let's look at an employee who has a 40-hour work week for 52 weeks a year. That is a total of 2,080 hours. However, no employee ever actually works 2,080 hours. From that amount you have to deduct the following:

- 88 hours for holidays (the average number of holidays in Canada is 11 per year);
- 80 hours for the minimum two weeks' vacation (three weeks in Saskatchewan);
- 40 hours for the average time off sick or for personal reasons.

Therefore we can calculate the hours that our typical employee works during a year as:

Total available	2080
Less – holidays	-88
vacation	-80
sick time	-40
Actual hours	1872

If the hourly rate for this employee is $20, the annual base salary is $41,600. However, the cost per hour worked is not the nominal $20, it is:

$$\frac{\$41,600}{1872} = \$22.22$$

If you are looking at your compensation costs this way, they are over 10% higher than if you look at the annual or nominal hourly cost. This is not necessarily a better way but it is possibly more realistic. It is also often overlooked by many executives in Canadian business.

ADDING STATUTORY AND NON-STATUTORY BENEFITS

Adding vacations, holidays and sick time to the calculation was just the beginning. To get your total compensation costs you have to add three other items:

- other legislated payments;
- benefits; and
- work-related pay, such as overtime and shift premiums.

Let's take the same employee and start with his or her pay at $20 per hour for 2,080 hours per year, therefore including vacation, holiday and sick or personal time off. For this example, I will assume our employee is in Ontario and the employer is subject to Employer Health Tax and provincial Workers' Compensation premiums:

Base pay	$41,600.00
Canada Pension Plan (2.925%)	1,216.80
Employment Insurance (4.06%)	1,688.96
Ontario Health Tax (0.98%)[1]	407.68
Workers' Compensation (2.85%)[2]	1,185.60
Benefits	5,500.00
Total Cost	$51,599.04

If you divide this amount by the 1,872 hours that the employee actually works, you can see that your cost per hour of production is $27.56. This is 37.8% more than the $20 the employee believes he is receiving.

Looking at your compensation costs this way does two things. First, it gives you a more realistic picture of the labour costs involved in producing the goods and/or services that keep you in business. Secondly, you obtain information which should be communicated to your employees. Generally speaking, they will be astonished when you show them a calculation like the one shown here. Most of your management people will be as well.

COSTING WORK-RELATED PAY

These costs include:

- overtime;
- shift premiums;
- weekend premiums;

---

[1] Some provinces charge a premium based on the family status of the employee. For example, Alberta charges $44 for family and $22 for a single employee.

[2] Assuming the minimum rate in Ontario as of January 1, 2002.

- call-in pay; and
- standby pay.

These items are often ignored in calculating compensation costs but can be quite significant. There are two ways you can do this.

The first is to make an assumption, or some sort of rough estimate, of how many employee hours are paid for these items and then translate that into a per employee cost. The second method, which I find more realistic, is to determine your actual costs for these items for the last year or some other representative period. Your payroll department should be able to provide this data quite readily. You can then divide this by the number of full-time equivalents ("FTEs") to arrive at a per employee cost to insert in the previous sample calculation.

COSTING A NEW SALARY PROGRAM

If you did not have a formal salary administration program before starting this book and have proceeded to follow my guidelines in Chapter 7, "Putting it All Together — Basic Salary Administration", you will have chosen either a step-rate or 3M system. Once you have made your choice you will want to establish the cost of making the transition from your current salaries to the new program. Obviously, you need to calculate this before you actually announce the program and then find out that the cost is unacceptable. The method of calculation is slightly different for each salary administration system so I will discuss them separately.

Step-rate System

Let's quickly review what a step-rate salary range looks like. Here is a typical set of steps with 12 months elapsed time between steps:

STEP	A	B	C	D	MAXIMUM
Percentage	80	85	90	95	100
$/Year	$25,600	$27,200	$28,800	$30,400	$32,000
Time in Job		12 months	24 months	36 months	48 months

When you convert to a step-rate system, you have to get all employees "on-step". For example, if one person is earning an annual salary of $26,000 she is between Steps A and B. She is not on-step. There are two ways to get employees on-step, assuming decreasing an employee's salary is not an option. You can move them to the first step above their current salary, or you can place them at the step that they "should be" at given their length of time on the job.

Choosing the first approach with our sample employee means moving her to Step B. If you choose the second option you have to know the length of time she has been in that particular job. Please note that it is time in the job that is the determining factor here, not time with the organization. As an example, let's assume that she has three years and two months on the job. If you look at the preceding table you can see that she "should be" at Step D.

Below you can see a condensed version of a spreadsheet[3] which can assist you to calculate the costs of moving each employee to the next step above his or her current salary:

Name	Title	Job Code	Salary Grade	Current Salary	Maximum
G.D. Smith	Analyst	F1	05	26,000	32,000
A	B	C	D	E	F

Difference	Positive Change	Next Step Up	Next Step Up $	Difference	Positive Change
		B	27,200	1,200	1,200
G	H	I	J	K	L

In order to use this spreadsheet, complete the following steps:

- Fill in columns A, B, C, D and E with the employee's name, title, job code, salary grade and current annual salary.
- In Column F enter the maximum of the new salary range at that salary grade.
- Using the new set of salary ranges that you developed in Chapter 7, enter the letter value (A, B, C, D, maximum) of the step which is the first one (in dollar value) above the current salary.
- You will have earlier set up the table in the top right corner of the spreadsheet which will show the steps in your new ranges expressed as a percentage of the maximum. In the example, I am using those in the table immediately before the spreadsheet. Using this table, in Column J enter a formula to calculate the exact step for the employee. For example, if the employee will move to Step B (and Step B is 85% of the maximum), enter the formula +E9*0.85. The spreadsheet will calculate the difference.

---

[3] This spreadsheet is on the accompanying CD-ROM.

- Look at the totals for Columns H and L.[4] The total in Column H is the increase that will result when everybody gets to the maximum, which they all do in a step-rate system. The total in Column L is the annual increased cost of each employee going to the next step above his current salary when you implement the new system.
- The process is essentially the same if you want to use the other method of getting your people on-step: moving them to the step that reflects their length of time on the job. Just fill in Column J using the same procedure except you will determine the step by the time the employee has been on the job. Look at the total in Column L.
- If the cost is not acceptable, you can lower it by adjusting the maximums in Column F.

3M System

If you have decided on a 3M system of salary administration you will have constructed ranges with a midpoint, minimum and maximum and divided them into sections such as thirds or fifths. For the sake of illustrating this procedure I will assume that you have constructed a range that looks like this:[5]

	MINIMUM	MIDPOINT	MAXIMUM
Percentage	80	100	120
$/Year	25,600	32,000	38,400

I will also assume that you have divided the range into thirds as follows:

SECTION OF RANGE	LOWEST POINT (percentage of mid)	HIGHEST POINT (percentage of mid)
Upper third	107	120
Middle third	93	107
Lower third	80	93

Methods of Making the Transition to a 3M System

As with the step-rate system there are two ways to move employees into the new ranges. You can place the employee at the point in the range where he or she "should be". This is much more of a judgment call with a 3M system than with a step-rate system because there are no precise points in the salary range which correspond to the steps. However, you can use rough guidelines like the following table; simply place the employee at a point in the salary range which

---

[4] Found in Spreadsheet A on the accompanying CD-ROM.
[5] See Chapter 7 for more details.

reflects his or her performance. If you have a performance appraisal system (you probably don't but if you do I suggest you read Chapter 16, "Performance Management and Rewards", before using it for this purpose), it may be possible to use it.

SECTION OF RANGE	EMPLOYEE PERFORMANCE
Upper third	Outstanding
Middle third	Meets job requirements
Lower third	Needs improvement *or* is new on job

If you choose to go this route you can use Spreadsheet B on the accompanying CD-ROM. It is very similar to Spreadsheet A except that in Column F you enter the midpoint of the appropriate salary range and in Column I you enter the point in the range that you assess is justified by the performance of the employee. For example, if you think that the employee should be at 102% of the midpoint, enter 102 in that column. The calculation is then automatic. See the total at the bottom of Column L for your increased annual cost of the new program.

The other choice about how to make the transition to the new system depends on what method of determining salary increases you have chosen for your 3M system. If you have decided to use a Salary Increase Table, like the one in Chapter 7, you can simply start applying it. Pick a start date for your new program and use the table to establish each person's new salary. Of course, the table in Chapter 7 is not complete. You have to determine a number of variables, such as the amount of X, and the pluses and minuses built around X.

At this point, the calculation of X is different than the method I described previously. In Chapter 7, I suggested that X for this table would be the amount of increase in the labour market. In other words, if you have done a salary survey and found that the labour market had moved by 5% since you last adjusted your range control points, X would become 5%.

However, when you are making the transition to a new program, you should use a different approach to establishing X. For this purpose, you need to assume that, on average, all your employees are performing satisfactorily (*i.e.*, meeting job requirements) and have been on the job long enough to justify being at the midpoint of the new salary ranges. On this basis you can calculate the compa-ratio for your current salaries compared with your new salary structure. The compa-ratio is simply the ratio of the current salary of an employee (or any group of employees) compared to the midpoint of the relevant salary range. Here is an example. Assume the following facts:

- salary = $42,000;
- midpoint of the salary range = $45,000.

Here is the calculation for the compa-ratio:

actual salary/midpoint = 42000/45000 = 0.93

Spreadsheet C can be used to calculate your compa-ratio. Simply fill in the salaries of the employees in Column E and the new midpoint of the respective salary range in Column F. The spreadsheet will calculate the compa-ratio for each individual and for the total employee group.

The compa-ratio will tell you how much your actual salaries are behind the range control points (which reflect the market). This number may be significantly different from the movement in the labour market over the past year, or whatever period you are looking at, when you set the X in the middle of the table under normal circumstances. Suppose your calculation shows that the compa-ratio for the group is 0.91. This means that, on average, your employees are 9% below the control or midpoints of the new salary ranges that you have established. Therefore, if you are going to follow this second approach to installing your new 3M system of salary administration, you will have to set X, in the middle of the table, at 9%. The other amounts in the table will be set around 9% as described in Chapter 7.

CONCLUSION

In this chapter we have reviewed the major methods you can use to make the transition from your current unstructured salary administration program to the new system you have chosen. We have also looked at ways to calculate the cost of implementing your new program. Using these methods will allow you to install your new salary program with some assurance that your organization will not go broke during the process. We also examined some alternate ways to calculate compensation costs to ensure that you have a complete picture of the financial impact of any salary increase.

11

Designing a Group Incentive Plan

INTRODUCTION

In Chapter 2, "Strategy", you made at least a preliminary decision about whether or not to have a large group incentive plan for your employees. This chapter covers the general principles involved in designing such a plan. There are four major types of such plans: broad-based profit sharing; productivity gainsharing; team-based plans; and employee share ownership plans ("ESOPs"). These will be discussed in detail in the four chapters which follow.

However, there are a number of issues that are common to all four types of group incentive plans and these will be reviewed in this chapter. These plans all share one common characteristic. The payments, in whatever form, all result because of the performance of a group of employees. This group can be the whole company, a production unit, a division, a team or a section. This chapter will review:

- the conditions required before starting a group incentive plan;
- membership;
- how the funds are generated; and
- how the bonus pool is divided.

At the end of the chapter, I also provide a comparison of all four types of group plans.

CONDITIONS REQUIRED BEFORE STARTING

There are several conditions which should exist, in whole or in part, before you get very far in the design of any group incentive plan. You, or a trusted advisor, should carefully examine your situation to see if the following are in place:

- reasonable employee relations;
- base salaries that are externally competitive and internally equitable;
- expectation of income to share;
- stability;
- good communications;
- need for additional production; and
- management commitment.

Reasonable Employee Relations

The relationship between management and employees should be in reasonably good shape. Relations do not have to be fabulous but, on the other hand, they should not be awful. Group incentive plans, especially profit sharing, are often considered magic bullets that will cure all the ills that afflict management/employee relations. They cannot do this. Management has to do it.

Base Salaries

Your salaries and wages need to be both externally competitive and internally equitable. Externally competitive means that they should be comparable to those paid in the industries and/or companies that you consider to be competitors for labour: where you are likely to hire employees and where they are likely to go. If you have followed the procedures laid out earlier in this book, especially in Chapter 7, "Putting it All Together — Basic Salary Administration", this should not be a problem. It is difficult to use incentives as a substitute for reasonable base salaries since there will be, as we all know, years in which the incentive plans produce nothing. Employees need a reasonable base salary on which they can live when there are no bonuses to share.

Internal equity is a related but different concept. This means that the pay for jobs (not individuals) should reflect their relative value within the organization. If you have followed the procedures set out in Chapter 3, "Selecting a Job Evaluation Plan", and Chapter 5, "Conducting Job Evaluation", you will have already established internal equity.

Expectation of Income to Share

It is pretty obvious that profits are needed before you start a profit-sharing plan. Similarly, with all the other types of group incentive plans, it is important to make sure that there is a medium to high probability that, when you announce the plan, there will be something to share. To the extent possible, this should also be true of the next year or two. If you go back to Chapter 1, "Assessing Your Situation", in the section on expectancy theory, you will notice that the third pillar of that theory is the expectation, by employees, that they will actually be paid if they achieve the desired results.

However, and this is an important point, you must recognize that there will be periods in which the plan in question produces nothing and that this will be acceptable to the employees. If you communicate enough, and train them enough in business literacy, they will understand. Many clients have expressed the concern that their incentive plan will be a failure if there is a year, or more, with no payout. Do not worry about this issue if you are prepared to explain to your staff how and why this happened.

Stability

Stability is another condition that should be present before introducing any group incentive plan. Obviously, at the start of the 21st century, very few things in Canadian business are completely stable. What I mean by stability is that your company should not be undergoing massive change, such as moving the head office from Montreal to Calgary, introducing ISO 9000 or divesting itself of a complete division. Some change is pretty well a constant but, since introducing a new group incentive plan is itself a form of change, you should try to ensure that other factors are relatively constant.

Communications

Communications are also important. It is critical that management and employees have regular and dependable channels of communication. Employees should have faith in what management tells them. The only way they will have such faith is if there is a corporate history of management consistently and openly reporting on the state of the business. It is quite common for management to believe that they are good communicators when such is not the case. A survey reported in *The Financial Post*[1] said that 61% of senior executives believed that they were doing a good job of communicating with their staff. However, only 33% of managers reporting to them agreed. Further down the ladder it gets worse. Only 22% of hourly employees and 27%

---

[1] L. Ramsay, "Communication Key to Workplace Happiness", *The Financial Post* (December 6, 1997), p. 58.

of clerical employees believed that senior management did a good job of communicating with them.

Need for Additional Production

This condition varies quite a bit depending on the type of group incentive plan you are considering. However, the most obvious example is any form of a productivity gainsharing plan. The Scanlon Plan and the Rucker Plan,[2] in particular, reward a specific group of employees for increased production. These plans measure the value of production compared with the inputs (labour and materials) and, if they produce more with less, or improve the ratio of output to input, there is a gain to be shared. That's fine, as far as it goes, but if the company cannot sell the additional products (most gainsharing plans are in manufacturing) because there is no demand for them, you have only served to increase your inventory and your variable labour costs.

Management Commitment

The final item on the list of conditions is management commitment. There are two parts to this requirement. The first is simply to put in the effort required to have a plan. It is not enough to design and announce a wonderful new incentive plan and leave it alone to work its magic. It has to be managed. Administration and communication is required, especially with deferred plans (whether profit-sharing or stock-based).

The second part of management commitment is the issue of involving employees. This is not the same kind of involvement that I talked about in Chapter 1. That was involvement in the process of designing a compensation system. In this case, I am talking about involvement in the management of the enterprise, corporation, division or section that the group incentive plan will be used in. Since the purpose of group incentives is to reward employees for their performance as a group, it is logical to include them in the decision-making process. This is where many managers, especially the entrepreneur, who has built the company from the ground up and is used to making all the decisions, fail the test of management commitment. Such people are often extremely resistant to employee involvement and reject it totally. However, without such involvement, the group incentive plan is just another mechanism to hand out money.

---

[2] See the discussion of these plans in Chapter 14, "Productivity Gainsharing".

MEMBERSHIP

In general, the question of membership involves asking the question: "Who is in the plan?" or "When it comes time to divide up the money — who gets to share in the pool?" There are four criteria you can use to determine whether or not a person becomes a member of the plan:

- occupation or employee group;
- length of service;
- type of plan; and
- leaving the plan.

These criteria can be used separately but are often used in combination. The way they are used, either separately or in combination, can vary with the type of plan and these variations will be discussed in the following four chapters on each of the specific types of group incentive. However, here are some general guidelines.

Occupation or Employee Group

Occupation or employee group means that membership in the group incentive plan is defined by the type of job, department or employee group. The most obvious example of this is the sales force. Sales representatives are the group that is probably the second most likely to be identified as an appropriate group for having its own incentive plan. Executives are the most common group to have their own incentive or bonus plan. Many productivity gainsharing plans include only direct labour in their membership. As you will see in Chapter 12, "Team-Based Incentives", many teams are defined by the department or section, although they can also be defined as the group which is assigned to a particular project.

Union membership is often another membership issue. If a number of your employees are unionized, and you are developing a group incentive plan that would include them if they were not members of a union (*e.g.*, a broad-based profit-sharing plan), you have to consider whether to include or exclude them. Many productivity gainsharing plans only include union members. This may be appropriate, since the original Scanlon Plan[3] was developed by a former union executive, Joseph Scanlon. Some profit-sharing plans exclude the executive group. For example, ABC Manufacturing in Guelph, Ontario, with about 40 employees, set up a broad-based profit-sharing plan which included all employees with 12 months of service but excluded the three senior executives of the Canadian company, as they were members of the corporate bonus plan.

---

[3] The Scanlon Plan was the first productivity gainsharing plan.

Length of Service

Many plans allow employees to join the plan the first day they are on the job. Others restrict membership to those who have been with the company, or part of the group, for a specified period of time. For example, Dofasco, the Burlington, Ontario steel manufacturer, does not allow employees to join its profit-sharing plan until they have been with the company for two years. Dofasco is considered to have one of the best (most successful) profit-sharing plans in Canada and is consistently rated as one of the best employers in the country.

There are two ways to look at this issue. First, you should identify how long after joining the company, or the group, it will take the employee to actually contribute to the success of the group. Every job, or group of jobs, has its own learning curve or break-in period. Although it is difficult to be precise about this, try to identify this length of time for a new employee (new to the group, not necessarily the organization). This can be your length of service requirement. It is important to have the same criteria for all employees in the incentive plan even though the amount of time before they start to be effective may vary. Do not have a different length of service requirement for managers and production workers, for example, even though it is possible to argue that managers and the lowest level of production worker obviously have different learning curves. Average it out for the group.

Another way to establish your length of service requirement is to look at when most of your turnover takes place. If you observe that 70% of the employees who quit do so within the first three months of employment, you could set your length of service for entry to the incentive plan at three months. This would save a lot of administrative effort as well as eliminating from the calculation those who will not contribute.

Type of Plan

The type of plan often dictates, or strongly influences, the rules for membership. Productivity gainsharing plans are usually restricted to direct labour (production and warehouse workers — hourly paid), although sometimes indirect labour such as maintenance staff is included. Cash profit-sharing plans, if they are "broad-based", include virtually all employees although sometimes this is restricted to full-time employees. Deferred profit-sharing plans ("DPSPs") are often reserved for more senior (in level) employees or those with longer service than the cash plan might require. Membership in team plans is a function of the type of team; the different types are reviewed in Chapter 12.

Leaving the Plan

Employees will leave the plan for various reasons. They can leave the organization by quitting, retiring or, more drastically, dying. They can be fired or quit of their own volition. If the plan is not organization-wide, as with productivity gainsharing, sales incentives or team incentive plans, the employee can transfer or be promoted out of the group to which the plan applies. It is necessary to define when such employees have left the plan and what share, if any, they will receive of the bonus pool.

There are several sub-issues involved. The first is whether the employee will be considered part of the group if he leaves before the last day of the fiscal period for which the calculation is being done. For example, all Scanlon productivity gainsharing plans are calculated and pay out monthly. The payment will not be issued on the last day (the accountants will need a few days, even with computers) but the calculation of the gain to be shared will be made as of the last day of the month. If the employee quits on April 25th, having given proper notice and serving adequate time, will he be considered a member of the group for the 25 days that he worked there?

For this issue it is useful to divide reasons for leaving the group, or the organization, into two somewhat arbitrary categories: acceptable; and unacceptable. Here is a list:

ACCEPTABLE REASONS	UNACCEPTABLE REASONS
Retirement	Termination for cause
Death	Termination for poor performance
Quitting amicably	Quitting with hostility
Transfer	Demotion
Promotion	

You may wish to further refine these two categories but they will serve for the moment to discuss the issue. Most employee groups that I have worked with take the approach that those who leave the group for any of the preceding "acceptable" reasons will be considered to have contributed for the time they were there and therefore should receive a share proportionate to their length of time in the group. Our employee who quit on April 25th would receive 25/30s of the amount that an employee who worked the whole month of April would receive. They also take the view that employees who leave for any of the "unacceptable" reasons will not receive any share.

Some companies do take the view that the employee has to be employed on the last day of the fiscal period in order to be considered for a share, in spite of the reason for leaving. Some take an even harder stance in that they insist that the employee still be employed when the payment is made. For example, XYZ Company has a profit-sharing plan which is calculated and paid annually. Payment is not usually made until after audited financial statements are received, about three months after the year end. XYZ Company insists that the employee has to be on the payroll at that time in order to receive payment.

Another issue regarding leaving the plan is whether the employee will receive a full share or one that is in proportion to the fraction of the fiscal period he spent as a member of the group. In the preceding example, the employee who quit on April 25th was given 25/30s of a full share. Although this is by far the most common practice, it is not absolutely necessary. Some organizations would consider the employee to be eligible for a full share.

There is also the consideration of whether the employee has to be around for a minimum number of days or months during the fiscal period in order to get anything. Some plans say that, if the employee leaves, for any reason, before he has completed a minimum portion of the period, such as one-half, he will not be eligible for any payment.

GENERATING THE FUNDS

Every incentive plan needs a methodology by which the pool of money that is to be divided among the members is established. The three specific types of plans discussed in Chapters 13, 14, and 15 (respectively, profit sharing, productivity gainsharing and ESOPs) have quite specific methods of doing so. Scanlon gainsharing plans, for example, take the value of production added during a specific month and compare it with an historical standard. This results in a pool of funds which is then split between the company and the employees and allocated to them as a percentage of their base pay. These details will be covered in the following chapters related to each specific type of plan.

However, in the case of team-based incentives, which are relatively new in the compensation field, the methodology of generating the funds for distribution is not as clearly established. Therefore, in the following paragraphs, I have outlined some general principles. These include that the plan should:

- reinforce desired behaviour;
- be within the control of the members of the group;
- be simple;
- be compatible with other groups;
- be large enough to be interesting to the group;
- generate a satisfactory return on investment; and
- be related to specific results.

There are two major ways by which you can establish the pool of funds. The first is to arbitrarily set aside an amount that will meet at least one criteria — be large enough to catch the eye of the group members. Remember that it should be about 3% to 5% of their base pay to meet this test. Suppose you had a team of ten employees averaging about $50,000 in base salary. This would mean that your bonus pool should be at least $15,000 to $25,000. This is the minimum you need to get their attention. It can, and possibly should, be larger than this.

Your arbitrary amount should also be tied to specific results that you expect or want the group to achieve, such as the implementation of a new system at a client company (for a systems implementation team) or the achievement of a specific market share in a new product line for a sales and marketing group.

The other major way to establish the bonus pool is to make it a portion of specified financial results. Cash profit-sharing plans are the best examples of this approach. One seafood products company in Newfoundland takes 10% of net profits before taxes. There are an endless number of ways to do the same but here are a number of examples to give you an idea of how to proceed:

TYPE OF PLAN	BONUS POOL
Sales	Percentage of increase in dollar volume
Mining production	$ per ton of ore produced
Management consulting	$ per hour billed to clients
Clerical group	Percentage of reduction in overhead costs

DIVIDING THE BONUS POOL

The third major issue you need to address in any group incentive plan is how to divide the pool of money that you established in the last section among the members you identified in the section before that. This is called the allocation formula.

The allocation formula can be the most significant variable of any group incentive plan. It probably has more effect on the members' perception of fairness and equity than any other factor. Each of the specific types of plans in the following chapters, profit sharing, gainsharing and ESOPs, have allocation formulas that are most common to that type of group incentive plan. However, as with the bonus pool determination, there are a number of common principles that can be followed. Here is a list of the major possibilities that can be used in an allocation formula:

- earnings;
- seniority or length of service;
- equal distribution;
- merit ratings;
- attendance;
- job levels;
- contributions by the employees; and
- combinations of two or more of the above.

I will discuss each of these in a little more detail below.

Earnings

The rationale for using earnings is that a person's pay can be considered a good approximation of his or her relative contribution to the success of the group. The manager who is paid $75,000 per year probably contributes more to the performance of the systems-implementation team than the junior programmer at $35,000.

Earnings are usually taken to mean base salary but do not have to be. They can be defined to include other items such as overtime, shift premiums or sales commissions. The important item to remember is to count only forms of earnings for which all members of your group are eligible. Management employees do not normally receive overtime but their employees can. If the group includes sales staff who can earn commission, and other administrative staff who cannot, you should probably not count commissions in earnings.

Seniority or Length of Service

Length of service or seniority (I will use the terms interchangeably although technically they are somewhat different) is used in allocation formulas for three reasons:

- The longer an employee has been with the group or the organization the more he has contributed to the achievement of the results of the group.
- Employees engage in many activities which do not produce results in the fiscal period in which they occur. This could be simply because they take place too late in the period or the nature of the improvement takes some time to come to fruition.
- The employee simply acquires skills and knowledge that make his contribution to the group more valuable as time goes on.

Length of service is connected to the membership issue in that it is affected by the minimum period of employment established for membership. If each member of the group is a member of the incentive plan as soon as they join the group (*i.e.*, there is no minimum length of service) you can start counting service right away. On the other hand, if you have a minimum period of 12 months, a number of other issues arise. Using an example will make this easier to understand. Suppose an employee starts at this company on April 1, 2002. The company requires that employees have 12 months of service before they are members of the plan, which pays out annually after the end of the fiscal year which is December 31st.

▽	▽	▽	▽

Start	**End of Fiscal Year**		
April 1 2002	Dec. 31, 2002	April 1, 2003	Dec. 31, 2003

According to this chart there are two points at which the employee can be considered to have completed the requisite 12 months of service. On April 1, 2003, she will have completed 12 months of service. However, some organizations insist that the 12 months must be achieved as of the last day of the fiscal year, in other words, within the fiscal year. In this case, she will not have fulfilled the requirement until December 31, 2003. This is a somewhat technical glitch. The only practical purpose it serves is to extend the length of service requirement for membership.

Another major issue about using length of service is whether it can be accumulated indefinitely or whether there should be a cap on the amount of service that will be used in the allocation of the bonus pool. The question is whether the reasons, cited above, for using length of service are open-ended. Does the employee continue to become more valuable to the operation of the group, and therefore contribute more and more, or does this eventually taper off. For the purpose of this discussion, let's consider two caricatures of employees. Both start in the lowest-level job in the organization. Both are exemplary employees — loyal, productive and co-operative. Employee A stays in the same, entry-level job for his entire career with the company. Employee B progresses steadily and ends up as the president of the company. (I am not implying that one of these employees is a better human being because of his career path; although the example is extreme, this happens for very good reasons.)

You can argue that Employee A, although a valuable employee, does not increase in contribution as he accumulates seniority beyond a certain point, and therefore allowing unlimited use of length of service in the allocation formula is not equitable. To solve this problem, many organizations place a cap on the amount of service that will be used in the allocation formula. Five or ten years is often set as a maximum.

Another variation on this issue is when to start counting if you are establishing a new plan. This only happens with a new plan. The question is whether or not you recognize seniority accumulated before the plan started or only after the start date. Virtually all companies choose the former approach.

Equal Distribution

Some organizations like to divide the bonus pool equally among the members of the plan. If there are 20 employees in the group and the pool of funds is $5,000, each employee gets $250. The rationale is: everybody is in this together, this is a joint effort, everybody works equally hard, any difference in basic contribution is recognized by differences in base salary. Equal distribution can be quite effective where the group is relatively small and there is not much difference in level of responsibility and/or base salaries.

Merit Ratings

Some organizations use merit ratings, an assessment by somebody, usually one or more levels of management, about the performance of the individual employee. The design and implementation of performance appraisal systems for use in compensation programs is covered in detail in Chapter 16, "Performance Management and Rewards", but I will provide some general comments here.

In this, and the following four chapters, we are talking about group incentive plans. The major feature of such plans is that they produce some financial result which is determined by the performance of the group. The basic premise of all such plans is that the group will do better than the individual, simply because of the characteristics of group behaviour.

Therefore, in my opinion, it seems counterproductive to introduce an element of individual performance into the group situation. Performance appraisal systems are designed to motivate individual performance, which may, or may not, be a contribution to the performance of the group.

Attendance

Counting the hours an employee is actually at work and including that number in the allocation formula can be done. It obviously will contribute to improved attendance. However, I do not encourage this for two reasons. First, it is similar to an individual merit assessment program, with only one performance factor, and should not be used for the same reasons as I am opposed to the use of merit ratings (see the previous section). The other reason it should not be used is that attendance is more appropriately treated as a management or disciplinary problem. Dealing with attendance problems should be part of your managers' daily routine as issues arise.

Job Levels

Jobs levels are a variation on using earnings in the allocation formula. If you have not followed the prescriptions laid out earlier in this book and do not have a reasonably (internally) equitable program of base salaries, you can use job levels. Jobs are grouped into categories, a predefined portion of the bonus pool is assigned to each category, and those funds are then allocated another way (*e.g.*, equally or by length of service) within the job level. Here is an example of job levels:

GROUP	PERCENTAGE OF POOL
Senior management	10
All other managers	20
Professional and technical employees	20
All other employees	50

Contributions by Employees

Some plans, such as group registered retirement savings plans ("group RRSPs") based on profit sharing, require employees to make contributions to the plan for exactly the same reasons that they require employee contributions to registered pension plans. The organization expects employees to at least partially pay for their long-term security, like retirement. In such cases it is not unusual for the employer to use the size of the payment by the employee as part of the allocation formula. For example, if the employee contributes $100 to the plan, they could be given one point which would be equal to the one point they receive for each year of service. This assumes the company is using employee contribution and length of service as the two components of its allocation formula. This practice used to be quite common with DPSPs prior to changes to the *Income Tax Act*[4] in 1991, which eliminated employee contributions to DPSPs.

Using employee contributions as part of the allocation formula will obviously encourage employees to save. It is debatable to what extent it will motivate them to work harder and/or smarter in support of the objectives of the group incentive plan.

Combinations

Any of the preceding options can be used by itself. In fact, all the classic productivity gainsharing plans (Scanlon, Rucker and Improshare) use only earnings in their allocation formulas. That does not mean they are right; it is just the way they have always been done.

Any of the factors discussed here can be used in combination with one or more of the others, although earnings and job levels are not usually combined as they are essentially the same factor. Earnings and length of service are frequently combined.

Choosing an Allocation Formula

Given all these choices, how do you select an allocation formula? There are three criteria. The first is that the formula should reinforce the objectives set for the plan early in the process. If, for example, your objective was to encourage employees to stay with the company, you should use length of service in the formula. If you want to ensure that the payout is proportionate to the employee's contribution to profitability, you have to use either earnings or job level.

The second criterion is that the formula should reflect the values of the employees. The best way to ensure this is to use an employee committee, as discussed in Chapter 1, to develop the formula. Finally, try and keep the formula as simple as possible while fulfilling the first two criteria. Simplicity is

---

[4] R.S.C. 1985, c. 1 (5th Supp.).

a major virtue in designing plans since it makes them much easier to communicate and administer.

COMPARISON OF PLANS

In the following table, I have summarized the major features of group incentive plans and provided an analysis of each type of plan. This may help you assess the relevance of each type to your situation. I use the terms low, high and moderate in the relative sense, not in absolute terms.

Criteria	Team Plans	Productivity Gainsharing	Cash Profit Sharing	Non-Cash Profit Sharing	ESOPs
Effort to implement	Low	High	Low	High	High
Effort to administer	Low	High	Low	High	High
Needs performance appraisal system	Possible	No	Possible but rare	Possible but rare	Possible but rare
Connection to "line of sight"[5]	High	High	Medium	Low to Medium	Low to Medium
Motivates inter-group rivalry	Yes	Yes	No	No	No

CONCLUSION

In this chapter we have reviewed the general principles involved in the design of a group incentive plan which can include team plans, productivity gainsharing, profit sharing (cash and deferred) and ESOPs. It is important to remember that this discussion has been about general principles. There are significant variations between the four types, and even among types when you get down to the specific organization in which they are implemented. In the next four chapters we will look at each of these four types of plans in more detail. You may wish to review this chapter after you have read them.

---

[5] "Line of sight" refers to the connection between the employee's performance and the corporate reward.

12

Team-Based Incentives

INTRODUCTION

There is a great deal of interest by Canadian employers in incentive pay for teams or small groups. This chapter will explore the reasons for the interest in teams, look at the types of teams, examine some models and discuss the compensation issues involved in paying teams, both in terms of base salaries and any other compensation plan.

WHY TEAM-BASED INCENTIVES?

Team-based incentives are appealing for two reasons that are quite closely connected. First, traditional individual incentive plans (such as piece work or sales commissions) encourage and reward personal behaviour that is often in conflict with the objectives of the group to which the employee belongs. The nature of work in the modern organization is more closely tied to group performance than ever before. Secondly, incentive plans that operate at the corporate or division level, such as employee share ownership plans ("ESOPs") or productivity gainsharing plans (*e.g.*, the Scanlon Plan or the Rucker Plan),[1] often lose the connection between the performance of the employee and that corporate reward. This is called the "line of sight". Employees cannot see the relationship between their personal productivity and the operating profit produced by the division in which they work.

---

[1] See the discussion of these plans in Chapter 14, "Productivity Gainsharing".

PREVALENCE OF TEAM-BASED INCENTIVES

Although there appears to be a great deal of interest in the subject, it is very difficult to determine exactly how many employers are actually implementing such incentive plans. The surveys differ quite widely on the subject.

For example, one survey reported that between 6% and 11% (depending on the employee group) of the companies claimed that they already had team-based or group incentives. Approximately 2% of the same companies reported that they were considering installing such plans.

Another survey showed that over 27% of about 300 companies had group or team incentive bonuses for their executive, management and professional employees. A third survey organization found that about 13% of the companies reporting had team/small group incentives for executive, middle management and sales personnel, but almost 22% had these plans for their office, professional and production staff. The same survey showed significant differences in the incidence of team incentives by industry. Small group incentives were quite common in durable goods manufacturing and banking/finance. Apparently, they do not exist at all in health care.

WHAT IS A TEAM?

A major problem with tracking the incidence of team incentives is the wide range of possibilities regarding exactly what constitutes a team. Katzenbach provides the following definition, which is useful as a starting point: "A team is a small number of people with complementary skills who are committed to a common purpose, set of performance goals, and approach for which they hold themselves mutually accountable."[2]

However, this still leaves an enormous amount of room in the corporation for teams. Any grouping below the corporate or division level, and above that of the individual employee, could constitute a "team" according to this definition. Stephen Gross, in his book about incentive pay for teams,[3] identifies three types of teams: parallel; process; and project.

Parallel teams are usually part-time teams, such as safety or suggestions. The members of the team have other jobs and the team can be either permanent or temporary in duration. A process team, on the other hand, is normally permanent and employees are permanent members of the team. They are also in the same job family. Examples of process teams are groups in the assembly of a product and an order-processing operation. In my opinion, a sales force can be considered a process team. Project teams are also described as time-based. They are set up for the purpose of a particular project, such as the design of a

---

[2]   J. Katzenbach and D.K. Smith, "The Discipline of Teams" (March-April 1993), Harv. Bus. Rev., at p. 111.

[3]   S. Gross, *Compensation for Teams – How to Design and Implement Team-Based Reward Programs* (New York: American Management Assn., 1995).

new photocopier, the installation of a computer system for a client or the re-engineering of a manufacturing assembly line. The members of a project team are full-time, but only for the duration of the project.

TYPES OF TEAMS

TYPE OF TEAM	SPORTS ANALOGY	CORPORATE EXAMPLE	CHARACTERISTICS
Parallel	gymnastics/skiing teams	safety committee suggestion plan committee	part-time, can be temporary or permanent members have other jobs
Process	soccer/basketball teams	assembly cells order processing sales	employees in same job family measure group results
Project (time-based)	rare – both the men's and women's Canadian hockey teams at the 2002 Olympics are good examples	design a new car or computer re-engineer a process	members are full-time, but only for the length of the project

TRADITIONAL DESIGN ISSUES

The design of any type of incentive plan for a group (*i.e.*, two or more individuals) always involves the following three main issues:

- identifying the members of the group;
- measuring the performance of the group; and
- dividing the funds generated by the group performance.

DESIGN ISSUES FOR TEAMS

Here are some of the issues which need to be addressed in the design of team incentive programs in addition to the traditional topics:

- Will teams receive incentive pay when the company does not make a profit?
- How do you compensate employees who are not members of teams, but hold jobs comparable in value to team members?
- Who defines a team — human resources, compensation, line management?
- How will total cash compensation be divided between base salary, corporate incentives and team incentives?
- Should all team members receive the same base salary?

- How do you avoid team incentives that discourage co-operation between teams or between other parts of the organization, including other teams, departments, sections, divisions and even individuals?
- How do you adjust the performance management system to account for the performance of the individual on the team?
- Can an employee be a member of more than one team?
- Do team members share the "team reward" equally, or is it divided according to performance, time spent on team work, base salary or some other criteria?

No Profit

In my opinion, you cannot tie most teams' incentive pay to the profitability of the overall organization, especially if you are a not-for-profit one, unless the team is a process team as defined earlier. If we look at a sales team, for example, it is not unusual to require that the company be profitable before any sales team bonuses or commissions are paid. This intuitively makes sense as there is not much point in selling your products or services unless it is profitable to do so. However, in the case of the other two types of teams, parallel and project, it does make sense to pay them for the achievement of objectives which have an impact beyond the current fiscal year. It is possible to have teams that actually reduce the profitability in the current year.

Base Salary

Should members of a team all receive the same base salary? This is more a question of whether they should be in the same salary grade. With all three types of teams, each person has a basic job. For process teams, the job is part of the team although there may be different types of jobs in the team. Look at a sales team; it could be comprised of the sales manager, senior sales representative, junior sales representative and sales trainee. They all come from the same job family. On the other hand, a project team implementing a human resource information system may come from a variety of different job families, such as payroll, systems, accounting, human resources and operations. They could also be from a wide range of levels in the hierarchy, from vice-president to analyst.

The bottom line regarding base salaries is that, with all types of teams, base salary should be determined by the primary job of the individual, using the methodologies provided earlier in this book. This sounds pretty straightforward, except that it raises the question as to when the responsibility of being a member of a team affects the evaluation of the basic job. Again, we have to look at this question according to the type of team. For process teams, the basic job is to be part of the team and this is not an issue. For project teams, the team responsibilities are clearly above and beyond the basic job, but are of limited duration, so they need to be paid for separately from base salary. For parallel teams, the team functions of the individual are usually considered part of their ongoing job responsibilities and should be written into their job description. The following table may help clarify these questions:

TYPE OF TEAM	TEAM FUNCTIONS INCLUDED IN BASIC JOB?	GROUP PLAN REQUIRED TO PAY FOR TEAM FUNCTIONS?
Parallel	Possibly	No
Process	Yes	Possibly
Project	No	Yes

Number of Teams

How many teams can one employee belong to? This is not really a compensation question. It is more a practical question of workload and job design which is beyond the scope of this book. I would only caution that there might be a tendency for executives to add their favourite employee to teams in order to get him or her more pay than could be obtained by legitimate means. This, of course, is a waste of money and will create a number of issues regarding the equitable treatment of employees.

Dividing up the Team-bonus Pool

In Chapter 11, "Designing a Group Incentive Plan", we discussed the major ways in which group incentives can be divided among the members of the plan. Since teams are, by definition, much smaller than the groups covered by ESOPs, gainsharing or profit-sharing plans, I believe the options can be limited to three factors which are:

- merit rating;
- prorate to base salary; and
- equal division.

The advantages and disadvantages of merit ratings are discussed in detail in Chapter 16, "Performance Management and Rewards". I question the usefulness of merit ratings in team incentive plans for the simple reason that they create a win-lose situation and can be very difficult to administer fairly and equitably. I have similar but less vigorous objections to the use of merit ratings in the allocation formula for large group incentive plans. However, they have been used successfully in such situations.

Prorating to base salary is easy to do and simple to communicate. However, it can have several disadvantages. In the case of process teams, where all the jobs may be quite similar in salary (*i.e.*, there are small differences in actual base salary because all the team members are in the same, or closely related, salary ranges), prorating to base salary will result in small differences in payout which bear little or no resemblance to the actual, relative performance of the individuals.

The argument against using prorating in project teams is quite the opposite. In such teams you may have team members who have quite different base salaries because of their basic jobs (vice-president to trainee). On the other hand, their contribution to the team, in terms of time, may be inversely proportionate to their base salary. The vice-president may spend very little time on team functions, while the systems analyst might spend a large proportion of her time on it.

Dividing the pool equally among the members has more appeal with teams than it does with other types of group incentive plans, where it is used in about 10% of plans. The general reason for using equal distribution in profit-sharing plans is that the group is small, everybody contributes equally, and there is little difference in rank or salary. Equal distribution is therefore the most equitable option for allocating the bonus pool.

Employees Who are Not Team Members

There may be questions raised by employees who are not members of any team, of any type, and are not eligible for any extra payments beyond their base salary or any organization-wide incentive plan. They may look at fellow employees, who are in jobs that are essentially the same as their own except for the team responsibilities, and perceive that they are being treated unfairly. Let's look at this according to the three types of teams.

Members of parallel teams will have the team functions included in their basic job and, if these functions are significant enough, they will produce a salary grade above that of the complaining employees. Members of project teams will have responsibilities that exceed those of employees in jobs that don't include the team functions and additional compensation is therefore justified. Members of process teams have their team functions built into their basic job responsibilities and this should not be a problem.

Models

Here are three separate models of a team incentive plan that could be used for discussion purposes in your organization. They vary according to their purpose, their membership, how the total funds are generated and how the funds are divided amongst the members of the team.

Model A

- *Type/purpose of team* — Cost reduction.
- *Membership* — All team members who work six weeks or more during the quarter.
- *Generate pool* — 50% of savings created by the team, payable on first dollar on savings.

- *Allocation* — Divide equally in dollars among the team members.

Model B

- *Type of team* — Product development.
- *Membership* — Team is formed at the start of the project and those still employed at the end are eligible.
- *Generate pool* — Management determines a dollar amount to be paid if the team reaches its target completion date with acceptable quality.
- *Allocation* — Prorate to base salaries of team members.

Model C

- *Type of team* — Systems implementation team.
- *Membership* — All team members who work on the implementation in proportion to the time they spend on the assignment.
- *Generate pool* — A percentage of the fees paid by the client for the systems implementation scaled according to the degree of client satisfaction.
- *Allocation* — Give each team member 1 point for each day on the project plus 1 point for each $1,000 of base salary multiplied by his or her performance rating. Divide the pool according to the points.

CONCLUSION

Although it is a relatively new concept and needs more conceptual development, team-based incentives offer significant potential for motivating and rewarding employees for group behaviour below the corporate level. Since a significant proportion of corporate effort is carried out by teams or groups rather than individuals, this aspect of compensation needs to be developed further by compensation professionals.

13

Profit Sharing

INTRODUCTION

Profit sharing is one of the oldest forms of group incentive plans reported in the business literature. The first plan, according to most sources, was created by Jean Leclaire, who ran a house-painting business in Paris, France. He announced the plan to his workers in 1842 and distributed 12,266 gold francs among them the following year. Apparently his staff, like employees everywhere, were quite skeptical until he actually gave out the money. In Canada, the earliest reported profit-sharing plan was that of the W.F. Hatheway Company of Saint John, New Brunswick, which was established in 1888.

This chapter will discuss the following aspects of profit sharing:

- definition and types of plans;
- objective(s) of plans;
- strategic issues to be decided by management; and
- major design issues.

DEFINITION AND TYPES OF PLANS

Profit sharing can be defined as "a compensation program which makes payments to employees, over and above their base salaries or wages, which are determined by the level of profits of the corporation". For example, Atlas-Graham Industries of Winnipeg, Manitoba, a small manufacturer of mops and brushes, has a classic cash profit-sharing plan. The company deducts 2% of sales from net profit before taxes and distributes 30% of the remainder equally among the employees.

One other distinction is important. In this chapter, I am talking about "broad-based" profit-sharing plans. These normally include virtually all the employees of a company and should be distinguished from "top-hat" plans which are usually reserved for the senior executives.

In Canada, there are four major types, and one minor type, of profit-sharing plans. The four major types are:

- cash;
- deferred profit-sharing plans ("DPSPs");
- employee profit-sharing plans ("EPSPs"); and
- combination plans.

The minor sort of profit-sharing plan is a group registered retirement savings plan ("RRSP") which is based on profitability. These are still quite unusual and are basically a variation on a DPSP.

Cash

In cash plans all payments are made to the employees "in cash" and are fully taxable to the employee. The payments are deductible for the employer and there is no limit on the amount of the deduction. Income tax must be withheld at source. Cash plans are the most common type of profit sharing.

Deferred Profit-Sharing Plans

Deferred profit-sharing plans are primarily governed by s. 147 of the *Income Tax Act*[1] ("the Act"). The employer may make contributions to a trust fund on behalf of employees up to certain maximums. The Act limits both the total contribution made by an employer and an employee to DPSPs, registered pension plans ("RPPs") and RRSPs, and the total contributions made by the employer to a DPSP.

All contributions, within these limits, are deductible expenses for the employer. Earnings and capital gains of the trust are not taxed until they are withdrawn — exactly like RRSPs. The funds can be used for most types of investments although there are some limitations.

Employee Profit-Sharing Plans

Section 144 of the Act is the legal basis for EPSPs. The use of the term "employee" is unfortunate, since all types of profit-sharing plans include employees. EPSPs are similar to DPSPs in that funds are placed in a trust, on behalf of the employee, by the employer without any limits. One difference is that income tax must be withheld by the employer. Another difference is that

---

[1]   R.S.C. 1985, c. 1 (5th Supp.).

there are no limits on the types of investments, but the earnings and capital gains of the trust are taxed each year. EPSPs are very rare.

Combination Plans

Obviously, you can set up a profit-sharing plan which combines any two, or all three, of the preceding options. For example, you could have a plan that is part DPSP and part cash. The company would pay the maximum allowable under the Act to the DPSP and any amount left over from the employer allocation (X% of profits) is paid in cash. Another possibility is to pay 50% of the company contribution to the DPSP and 50% in cash. The major features of any combination plan will depend on the exact proportions of the major components. Combination plans are able to achieve a lot of the objectives of all types of plans.

Group Registered Retirement Savings Plans

Normally, group RRSPs are set up instead of, or in addition to, a pension plan. Some employers, such as Almag Aluminum of Brampton, Ontario, use a group RRSP instead of a DPSP since they cost less to administer and register. The primary difference between a DPSP and a group RRSP is that in the former you can control employees' withdrawals from the plan. With a DPSP the employer is allowed to restrict withdrawals to death, retirement or the attainment of age 65. An employer cannot do this with a group RRSP, except by withholding future company contributions to the plan when an employee withdraws moneys.

OBJECTIVES OF PLANS

Profit-sharing plans can be used to achieve many objectives. One of the first steps when considering a plan is to determine what you are trying to achieve with it. Here is a list of the major objectives for a profit-sharing plan that companies have established in the past. The objective is just the answer to the apparently easy question: "Why do I, the employer, want to establish a profit-sharing plan?" The major objectives are to:

- provide an incentive for employees to increase productivity;
- provide retirement income;
- reduce turnover;
- improve the ability to attract high-quality employees;
- reinforce teamwork;
- encourage employee savings; and
- enable employees to acquire "ownership" in the company.

Some of these objectives dictate the type of plan you will need. For example, if you wish to provide retirement income for employees, you will have to go with a DPSP or possibly an EPSP. On the other hand, if you need to attract high-quality employees, a cash plan with a short length of service requirement will be more suitable. If you wish to encourage employee savings, either a DPSP or EPSP can do the job (with different tax implications), while promoting employee ownership in a private company can only be done with an EPSP.

Your choice of objective will influence nearly all the decisions you make about the design of your profit-sharing plan.

STRATEGIC ISSUES TO BE DECIDED BY MANAGEMENT

In preparation for designing a plan, the following issues must be addressed by management before starting to involve the employees:

- objective(s) of the proposed plan;
- type of plan;
- nature and degree of employee involvement in the design process; and
- definition and amount of the employer contribution to the plan.

It is critical that you have a clear idea of what you want to do with your profit-sharing plan. Plans can perform a number of different functions. The choice of objective will influence virtually all of the design decisions that you make later on. Three brief examples will illustrate this point but it will become much clearer as you progress through the procedure. If your purpose in introducing profit sharing is the provision of retirement income (either in addition to, or instead of, a pension plan) then it is pretty clear that you will have to use a DPSP. If you are a private company and want employees to become owners, it will be necessary to use an EPSP. If you want to attract high-quality employees you will have to make your waiting period to join the plan very short or eliminate it entirely.

Some employers know in advance what type of plan they want to install. They have decided, for example, that they want to use profit sharing to provide retirement income and therefore they have to use a DPSP. Others only know that they want to have some form of profit sharing, believing that it is "a good thing", but are open to the exact type of plan. If you are in this second category it is useful and practical to go to the employees and seek their input regarding what type of plan will be most effective. On the other hand, if you know what type of plan you want, simply advise the employees of that decision and get on with it. In my experience, they will readily accept this. What they will not accept is being asked their opinion when you have already decided and then having that opinion ignored. My experience has been that virtually all employees prefer a cash plan if they are given a choice. Therefore, if you are sure that you want something other than a cash plan, just make that decision and communicate it.

One of the most critical decisions you will make at this stage is the extent to which you will involve rank-and-file employees in the process of designing your profit-sharing plan. Basically you have two choices. You can sit down by yourself, or with a few trusted advisors, design the plan and then announce it. Most employers who have done this expect the employees to be both pleasantly surprised and grateful. What usually happens is that the employer is shocked to find that her employees are surprised but very suspicious of her motives; they are also often hostile. In these circumstances they will question every design decision you have made. The only way I know to counter this is to get employees involved in the process as early as possible.

By far the best way to do this is to form a committee comprised of a representative cross-section of employees (between five and ten). It should represent all the major divisions, departments, levels, occupational groups and the demographics of the employee population. I recommend that you choose employees who are:

- viewed as "opinion leaders" by the group they are supposed to represent;
- able to understand the concepts involved; and
- willing to act as spokesperson for their group and are articulate enough to do so.

At this stage I suggest that you select the committee members instead of having them elected, primarily because it is easier to obtain the characteristics mentioned if you make the choice. You may decide to have an ongoing committee to help administer the plan to which employees will be elected, but this is a separate issue.

The final and most significant decision that you must make, and have a good grasp of, before proceeding with an employee committee is that of the size and definition of the company contribution to the profit-sharing fund. In other words, how much money will you, the employer, put into this plan? The sub-issues in this question involve: the definition of profits; the proportion thereof that will be available for distribution to the employees; the type of formula; and the timing and frequency of the payments.

Profits can be defined in two ways: net profits before tax; or net after tax. Over 80% of companies use net profits before tax. A related question is whether or not to include extraordinary gains or losses (such as the sale of a building), and investment gains and losses, in the calculation. In making this decision, determine whether the employees have a significant influence on the activities in question and, if so, include them. The opposite also applies. Some companies, such as Algoma Steel, use operating profit as the basis for their calculation.

You can decide to use either a "specified" or "discretionary" formula. Discretionary means that you decide each year what proportion of profits will go into the plan. Specified means that you declare, when the plan is introduced, what percentage of profits (however defined) will be contributed by the company. I do not recommend the use of a discretionary formula for a broad-based, employee profit-sharing plan. Discretionary formulas are more appropriate for executive bonus plans than for the broad-based profit-sharing plans that we are discussing here.

The actual formula can be a straight percentage of all profits, such as 15% of net profit before taxes. Alternatively, it can be a specified percentage above a certain minimum level of profit. For example, it could be 10% of net profit over $100,000 after taxes. A formula can also be graduated so that the percentage of profits to be paid out increases at various points. It could provide for 10% of the first $1 million, 15% of the next million, and 20% of any profits over $2 million.

The final decision is the actual percentage that will be used. The two most common are 8% to 10% of net profit before taxes and 15% of the same amount. You have to look at your own requirements for capital and cash flow in making this decision.

The other approach to answering this question is to look at your proposed percentage of profits as a percentage of your cash payroll. Psychologists tell us that any payment to employees should be at least 3% to 5% of their base pay, just to get their attention. However, you have to think of this as a very rough rule of thumb. Remember, 2% of annual pay is more than one week's pay and some would consider this significant. I know at least one company president who claims he has never paid out more than 2% but has a very successful profit-sharing plan. If you are just starting your profit-sharing plan and you are not totally sure about what percentage of profits to contribute, start with an amount that meets the criteria mentioned above but on the low end. You can always increase the percentage later. It is much more difficult to decrease if you find you are not able to sustain that level of contribution to the plan.

MAJOR DESIGN ISSUES

If you have decided to follow my recommendation to involve the employees in the design process, you are now at the point where you can select and meet with your committee. You have made the decisions necessary in the previous section to get to this point. There are two major design issues that you can take to the committee — membership and allocation.

Membership

Membership is simply the answer to the question: "Who will be in the profit-sharing plan?" or "Who will be eligible to receive a share of the profits when they are distributed?" This question must be answered for all types of plans, whether they are cash or deferred. There are five ways to define membership:

- category of employment;
- length of service;
- employees who leave the company;
- union status; and
- employees who are already in an incentive plan.

The first two topics, category of employment (full-time, part-time, occasional, temporary or contract employees) and length of service, are quite intertwined. All plans include full-time employees subject to a length of service requirement. The evidence is more mixed regarding part-time employees; some companies include them while others do not. Those that do require the same length of service that they do of full-time employees, except that they allow the employee more elapsed time to achieve it. For example, if an employee works half-time and the normal length of service is three months, the part-timer will have to work six months before being admitted to the plan. Occasional and temporary employees are never included in a plan, at least to my knowledge. The inclusion of contract employees has become more of an issue in recent years since many more companies are using them. One can argue that contract employees are simply temporary employees with somewhat different characteristics and they should no more be included than any other temporaries.

However, two characteristics of contract employees do separate them from the temporary employee who is hired as a summer replacement. They tend to work longer, say six months to one year or even more, and they also tend to be in professional occupations. Their use is extremely prevalent in the information technology ("IT") field. A payroll services company in Winnipeg includes contract employees in its plan as long as they meet the minimum service requirements and are on the payroll on the last day of the fiscal year. What you should really consider is whether they are at a high enough level, and are employed long enough, that they become very much a "part of the team". If so, you should probably include them in the membership of the plan.

If you have bargaining units at your company, you will have to decide whether or not to include those unionized employees in the profit-sharing plan. In general, Canadian labour law does not obligate you to negotiate profit sharing with the union unless the recognition clause in the collective agreement includes profit sharing. My first approach to this issue is to consider the unionized employees members of the plan unless there is some reason not to do so. My rationale is that profit-sharing plans are, by definition, "broad-based" and therefore should be all inclusive. On the other hand, there are two major reasons why they are excluded. One is that they often already have some sort of group incentive plan, such as a Scanlon productivity gainsharing plan[2] or even an old-fashioned piece-work system. The other reason may be that the union leadership, either local or national, is philosophically opposed to the idea of profit sharing. Officially, organized labour in Canada is vehemently opposed to profit sharing or any other form of "variable" pay.

The last membership issue that should be addressed concerns those employees who are already involved in some sort of incentive plan. As discussed, these could be union, or non-union, employees in a productivity gainsharing plan. The other most common such group are sales representatives on commission or other sales incentive plan. There are two points of view about this issue. One is that such employees are already included in a "bonus" plan and including them in profit sharing would tend to reward them twice for the same effort. The other viewpoint is that profit sharing is all-inclusive and therefore everybody should be in the plan; commissions or similar payments are really just part of the employee's regular earnings. This is not a technical issue in the strict sense of the term; it is more of a philosophical question. To what extent do you really believe that a profit-sharing plan should involve as many employees as possible?

Allocation

Allocation is simply "how you divide up the available profits among the members of the plan". These are the major factors used:

- earnings;
- job levels;
- attendance;
- length of service;
- merit ratings; and
- contributions by the employee.

Combinations of these factors are also often used.

To use earnings, you simply divide the employer contribution into the total cash earnings of the members of the plan; the technical term is "prorate to earnings". Using earnings means that an individual's share of the profits is roughly comparable to his contribution to their creation, assuming that you have a reasonably equitable salary administration program. If you do not have such a salary program you can use a variation of earnings: job levels. All jobs are grouped into categories such as executives, all other management, and non-management. A portion of the fund is pre-allocated to each group and then

---

[2]   See Chapter 14, "Productivity Gainsharing", for a complete review of productivity gainsharing plans.

is divided within the group using some other criteria. It could be divided equally, or prorated to the earnings, within each group.

Attendance can be used if you want to improve or maintain attendance levels. Points are given for each hour worked and the fund is allocated to each individual in proportion to the number of points held. Be sure to give points for hours of vacation. Otherwise, you will discriminate against employees with longer service who usually get more vacation. You may also wish to include overtime hours. The main point is to clearly identify which hours will be counted. Some believe that counting overtime hours discriminates against employees who are not eligible for overtime, such as managers.

Length of service or seniority is very often used, especially if you are trying to encourage employees to stay with the company and/or reduce turnover. Points can be given for each year of service, usually counted as of the last day of the fiscal period for which profits are calculated. One critical decision is whether or not you will place a maximum on the number of years that can be recognized. Most companies do, at about ten years, on the theory that most employees do not continually increase their contribution to profitability.

Merit ratings, that is, evaluations of the performance of the employee by one or more levels of supervision, can also be used. The essential ingredient for this to work is an effective performance management system. Since most companies do not have such a system, and they can be extremely difficult to develop, I generally do not recommend the use of merit ratings in your allocation formula. I am also opposed for another, more philosophical reason: such systems reward individual performance. Since profit sharing encourages, and rewards, group behaviour it is counterproductive to encourage the opposite.

Some profit-sharing plans are established to encourage employee savings and/or investments. Such plans often try to reward employees for their own contributions to a fund by partially or wholly matching what the employee puts in. For example, if the employee contributes $1 the employer may allocate 50¢ to the fund. Alternatively, the employee could be given one point for each $1 contributed and the funds would be allocated according to the points of each employee. This feature of plans was much more common before revisions to the Act in 1991 eliminated employee contributions[3] to DPSPs. However, it is still possible to have such a feature in a group RRSP which is based on profit sharing. The concept is virtually identical to that of employers matching employee contributions to a registered pension plan.

The final option regarding the allocation formula is to use combinations of these factors. Combinations are appropriate when you have multiple objectives for the plan or you simply want to reflect different demographics of your employees. You may have decided that the plan will be a retirement vehicle with employees contributing, but you also want the formula to reflect their

---

[3] These were not tax-deductible but any earnings and/or capital gains were not taxed until they were withdrawn.

relative contribution as indicated by their base salary. You could therefore give an employee one point for each $1,000 of base salary and two points for each $100 he contributes to the group RRSP. The most common combination formula includes earnings and seniority or length of service.

In my opinion, the allocation formula has the most influence on the employees' perseption of the fairness of the profit-sharing plan. When you are considering the various choices I suggest you review the section "Choosing an Allocation Formula" in Chapter 11, "Designing a Group Incentive Plan". In summary, that section says that the allocation formula should:

- support the objectives of the plan;
- recognize the opinions of the employees; and
- be simple.

CONCLUSION

In this chapter we have covered the major types of profit-sharing plans, the reasons for creating such plans, and the primary design issues, including the questions of the type of plan, employee involvement, membership in the plan and the allocation of the funds.

14

Productivity Gainsharing

INTRODUCTION

Productivity gainsharing is another form of group incentive plan with many similarities to profit sharing. In fact, it is often confused with profit sharing. There are some significant differences between the two types of group incentive plans which will be discussed later in this chapter.

Joseph Scanlon is considered to be the inventor of gainsharing, or "productivity gainsharing", which is the original name of this type of incentive plan. Mr. Scanlon was a union leader working for the Erie Steel Company in the 1930s. The company was in serious trouble and he apparently came up with the concept of sharing productivity gains between the company and the employees. The result was that the company returned to profitability and the term "Scanlon Plan" became part of the lexicon of compensation professionals.

In Canada, a review of a number of compensation surveys shows that 2% to 7% of companies have some sort of gainsharing plan. Unfortunately, the surveys do not distinguish between types of plans such as Scanlon or Rucker.

CHARACTERISTICS OF PRODUCTIVITY GAINSHARING PLANS

All gainsharing plans have the following characteristics:

- A productivity standard is established at a point in time.
- Productivity gains above this standard are shared between the employees and the company.
- Payments are made monthly.

- The funds are prorated to base salary for the purpose of allocating them to employees.
- Members of the plan are usually direct labour.

Gainsharing plans also differ in the following areas:

- the division of the gains between the employees and the company;
- the basic formula; and
- the amount of employee involvement.

The three major, traditional types of gainsharing plans, Scanlon, Rucker and Improshare, are described in the following sections.

SCANLON PLANS

An example of the calculation involved in a Scanlon plan is shown in the table which follows. The total value of production during the period is calculated by adding the actual sales, less returns, and any additions to inventory of finished goods. In the example, the value of production is $1,930,000. The "allowed payroll costs" are usually calculated using historical data although they can be calculated with industrial engineering techniques. In this case we have used 25% of the value of production as the standard, so that the actual allowed payroll costs in this period are 0.25 x $1,930,000 = $482,500.

In this example, the actual payroll costs are $400,000 and the difference between the "allowed" and actual costs is $82,500. This is the bonus pool. In classic Scanlon plans, 75% of the bonus pool is distributed to the employees.

The bonus pool is distributed on a *pro rata* basis according to the employee's earnings. In the example, each employee will receive 15.5% of his or her base pay as a bonus.

EXAMPLE OF A SCANLON PLAN CALCULATION

Sales	$2,000,000
Less returns	100,000
Net sales	1,900,000
Additional inventory	30,000
Value of production	1,930,000
Allowed payroll costs	
(25% of production)	482,500
Actual payroll costs	400,000
Bonus pool	82,500
Employee share of pool (75%)	61,875
Payout	61,875/400,000 = 15.5%

An essential feature of Scanlon plans is the establishment of a two-tier committee system. Production committees are formed in each major department and are comprised of employees and management (usually the supervisor of the section). The main purpose of these committees is to review and develop suggestions by the workers to improve quality, reduce costs or increase productivity. These committees meet twice a month.

There is also a screening or plant committee consisting of members of plant management and worker (usually union) representatives, who meet monthly to review reports by the production committees and, in general, to manage the gainsharing plan.

This level of employee involvement is an essential part of the Scanlon philosophy. It is not necessarily required in either of the other two types of gainsharing plans.

RUCKER PLANS

The table in this section provides an example of the calculations used in a Rucker gainsharing plan. As with Scanlon plans, there is a determination of the "value of production" but with a different methodology. There is also a determination of "allowed payroll costs" which can, as with Scanlon plans, be determined either historically or by industrial engineering methods.

The difference between the allowed payroll costs and actual costs form the bonus pool, just like the Scanlon plan. However, classic Rucker plans pay two-thirds of the pool to employees while one-third is kept by the company. In the example, this results in a bonus payment of 8% of the employee's base pay.

EXAMPLE OF A RUCKER PLAN CALCULATION

Value of production	$1,000,000
Less outside purchases	600,000
Value added	400,000
Allowed payroll costs	
(35% of value added)	140,000
Actual payroll costs	125,000
Bonus pool	15,000
Employee share of pool (2/3)	10,000
Payout	10,000/125,000 = 8%

IMPROSHARE™

Improshare was designed in the mid 1970s by an industrial engineer and management consultant, Mitchell Fein. This type of gainsharing uses quite a different productivity standard than either Scanlon or Rucker plans. The table which follows shows a sample calculation of the Improshare formula.

The first step in making an Improshare calculation is to establish the base standard. In the example, it is four hours. This is the number of labour hours required to produce one unit of product (for example, a hair dryer).

Next, you calculate the number of standard hours earned, which is the product of the standard hours per unit times the actual number of units produced. In this example it is 5,200 standard hours.

The actual hours worked are then compared with the standard hours and, if the standard hours exceed the actual hours, there is a "gain to be shared". In the example, this amounts to 1,120 hours. In Improshare plans any gain is split 50/50 between the employees and the company. Thus the 1,120 hours are divided in two and the result expressed as a percentage of the actual hours worked. Each employee will receive 13.7% of his or her base pay for this period. Improshare plans do not require any formal employee involvement as in Scanlon plans.

EXAMPLE OF AN IMPROSHARE CALCULATION

Base standard = average time to produce a unit
              = 4 hours

Actual example
  • 102 employees
  • 40-hour week
  • 1,300 units produced

Standard hours earned = 4 x 1,300   = 5,200
Actual hours   = 102 (employees) x 40 = 4,080
Difference   1,120

Payout $\dfrac{1,120}{2}$ = 560

              $\dfrac{560}{4,080}$ = 13.7%

OTHER GAINSHARING PLANS IN CANADA

There is a wide variety of incentive plans that are called gainsharing in Canadian businesses. Unfortunately, there is no central registry of such plans similar to the Profit Sharing/401(k) Council of America. However, it is possible to show several examples of such plans that are not necessarily one of the three classic types. Here are several examples found in collective agreements:

• *Employer* — Workers' Compensation Board of British Columbia
  Union — Compensation Employees' Union
  Date of agreement — April 1, 1998 to March 31, 2002

Number/type of employees — 2,400 office technical and professional employees

Plan — One per cent of payroll is set aside to be paid as a lump sum based on "planned productivity improvements". In the third year of the contract the lump sum will be converted to a general increase.

* *Employer* — Western Star Trucks, Kelowna, British Columbia
Union — International Association of Machinists and Aerospace Workers
Date of agreement — January 1, 1998 to June 30, 2002
Number/type of employees — 820 employees assembling heavy-duty trucks
Plan — If labour hours per truck fall below threshold and quality meets or exceeds acceptable levels, employees are eligible for additional adjustments of as much as 2% of annual salary.

* *Employer* — Ontario Hydro Services Company
Union — Canadian Union of Public Employees, Local 1000
Date of agreement — April 1, 2000 to March 31, 2001
Number/type of employees — 4,000 general trades and office/clerical employees
Plan — This is a new plan. During the contract a joint committee will develop an incentive plan designed to provide employees with the opportunity for financial gain from improved operational performance.

COMPARISON OF GAINSHARING AND PROFIT-SHARING PLANS

Some of the literature on incentive plans unfortunately uses the terms profit sharing and gainsharing almost interchangeably. Others describe profit sharing as a type of gainsharing. This confusion is somewhat unavoidable since they are both a form of incentive plan for groups of employees. However, they are quite different. Here is a summary of the differences.

A profit-sharing plan is obviously based on profitability. This alone makes it different from gainsharing plans which can pay out even when the overall company is not profitable. A further difference is that profit sharing is calculated each fiscal period as a portion of the profits for that period of time, *e.g.*, 10% of net profits after tax. Gainsharing plans calculate the bonus as the difference between the current level of productivity and the historical standard. The historical base is always the point of reference.

All gainsharing plans pay monthly. The vast majority of profit-sharing plans pay out annually. Very few profit-sharing plans are known to pay monthly, although some do make payments semi-annually or quarterly.

Gainsharing plans are generally organized at the plant or department level, often with just direct labour included as members. In contrast, profit sharing generally includes the whole company, division or profit centre, with some provision for a minimum length of service.

The final difference between the two types of plans concerns the allocation formula — how the bonus pool is divided among the employees who are members of the plan. All the classic gainsharing plans (Scanlon, Rucker, Improshare) prorate the bonus pool to base earnings. Profit-sharing plans also use this method but they frequently use many other methods of allocation.

The following table summarizes the differences between gainsharing and profit-sharing plans:

FEATURE	GAINSHARING	PROFIT SHARING
Membership	Usually direct labour at the plant or department level	Usually all employees of the company
Timing	Monthly	Most often annually
Calculation of bonus pool	Difference between historical standard and current period results	Portion of profits for current period
Allocation formula	Prorate to base salary	Variety of methods including prorate to base

EFFICACY OF GAINSHARING PLANS

In 1981 the General Accounting Office of the United States federal government did a major review of about 25 productivity gainsharing plans in the northwestern United States. It found that firms that had gainsharing plans for five years or more had labour cost savings averaging 29% per year.[1]

The most interesting result of this study was not the numerical results of the companies that provided actual, historical data. It was the fact that some companies would not participate in the study in any way because "they considered their productivity gainsharing plan to be a *competitive advantage*" and did not want other companies to have any information about their plan.

To my knowledge, there are no studies of the effectiveness of productivity gainsharing plans in Canada.

CONCLUSION

Productivity gainsharing plans can be an extremely effective way to motivate and reward employee contributions to productivity improvement at the

---

[1]   R. Long, *Compensation in Canada, Strategy, Practices and Issues* (Toronto: ITP Nelson, 1998), at p. 233.

local or department level. Like profit-sharing plans they need the following conditions:

- competitive base wages or salaries;
- commitment by management to the operation of the plans; and
- employee trust in management.

15

Employee Share Ownership Plans

GENERAL

Employee share ownership plans are generally known by the acronym "ESOPs". ESOPs, at least those that are broad-based, are a relatively new concept in Canadian businesses. Stock option plans for executives have been a staple in Canadian boardrooms for many years but the extension of such plans, or other forms of stock acquisition, to non-management employees is still not very widespread. ESOPs first appeared with Canadian subsidiaries of American companies around the time of the Second World War.

As with profit sharing, there is almost no federal government legislation specifically concerned with ESOPs, although one can consider deferred profit-sharing plans ("DPSPs") that purchase stock in the employer company as a form of ESOP.

There is some relevant legislation at the provincial level. The government of the Province of Quebec introduced the first ESOP legislation in Canada in 1979.[1] Its purpose was to create pools of capital for Quebec businesses. British Columbia enacted the *Employee Investment Act* in 1989.[2] This provides a 20% tax credit (provincial) for employees who purchase shares in companies that are registered according to the Act. There is also a labour-sponsored investment fund in Manitoba through which employees can purchase shares in Manitoba companies.

---

[1] P. Phillips, *Carswell's Compensation Guide* (Toronto: Carswell, 1996), at p. 34-17 (April 2000).

[2] R. Long, *Compensation in Canada, Strategy, Practices and Issues* (Toronto: ITP Nelson, 1998), at p. 255. See now *Employee Investment Act*, R.S.B.C. 1996, c. 112.

211

In November, 1990, a group of consultants, lawyers and actuaries with an interest in ESOPs formed ESOP Association Canada, which is a non-profit organization dedicated to promoting the concept of employee ownership for business.[3]

TYPES OF ESOPS

There are three primary types of ESOPs in Canada: stock-option plans; stock-grant plans; and stock-purchase plans.[4]

Stock-Option Plans

Stock options have been a cornerstone of executive compensation in Canada for over half a century. As in most countries, Canadian stock options allow the employee the chance to buy company stock in the future at the price on the day the option was granted. The Conference Board of Canada reports that 97 of the top 100 companies on the Toronto Stock Exchange provide stock options to the senior management team.[5] In the same document the authors report that, in the companies with a long-term incentive plan, 93% offer stock options to executives at the level just below senior management, 57% provide them to management staff and 22% give stock options to non-management salaried employees.[6]

Canadian federal legislation considers the benefit gained when a stock option is exercised to be a capital gain which is taxed at 50%. The Canadian government recently changed the rules so that this gain is only actually taxed when the shares are sold, not when the option is exercised. This change may have been in response to considerable lobbying by ESOP Association Canada and other industry groups like the Canadian Advanced Technology Association ("CATA"), who are concerned about the "brain drain" of talented and well-qualified people to the United States.

Stock-Grant Plans

Stock-grant plans involve the employer giving company stock to the employee at no cost. The major[7] variations of stock grants include performance-share/unit plans, restricted-stock plans and phantom-stock plans.

---

[3] Its website is www.esop-canada.org.

[4] R.N. Kanungo and M. Mendonca, *Compensation: Effective Reward Management*, 2nd ed. (Toronto: John Wiley and Sons, 1997), at p. 236.

[5] D. Hynes and J. Lendvay-Zwickl, *Assessing the Options: Stock Option Plans in Canada* (Conference Board of Canada, January, 2001), at p. 1.

[6] *Ibid.*, at p. 2.

[7] Kanungo and Mendonca, *op. cit.*, footnote 4, at p. 238.

In performance-share plans, participating staff receive performance "units" based on the attainment of specified objectives, such as a certain rate of earnings per share. The units are paid out in company stock instead of cash as in conventional bonus plans. Restricted-stock plans provide for the granting of blocks of company stock to employees to either attract or retain them. The plan usually limits the actions of the employee, such as requiring that he hold the shares for a minimum period of time or until the company reaches certain targets. Phantom-stock plans have units which correspond to a certain number of actual shares. At specified points in time the employee receives the cash equivalent to the value of the shares on that date plus any dividends that have accrued for the time period the "units" were held.

Stock-Purchase Plans

Stock-purchase plans allow employees to purchase company stock at a price that is usually somewhat (10%) lower than the market price. They may be assisted with company loans or allowed to conduct their purchase by payroll deduction.

EFFECTIVENESS OF ESOPS IN CANADA

Perry Phillips, President of ESOP Builders Inc.,[8] reports the following results from a 1986 Toronto Stock Exchange comparison of ESOP and non-ESOP public companies:

- five-year profit growth was 123% higher;
- net profit margin was 95% higher;
- productivity was 24% higher;
- the stock market favoured ESOP public companies with a 2% to 10% premium;
- return on average total equity was 92.26% higher;
- return on capital was 65.52% higher; and
- debt/equity ratio was 31.54% lower.

WHY HAVE AN ESOP?

ESOPs have several advantages over the other large group incentive plans that I have discussed in this book. Here are the major advantages of having an ESOP:

---

[8] P. Phillips, *Employee Share Ownership Plans — How to Design and Implement an ESOP in Canada* (Toronto: John Wiley & Sons Ltd., 2001), at p. 11.

- ESOPs create an ownership mentality because they turn employees into owners of the company.
- Employees can share in the success of the company through capital accumulation.
- There are tax advantages to owning shares that do not apply to cash incentive plans, such as profit sharing or productivity gainsharing.
- They can be used to create an orderly transition of ownership, either from one generation of a family to a succeeding one or from the founder to a group of employees.

DISADVANTAGES OF AN ESOP

ESOPs have many advantages and supporters. However, there are also some serious disadvantages which may make an ESOP unsuitable for your company. Here is a brief listing of them:

- The success of the plan, as measured by the growth in value of the shares, is significantly affected by the performance of the stock market. There are two problems with this. First, the performance of the stock market will often be different from the performance of the company; this can affect the motivation of your employees because their efforts will not be reflected by the changing value of their stock. Secondly, if the stock is considered a major part of the employee's capital accumulation (either in general or as part of their retirement planning), a major downturn in the stock market will adversely affect them if it occurs at a time when they were expecting or even depending on being able to cash in their stock to use the cash proceeds for other purposes.
- An ESOP in a private company can have a couple of problems. First, the value of the shares is not determined by an independent agency (*i.e.*, the stock market), but by professionals in the field such as business valuators, accountants and lawyers. I am not questioning the professionalism of such people but rather pointing out that the value they place on the shares is ultimately a judgment call. Secondly, the shares have virtually no liquidity. The only market for those employees who want, or have, to sell their shares is the company itself or other employees.
- They can be expensive to design, implement and administer.
- They are essentially a long-term form of deferred income and may have limited interest for younger employees, exactly like DPSPs.
- They are subject to the rules and regulations of securities regulators, such as the Ontario Securities Commission and the Toronto Stock Exchange. This means an additional regulatory and administrative burden on your compensation function.
- They tend to be complex and therefore difficult to explain to employees.

- The "line of sight"[9] can be obscure for most employees who are not at the executive level.

CONCLUSION

ESOPs are a proven method of creating a large group incentive plan which can be highly effective in motivating and rewarding employees. They are very effective in creating an "ownership" culture. They can be complex and difficult to implement and administer, but are definitely worth considering as a form of compensation, especially in a public company.

---

[9] "Line of sight" refers to employees' ability to see the relationship between their personal productivity and the operating profit produced by the division in which they work.

16

Performance Management and Rewards

INTRODUCTION

Performance appraisal systems are one of the most difficult subjects in the whole field of human resource management. The major purpose of this chapter is to help you develop a performance appraisal system that can be used for the *distribution or granting of rewards*. The rewards could be any of those discussed in this book, including merit increases, step increments or profit-sharing allocations. For this purpose, we will look at the following aspects of performance appraisal systems or performance management, as it is now called:

- major purposes of performance appraisals;
- types of appraisal techniques;
- performance improvement;
- selecting an appraisal technique;
- setting up a procedure; and
- attitude or behaviour.

MAJOR PURPOSES OF PERFORMANCE APPRAISALS

There are at least a dozen different types of performance appraisal systems. All of them can be used for various purposes. Here is a list of possible purposes of appraisal programs:

- give employees an idea of how they are doing;
- identify employees who are eligible for promotion;

- determine individual salary treatment;
- provide a basis for supervisor/employee communication;
- help supervisors to know their staff better;
- identify training needs;
- identify employees for lay-offs or recall;
- assist in placement;
- evaluate human resource department effectiveness;
- identify need for disciplinary action;
- determine whether probationary employees should be hired;
- provide input to other human resource processes, such as succession planning;
- provide data for use in grievance procedures; and
- determine the allocation of bonus pool among the members of the group.

However, the fundamental fact to recognize about the preceding list of purposes of performance appraisal systems is that they can be grouped into two major categories. Furthermore, some types of appraisal systems work well for one major purpose while others work well for the other prime function. None of them work well for both major purposes. The two major purposes are: (i) administrative; and (ii) coaching or mentoring.

Administrative purposes can include such actions as:

- salary increases;
- promotions;
- transfers;
- human resource planning;
- lay-offs; and
- bonus determination.

Coaching or mentoring, on the other hand, involves:

- identifying inadequate performance;
- advising the employee;
- selecting performance criteria;
- developing improvement plans; and
- advising on areas of improvement.

FIVE FEATURES AFFECTED

There are five features of a performance appraisal system that vary according to the major purpose thereof. These features are:

- role of the supervisor;
- timing of the appraisal;

- distribution of the information;
- basis of comparison; and
- type of appraisal instrument.

Role of the Supervisor

If the overall purpose of the appraisals is administrative, the role of the supervisor (or whoever is conducting the process) is that of judge. She is required to make a judgment about the extent to which the employee is performing his or her duties. If the overall purpose is coaching, the role of the supervisor is to help, advise and counsel. These roles are quite different and require different approaches by the supervisor.

Timing of the Appraisal

For administrative purposes, the timing of the appraisal is driven by the administrative process. For example, if all merit increases are granted on January 1st, it is imperative that the appraisals which support the size (if any) of the increase be done shortly before January 1st. Succession planning is often done at a specific time of year (often in the "off cycle" of a cyclical company, such as summer at a ski resort). Appraisals of employee performance are critical input and all have to be done at a certain time. The supervisor has no choice about the timing.

Conversely, for coaching purposes, the appraisal should take place when the supervisor observes behaviour or job performance that is not satisfactory. There is no point in telling the employee that she was rude to a customer six months after the event. Unless the supervisor makes a note of the event she is unlikely to remember it. You can be sure that the employee is highly unlikely to recall the situation six months later.

Distribution of the Information

In an administrative system the information generated by the appraisal process usually has to be provided to two or more levels of supervision. In one major, international, financial-services organization a salary increase form (with the appraisal attached) had to be approved by seven levels of management, two in Toronto and five in New York. Major departments, in addition to human resources, will also see the data. These can include payroll, accounting, budgeting, cost accounting and strategic planning.

In a coaching system the only people who *really* need to see the information are the supervisor (appraiser) and the employee. In many cases of coaching, the information does not even have to be in writing.

Appraisal Technique

For administrative purposes, such as the allocation of a bonus pool of money, each employee needs to be compared with each other employee. This means that you have to use some sort of scale of performance, such as:

Poor performance =   1
Needs improvement =   2
Satisfactory =   3
Better than satisfactory = 4
Outstanding =   5

On the other hand, for coaching purposes, appraisals are only useful to the employee if they are couched in terms of predetermined standards of performance. It is not enough to say that an employee's job performance is below everyone else in the section. Criticism has to be specific to the job.

Type of Appraisal Instrument

There are many types of appraisal instruments. Here are the major ones:

- behaviourly anchored rating scales;
- employee comparison or ranking;
- rating scales (single word, short phrase, paragraph);
- direct indices;
- management by objectives;
- 360 degree feedback;
- essay type;
- critical-incident method;
- checklist method; and
- forced choice.

Each of these methods, and their advantages and disadvantages, are discussed in more detail in the following section.

APPRAISAL INSTRUMENTS

Employee Comparison or Ranking

There are two variations of the employee comparison method, also known as ranking:

- *Ranking* — If you have 10 employees, you can simply rank them from highest performer = 10, to lowest performer = 1.
- *Paired comparison* — You can also used paired comparison ranking to evaluate a group of employees. Paired comparison was used in Chapter 3, "Selecting a Job Evaluation Plan", as a variation of whole-job ranking — a

major type of job evaluation. The techniques are identical except that here you compare the performance of people in their jobs instead of the actual jobs, separated from the person. Here is an example. In this example, I have rated George better than Brenda and Ricardo. Brenda is better than Monique and Ricardo. Monique is rated better than George, Brenda and Ricardo. The resultant rankings are shown in the right-hand column:

EXAMPLE OF PAIRED COMPARISON EMPLOYEE RANKING

Employee Name	George	Brenda	Monique	Ricardo	Total
George		✓		✓	2
Brenda			✓	✓	2
Monique	✓	✓		✓	3
Ricardo					0

Essay

Essay-type appraisal systems are also known as narrative systems. The person doing the appraisal simply writes out his comments about the performance of the employee. The form is literally a blank document, aside from identification data such as the name of the employee and supervisor, date of appraisal, and period being appraised. This method can be useful for helping the employee improve his performance but is of no use in the allocation of rewards.

Direct Indices

Direct indices are measurements of actual volume of production or effort. The best example of a job where these can be used is that of a sales representative. Her performance can be measured by unit sales volume, dollar volume or increase in either index over the previous period, such as year or month. Piece-work systems, which were once widely used and are now virtually extinct, used this method. It is also very useful in other fields such as mining (tons of ore produced per shift), warehousing (boxes shipped out the door) or vocational counselling (number of clients processed per day).

Direct indices are very useful because they are so specific to the job and/or person being appraised. However, this is also their major disadvantage for general use. It can be difficult to compare the sales volume with the responsibilities of other jobs, such as accounting manager or systems analyst.

Management by Objectives

Management by objectives, otherwise simply known as "MBO", has been around for over 30 years. It involves the mutual setting of goals (objectives) by the employee with the supervisor. MBO is considered quite motivational for this reason and also because it permits frequent feedback on performance. It can be used for reward purposes when several items are recognized:

- Some employees may tend to set easy goals, especially if rewards are at stake.
- The system only measures end results, not how they are obtained.
- It can be difficult to compare achievement of objectives between functions or departments when they are quite different.
- It may not recognize achievement, or non-achievement, of objectives for reasons that are beyond the control of the individual.

Rating Scales

Rating scales have four components:

- items to be rated;
- a numbered scale;
- a single word or short phrase which describes each number level; and
- a paragraph which describes each number in terms specific to the item being rated.

On the next page there is an example of an Executive Assessment Form developed for the executive group of a Canadian Great Lakes shipping company. It illustrates the various components of rating scales.[1]

---

[1]   This form is also available on the accompanying CD-ROM.

EXECUTIVE ASSESSMENT FORM

	1	2	3	4	5	A	B	C
	Completely Unsatisfactory	Needs Improvement	Generally Satisfactory – Some Exceptions	Exceeds Standards in Some Areas of Responsibilities	Outstanding Performance	Weight 0-1-2-3	Rating 1 - 5	Total A X B
Meeting Objectives of Job	Failed to meet even simple, easy objectives.	Met most objectives but only with frequent supervisory direction. Tends to set easy objectives.	Major objectives met with only a reasonable degree of supervision. Steady performance. Takes initiative under most conditions.	Met major objectives and most others with minimum supervision. Exceeded some major objectives. Met difficult objectives.	Exceeded most major objectives. Established a high number of difficult and distinctly different objectives.			
Self-development	Carried out no self-development plans. Displayed no interest in so doing.	Some development activities but questionable results on job and spotty on follow-through. Barely keeps up with current job.	Has completed a program based on present job assignment. Keeps up to date with developments in the field.	Is completely up to date in current job. Development plans include elements to prepare for a job of greater responsibility.	Extremely knowledgeable about own and related jobs. Development is at least 2 job levels higher than current position.			

EXECUTIVE ASSESSMENT FORM — *Continued*

	1 Completely Unsatisfactory	2 Needs Improvement	3 Generally Satisfactory – Some Exceptions	4 Exceeds Standards in Some Areas of Responsibilities	5 Outstanding Performance	A Weight 0-1-2-3	B Rating 1 - 5	C Total A X B
Supervisory Skill	Unable to establish even basic positive relationships with subordinates.	Maintains some acceptable relationships but there is little team feeling or cohesiveness in the section. Frequent intervention required.	Supervision is effective. Staff are generally well trained and work together well. May be some inconsistency or abrasiveness.	Staff is highly motivated and cohesive. Executive can handle almost all difficult situations.	Exceptional supervisory skills. Department is considered "the place to work". Staff are all well trained and motivated. Human resources are utilized to the maximum.			
Interpersonal Skill	Unable to initiate or maintain positive relationships with most people. Generally uncooperative.	Some relationships are effective but needs frequent supervision to avoid or correct abrasive areas.	Most relationships are satisfactory. Occasional problems arise but these are generally short-term and can be resolved.	Very few areas of weakness. Above average ability to deal with people.	Exceptional interpersonal skills. Inspires respect and recognition from peers and superiors throughout the organization.			

EXECUTIVE ASSESSMENT FORM — *Continued*

	1 Completely Unsatisfactory	2 Needs Improvement	3 Generally Satisfactory – Some Exceptions	4 Exceeds Standards in Some Areas of Responsibilities	5 Outstanding Performance	A Weight 0-1-2-3	B Rating 1 - 5	C Total A X B
Conceptual Skill	Unable to plan or organize beyond very short term. Very little conception of how department relates to total business.	Needs improvement in planning and organizing for the medium term. Doesn't always appreciate relationship of department to all other departments.	Plans and organizes effectively for the medium term. Understands relationship of department with most other units. Needs longer range and wider perspective.	All medium and short-term plans are appropriate. Needs improvement in some long-term activities or appreciation of developments in the industry.	Highly developed conceptual ability. Plans and organizes extremely well for both short and long-term objectives. Understands total industry from all viewpoints.			
					TOTALS			

The major components of any rating scale appraisal instrument are included in this form. They are:

- The numerical scale from 1 (lowest) to 5 (highest).
- The short phrases, which go with the numerical scale and provide additional information about the level of performance:
    - completely unsatisfactory;
    - needs improvement;
    - generally satisfactory, some exceptions;
    - exceeds standards in some areas of responsibilities;
    - outstanding performance.
- Short paragraphs further describe the level of performance. These take the numerical scale and the short phrase descriptors and expand on them for each item to be rated. For example, Level 2 — Needs Improvement for "Supervisory Skill" is: "Maintains some acceptable relationships but there is little team feeling or cohesiveness in the section. Frequent intervention required."
- The items for which the individual executive will be rated. They are:
    - meeting objectives of job;
    - self-development;
    - supervisory skill;
    - interpersonal skill; and
    - conceptual skill.

Ratings scales are the most commonly used method of performance appraisal for allocating or distributing rewards.

Behaviourly Anchored Rating Scales

Behaviourly Anchored Rating Scales ("BARS") were developed as an answer to some of the problems with rating scales. This mainly concerned the lack of job-specific behaviour which was being exhibited (or not) by the employee. For each element on which the employee is to be rated, there are a number of descriptions of various levels of behaviour. Here is an example of a three-point scale for the factor of customer contact for a cashier in a supermarket:

Number	Level of Performance	Behavioural Description
1	Needs improvement	Often ignores the customer. No verbal exchange or even eye contact.
2	Meets expectations	Always greets the customer pleasantly and comments on the weather or another neutral topic. Makes eye contact.
3	Exceeds job requirements	Greets the customer enthusiastically and engages her in pleasant conversation.

As you can see, BARS are very specific to a job and are therefore very useful in providing feedback to an employee about performance. However, they can be very difficult and time-consuming to develop. Since they are so specific to particular jobs, or occupations, they are not that useful for the purpose of allocating rewards.

Critical Incident Method

If this method is used, the supervisor keeps a diary or log of specific behaviours of the employee over the specified period of time. The behaviours that are recorded can be examples of effective or not effective job requirements. The general idea is to have a list of actual incidents that can be discussed with the employee. These can then be used for coaching and developmental purposes.

The critical incident method does not have much applicability to our purposes in this book. It also has serious deficiencies as a developmental tool, including:

- Employees may resent supervisors "keeping tabs" on them.
- The supervisor can only record what he actually "observes" even though what he does not see may be more important.
- Supervisors tend to be more diligent about recording incidents as the date of appraisal approaches and may miss important incidents early in the period.
- The feedback is provided after the behaviour in question has occurred, often very long after and is therefore of little use. The closer the feedback is to the occurrence, the more useful it will be.

DEVELOPING A RATING SCALE FOR YOUR ORGANIZATION

In the introduction to this chapter, I said that the primary purpose was to develop a performance appraisal system that can be used by your organization for one very specific purpose — allocating rewards. As you can see from the preceding discussion, rating scales are the most applicable form of appraisal technique for this purpose. They can be combined with other techniques, such as direct indices or management by objectives, but they must remain the dominant format.

In this section I will take you through the process of developing a rating scale that you can use for your organization. I will use the sample "Executive Assessment Form" found earlier in this chapter as the basis for this discussion. Using it I will review these topics:

- the numerical scale;
- general descriptors of performance levels;

- performance criteria;
- paragraph anchors;
- weighting of performance criteria and summary rating; and
- the performance appraisal process.

Numerical Scale

The sample assessment form shows a scale of one to five. There are two aspects to the numbers: the absolute number, *e.g.*, five, six or ten, and whether you use an odd or an even number of levels.

The number of levels that you use should be kept to a "reasonable" level. It is more a matter of common sense than scientific methodology. Most scales seem to go from three to seven levels.

The other question is whether to use an even number of levels (*e.g.*, four) or an odd number, such as five. Odd numbers are the most common practice, in my experience. Most people intuitively gravitate to odd numbers since they seem to fit a standard distribution of performance levels, with most people being in the middle category. Using a scale of one to five (five being the top of the scale) you would expect a normal distribution of performance ratings to be something like the following table:

RATING SCALE	1	2	3	4	5
PERCENTAGE OF EMPLOYEES	5	10	70	10	5

The issue here is the location of the greatest potential for improvement of employee performance. I maintain that this is in the group rated at Level 3. Employees rated at Level 1 are unlikely to move to Level 2; they will be terminated or they will elect themselves to leave the organization. Some of those in Level 4 might move to Level 5, but these will be few in number. However, think of the possibilities if you could move those employees who are at the low end of Level 3 to the upper end of Level 3. If you focus on this group, there is tremendous potential for improving the overall operation of the company.

There are two reasons for this. First, the number of employees is by far the largest. Secondly, moving employees from low Level 3 to high Level 3 is the easiest performance change to implement. You cannot move significant numbers of Level 3 employees to Level 4 or even 5 (on a five-point scale) except in unusual circumstances. It is quite possible to move low Level 3s to high Level 3s in relatively large numbers.

However, if you have an odd-numbered scale, you have a major impediment to doing this. Here is why. Consider that the 70% of employees in Level 3 really comprise two groups: the employees that you want to improve (Group A); and the employees that don't need improvement (Group B). With the odd-numbered scale they will all receive the same performance rating. This creates two problems. First, the members of the target group do not know that they need to improve, since they will be rated in the Satisfactory or Meets Job Requirements category. Obviously, they cannot change performance if they do not perceive that it is deficient or have been advised that somebody else (their manager) sees it this way.

Secondly, assuming you are using a merit-increase program, you are unable to reward Group A for improving. Under a typical merit increase system, both Group A and Group B (*i.e.*, all Level 3s) will receive the same salary increase or share of the bonus pool.

With the odd-numbered scale, you cannot identify the target group and you cannot reward them for improving their performance. That is my argument for using an even-numbered rating scale in a compensation program. Please recognize that odd-numbered scales are the most common type. They also work. However, I believe that there is significantly more potential for organizational improvement if you use an even number of points on the rating scale.

Descriptors of Performance Levels

Whatever the number of levels you decide to use in your numerical scale, you need to have a general description of each number. Technically, these are referred to as either short-phrase anchors or single-word anchors. The terms are pretty self-descriptive.

Here are some examples of both single-word and short-phrase anchors used in other performance appraisal forms:

Numerical Scale	Single-word anchor	Single-word anchor	Short-phrase anchor	Short-phrase anchor
6	Exceptional			Outstanding performance
5	Distinguished	Outstanding	Rarely achieved by others	Often exceeds standards
4	Notable	Excellent	Substantially exceeds position requirements	Fully competent
3	Competent	Satisfactory	More than fully meets requirements	Competent with some exceptions
2	Marginal	Poor	Meets most job requirements but does not meet some	Satisfactory with close supervision
1	Unsatisfactory	Inadequate	Does not meet most job requirements	Completely unsatisfactory

Performance Criteria

There are six types of items that can be listed on the left-hand side of the sample Performance Appraisal Form found later in this chapter:

- specific job duties;
- general job duties;
- objectives;
- behaviours;
- personal characteristics;
- work characteristics; and
- combinations.

Here are some examples of rating factors for specific occupations or types of occupation:

Management Consultant	Executive	Appliance Technician
• Engagement administration • Efficient task completion • Oral communication • Written communication • Analyzing problems • Developing solutions • Gaining acceptance of recommendations • Technical quality • Relations with clients • Relations with colleagues	• Self development • Supervisory skill • Interpersonal skill • Conceptual skill	• Basic knowledge of job • Quality of work produced • Quantity of work produced • Job-related characteristics • Care and maintenance of company equipment • Relations with customers • Relations with fellow employees

Possible Factors Used in Performance Appraisal

Here is an extensive list of factors used in a variety of graphic rating scales:

- plant knowledge;
- knowledge of supervisory requirements;
- safety knowledge;
- administrative knowledge;
- planning knowledge;
- leadership knowledge;
- company knowledge;
- planning and scheduling;
- training;
- delegating;
- written communications;
- verbal communications;

- problem solving;
- decision making;
- productivity;
- initiative;
- supervisory ability;
- interpersonal skills;
- knowledge of job;
- ability to learn;
- amount of work;
- daily supervision and leadership;
- foresight;
- people orientation;
- firmness and flexibility;
- work performance;
- dependability;
- relationships;
- safety;
- performance improvement;
- supervision/work direction;
- adaptability;
- attitude;
- personal appearance and habits;
- safety and housekeeping;
- potentiality;
- public relations;
- quality of work produced;
- quantity of work produced;
- job-related characteristics;
- capacity and ambition for future growth;
- attendance;
- punctuality;
- ability to get along with fellow employees;
- co-operativeness;
- people sensitivity;
- communication;
- organization;
- attention to detail;
- meeting basic job responsibilities;
- care and maintenance of company equipment;
- relations with customers;
- relations with fellow employees;
- independent action/thinking;
- meeting specific objectives;
- basic skills of management;

- judgment;
- leading and motivating;
- planning;
- organizing;
- controlling;
- using staff services;
- relating with other departments;
- relating with subordinates;
- other significant skills;
- appraising and developing subordinates;
- carrying out self-development plans;
- dependability and judgment;
- efficient task completion;
- analyzing problems;
- developing solutions;
- technical quality of output;
- relations with clients; and
- relations with colleagues.

Selecting Performance Criteria

How do you select performance criteria? Here are some guidelines:

- They should be job related.
- They should apply to all the jobs in the employee group.
- They should be discrete — they should not overlap.
- They should be clearly defined. Using a one-word definition, *e.g.*, communications, will normally lead to confusion and different evaluators will define the term in different ways. This will result in inconsistent ratings.

Writing Paragraph Anchors

Many graphic rating scales do not use paragraph anchors. They limit themselves to a numerical scale and either single-word or short-phrase anchors. However, I have found that it is much easier to use a scale if brief descriptions of each level of performance for each criterion or factor are provided. Actually, you don't necessarily have to provide definitions for all levels; you could just do every second one. For example, on a five-point scale you might limit the paragraphs to Levels 1, 3 and 5.

Here are some guidelines to use in writing your paragraph anchors.

- Avoid the use of absolute terms like always or never. These are often used at the ends of a scale but using them makes it impossible for anyone to be legitimately rated at that level.
- Do not use terms like average that compare the employee to other employees. Instead use words that describe the level of performance relative

to the job. "Normally expected" quantity of work is better than "average" quantity of work.

- Be sure that the paragraphs describe different levels of the performance factor and not another factor. This is quite a common problem. For example, in one company, the performance factor was listed as communications but one of the paragraphs talked about relationships with other employees.
- The words in the paragraph should clearly indicate that one level is higher than the other. There are two ways to test this. First, take away the numerical scale. The words themselves should clearly indicate a continuum. Secondly, arrange the paragraphs in random order and then have someone (your committee, perhaps) rank them numerically. It will be readily apparent if the words are not clear.

Weighting of Performance Criteria and Summary Rating

Once you have decided on the performance criteria discussed in the last section, you have to determine whether they are equal or not. Some techniques consider all criteria to be equal in their impact on the job. This is easier than the alternative but may not be as realistic. For example, let's look at two jobs — punch press operator and customer service representative. Let's compare them regarding two possible performance criteria — relationships with people and volume of work. Both of these are frequently found in rating scales in Canadian business. One could argue that the relative importance of the two factors is as follows:

Factor	Customer Service Representative	Punch Press Operator
Relationships with people	50	10
Volume of work	50	90

You can argue with the exact weightings that I have shown but hopefully you can see the point that they need to be quite different for these two very different jobs. Weighting the criteria equally would do a severe injustice to both jobs and certainly will not do your organization any good.

The Performance Appraisal Process

You need to determine the following elements of a process for the purpose of granting rewards:

- timing;
- who conducts the initial appraisal;
- who approves the initial appraisal;
- distribution of the completed form; and
- advising the employee.

Timing

The timing of the appraisal is driven by the compensation program it is being used for. Generally, as you have seen from other sections of this book, there are three main types of compensation programs that will include a performance appraisal element: merit salary increases; group incentive plans; and individual bonus plans.

Who Conducts the Initial Appraisal?

It is virtually universal practice for the immediate supervisor of the employee to conduct the initial appraisal. One manufacturing company, which recently made a major modification to its profit-sharing plan, set up its program so that appraisals were done by a committee comprised of the supervisor, the human resources administrator and one other supervisor, who was considered to be a customer of the department in which the employee worked.

Review and Approval of the Initial Appraisal

It is also universal practice for the initial appraisal to be reviewed and approved by the next level of management and the human resources department. Many have two additional levels of approval. Since we are talking about appraisals, which are conducted for the purpose of granting or distributing rewards, it is quite critical that there be a central control point to ensure consistency and general affordability. Remember that most incentive plans are zero-sum games. In the case of the company just mentioned that uses the three-person committee, the president also reviewed and approved all ratings.

Distribution of the Completed Forms

The completed performance appraisal documents will normally just be sent to the employee, the management staff who reviewed and approved the rating and the human resources department. It is not necessary to send it to payroll assuming that you have a separate Salary Increase Form as I discussed in Chapter 7, "Putting it All Together — Basic Salary Administration". If you have a human resource planning section they might require performance ratings for their planning purposes.

Advising the Employee

Obviously, the employee must be told the results of the appraisal and the financial rewards that flow (or do not flow) from it. It is common practice for the immediate supervisor to do this although it is often done by the next level of management and the immediate supervisor.

WORKSHEET TO DESIGN A PERFORMANCE APPRAISAL FORM FOR REWARD ALLOCATION PURPOSES

Here is a worksheet that you can use for the purpose of designing a performance appraisal form for allocating rewards as part of your compensation program. (It is also available on the accompanying CD-ROM.) Remember, this form will have a very specific use — the allocation of rewards (a zero-sum game). Actually, in your compensation program its function will be even more specific. It may be used to determine the size of a merit increase or as part of the allocation formula in a team-based incentive program. It *cannot* be used for coaching or mentoring purposes. You have to go considerably beyond this very basic appraisal technique if you actually want behaviour change to take place.

DAJATY ENTERPRISES LIMITED
PERFORMANCE APPRAISAL FORM — DESIGN SHEET

NAME _____

TITLE _____

SUPERVISOR_____

REVIEW PERIOD _____

FACTOR	1 Completely Unsatisfactory	2 Needs Improvement	3 Meets Job Requirements	4 Exceeds Some Job Requirements	5 Outstanding
A					
B					
C					
D					
E					

Decisions Required: 1. Numbered scale – 1 to 5 or 1 to 10?
                     2. Short-phrase anchors?
                     3. Paragraph anchors?
                     4. Factors?
                     5. Who does appraisals?

POINTS TO REMEMBER IN DESIGNING A PERFORMANCE APPRAISAL FORM

The following important points should be kept in mind when designing a performance appraisal form:

- *Average* — Avoid the use of the term average to anchor the middle point on a rating scale. Average is a statistical term and has many uses. Describing performance is not one of them. The problem is that it compares the employee with other employees. What if all your staff are "below average"? Rating another employee the same as all your other unsatisfactory employees does you no good. It is better to think in terms of comparing the performance of the employee with the requirements of the job. It is more useful to say that an employee "does not meet all the requirements of the job" than to say that he is below average.
- *Process or results* — In theory it is better to measure employees on the specific results that they achieve. These can be the actual results or those compared with some pre-determined target or objective. However, it is important to recognize that the way objectives or results are achieved can be at least as important as the final results. Consider a sales representative who achieves very high sales in his territory. If you just measure the results, he will receive a very high rating. However, suppose that the employee achieved those results by promising totally unrealistic delivery times or product performance. Although such behaviour may be detected quite quickly, it is also possible that it will go undetected for some time.
- *Job specific* — In designing the rating scales (word, phrase or paragraph) be as specific to the job or group of jobs as possible. Obviously, as a group of employees gets larger and more diverse this becomes more difficult to achieve.
- *Personal characteristics* — Avoid the measurement (which is probably impossible anyway) of personal characteristics, such as neatness or grooming.
- *Attitude* — Many performance appraisal systems include some measurement of "attitude". This is a major mistake and causes nothing but trouble. Many managers that I have worked with seem to have a particular affinity for this word. When challenged on the use of it, they are usually able to describe reasonably well what they are talking about. However, it is not attitude. It is unacceptable behaviour that gets labeled "attitude".
- *Measurable* — The factor has to be as measurable, or at least as observable, as possible. It makes it easier on the person doing the appraisal and it also makes the comments meaningful to the employee. It is much more informative to tell an employee by how much she has exceeded her quota, in units of production, than by assessing her personality.

PERFORMANCE IMPROVEMENT

The critical issue in a performance management system is: "How do you get employees to improve their performance?" Just doing an appraisal and telling them they are not satisfactory performers will not get the job done. You have to look at why they are not performing what you need or want them to do, and make sure that there is nothing forcing them to do the wrong thing and/or rewarding them for it.

Ferdinand Fournies reported on an extremely interesting study that provides a lot of insight into this problem. He asked 25,000 managers and supervisors this question: "Why don't subordinates do what they are supposed to do?" Their answers are listed below in descending order of frequency:[2]

1. They don't know what they are supposed to do.
2. They don't know how to do it.
3. They don't know why they should.
4. They think they are doing it.
5. There are obstacles beyond their control.
6. They don't think it will work.
7. They think their way is better.
8. They think something is more important.
9. There is no positive consequence to them for doing it.
10. There is a negative consequence to them for doing it.
11. There is a positive consequence to them for not doing it.
12. There is no negative consequence to them for not doing it.
13. They have personal limits.
14. They have personal problems.
15. They are afraid to do it.
16. No one could do it.

COACHING EMPLOYEES TO IMPROVE THEIR PERFORMANCE

The process you need to follow to help an employee correct a performance deficiency has been quite clearly laid out in several excellent books, including the one by Fournies just mentioned.[3] Here are the steps:

- Identify the performance problem. Be as specific as possible. Telling the employee he has a punctuality problem is not as effective as saying that he was one hour late yesterday, one-half hour late the day before and 15 minutes late the previous Wednesday.

---

[2] F.F. Fournies, *Coaching for Improved Work Performance* (New York: McGraw-Hill, 2000), at p. 94. (Reproduced with the permission of the McGraw-Hill Companies.)

[3] *Ibid.* See also R.F. Mager and P. Pipe, *Analyzing Performance Problems: Or You Really Oughta Wanna*, 3rd Rev. ed. (Center for Effective Performance, 1997).

- Determine if the deficiency is relevant. I once talked to a manager of a data entry department who complained that his "girls" wore the headsets for their Walkmans and listened to music while keying in data. He admitted, under duress, that actual work measures like number of keystrokes and error rate indicated they were performing to expectations. However, he maintained, and may do so to this day, that "they couldn't possibly be doing a good job while listening to music on their headphones".
- Does the employee know that the performance is not satisfactory? If not, simply tell him and give him time to fix it.
- Does the employee have the knowledge or abilities to do the job? If not, simply arrange for him to take the necessary training. Don't have a long performance appraisal discussion about his lack of performance. Give him the tools to do the job.
- Determine whether there are factors that prevent the employee from doing a good job. The reason piece-work systems often fail is that peer pressure from the work group prohibits the employee from producing beyond the normal level dictated by the group. Naturally, this group norm is not the same as the one established by the industrial engineering department.
- Review the situation with the employee.
- Set measurable and objective targets with dates for when they will be achieved.
- Get the employee to agree on these. If there is not agreement that he can do them, and that they need to be done, nothing will happen. (See the section on expectancy theory in Chapter 1, "Assessing Your Situation".)

CONCLUSION

In this chapter we have looked at the two major purposes of performance appraisal systems and identified the one that is most relevant for a compensation system. The differences between pure performance appraisal systems and performance management systems have been presented. There has been a brief discussion of why employees do not perform according to your expectations and how to coach them to improve their performance. Finally, and most directly, we have discussed the types of performance appraisal forms and prepared you to design your own form for the very specific purpose of granting or allocating rewards in your organization.

17

Pay Equity

INTRODUCTION

In various parts of this book I have talked about value-laden terms, especially with regard to describing jobs and writing job descriptions. Pay equity is one of those terms, except that it is usually used with capital letters and boldface type. Pay equity is about gender equality in wages. It is also about gender discrimination in wages. This chapter will provide a brief history of pay equity in Canada, a summary of major provisions of pay equity legislation, and detailed discussions of the legislation in Ontario and Quebec.

HISTORY OF PAY EQUITY IN CANADA

As late as the 1960s two practices were quite common in Canadian organizations. In fact, they are still carried on although not officially or openly. One was maintaining separate wage or salary structures for different occupational groups, such as clerical workers, typists or factory workers. It was not always explicitly stated but these jobs were often totally (or almost totally) comprised of one gender. Clerks were female, as were typists. Production workers in the factory were male. Some organizations had both male and female production workers but with different wage scales. It was quite common to refer to a particular job as a "man's" job or a "woman's" job. It was not unusual to hear the terms "light general labour" and "heavy general labour" referring to female and male jobs, respectively, in the factory. The other practice was hiring men and women for the same, or very similar, job and paying the women at lower rates of pay.

At some point, legislators were persuaded that the difference in pay for men and women was unjust and they passed "equal pay for equal work" laws. The first was an amendment to the Ontario *Employment Standards Act*[1] in the early 1970s. These laws prohibited employers from paying different rates to men and women who were doing the same or "substantially the same" work. The legislation usually included reasons which permitted paying men and women differently, such as seniority or merit.

However, this did not solve the problem. Macro statistics continued to show that there was a significant gap in pay between men and women. The reason that "equal pay for equal work" laws did not work was that men and women are often concentrated in specific occupations. These are also called "job ghettos" — a somewhat harsh term although there is a strong element of truth and accuracy in it. For example, the following table shows some of the percentages of men and women in various occupations:

OCCUPATIONAL GROUPS	PERCENTAGE OF WOMEN IN 1999
Nurses and health-related therapists	87%
Clerks and other administrators	75%
Teachers	62%
Sales and service	59%

Those people who were concerned about this came up with the concept of "comparable worth" or "equal pay for work of equal value". Essentially they meant that equal pay for equal work only applied when a man and a woman were working in the same job and were paid differently. Comparable worth advocates claimed that one had to compare jobs that were not the same occupation and establish their relative worth. If one did so, then the female job of secretary, which had traditionally been paid less than the male general labourer job in the factory, would be paid properly. This concept came to be known as pay equity, much to the relief of those who previously had to write out "equal pay for work of equal value".

PAY EQUITY JURISDICTIONS IN CANADA

As you have seen in Chapter 1, "Assessing Your Situation", there are 11 different jurisdictions in Canada for labour legislation. Not all have pay equity legislation. There are two major differences between the jurisdictions: the sectors covered; and whether it is proactive or complaint driven.

---

[1]   R.S.O. 1970, c. 147 [now *Employment Standards Act, 2000*, S.O. 2000, c. 41].

Some jurisdictions only apply pay equity legislation to the public sector, while others apply it to all employers with ten or more workers. If the legislation is proactive, it means that employers are required to take specified steps to comply with the law. If the legislation is complaint driven it means that the government will only act when an employee, or possibly a union, has submitted a complaint about pay equity discrimination.

The following table summarizes some aspects of the various pieces of pay equity legislation in Canada. It is important to recognize that pay equity only applies, at the time of writing this book, to the private sector in Ontario, Quebec and federally regulated employers:

Jurisdiction	Type	Private Sector	Civil Service	Municipal Government	School Boards
Federal	Complaint	Yes	Yes	N/A	N/A
British Columbia	Proactive	No	Yes	Yes	Yes
Manitoba	Proactive	No	Yes	No	No
New Brunswick	Proactive	No	Yes	No	No
Newfoundland and Labrador	Proactive	No	Yes	No	No
Nova Scotia	Proactive	No	Yes	Yes	Yes
Ontario	Integrated	Yes	Yes	Yes	Yes
Prince Edward Island	Integrated	No	Yes	No	Yes
Quebec	Integrated	Yes	Yes	Yes	No
Yukon	Complaint	No	Yes	Yes	Yes

PAY EQUITY IN ONTARIO

The Ontario *Pay Equity Act, 1987*[2] was the earliest, proactive legislation to apply to the private sector. It is widely considered to be the most proactive piece of such legislation in the world. It initially came into effect on January 1, 1988, and was subsequently amended, or had additional regulations added, several times in the 1990s. Here are the major provisions of the *Pay Equity Act*.

Coverage

All employers in Ontario are required to develop one or more pay equity plans if they have ten or more employees in the province. There must be a pay

---

[2] S.O. 1987, c. 34 [now *Pay Equity Act*, R.S.O. 1990, c. P.7].

equity plan for each "establishment" of the employer. Establishment is defined as all employees of the employer in a geographic division, which can be a county, regional municipality or territorial district.[3]

Male and Female Job Classes

Job classes, as defined in the *Pay Equity Act*, are essentially the same as the definition of job used in this book. Job classes can be identified as male or female by the percentage of each gender currently in the jobs, the gender stereotyping of the type of work or the historical incumbency of the job. A job class that has 70% or more male incumbents is a male job class, while one with 60% or more females is a female job class. Gender stereotyping simply means that, if you think of a job as belonging to a specific gender, it is considered to be that type of job for the purpose of the Act. For example, secretaries are generally female and therefore the job of secretary will be a female job class even if the incumbent is a male.

Comparison of Male and Female Job Classes using a Gender-Neutral Comparison System

The employer must compare the jobs using a job evaluation system which encompasses the four factors specified in the Act: skill; effort; responsibility; and working conditions. (These factors are not defined.) There is no requirement to use a formal job evaluation plan, such as the Tyson-Totten Plan provided in this book. In fact, whole-job ranking is permissible[4] as long as it is used in a gender-neutral manner.

Identification of Job Rates

Job rate is defined as "the highest rate of compensation for a job class" and compensation is "all payments and benefits paid or provided to or for the benefit of a person who performs functions that entitle the person to be paid a fixed or ascertainable amount". The Pay Equity Commission has defined four types of compensation systems to help in determining the job rate. These are:

- a straight seniority progression;[5]
- a merit compensation system where employees are expected to reach a reference point in the salary range;[6]

---

[3] For this purpose, these geographical terms must be interpreted in Ontario terms. They may have different meanings in other provinces.

[4] See Chapter 3, "Selecting a Job Evaluation Plan".

[5] What I called a step-rate system in Chapter 7, "Putting it All Together — Basic Salary Administration".

[6] The 3M system in Chapter 7.

- a merit compensation system in which the highest point of the salary range is the maximum; and
- a single-rate system.

In my opinion, the last two systems identified by the Commission are not of much use and do not need to be considered.

Identification of Comparator Job Classes

For each female job class you have to find the male job classes that are of equal or comparable value. Essentially, this means they are in the same salary grade. If you use whole-job ranking you will have banded them together into a salary grade. If you use a point-rating plan two jobs will be considered equal or of comparable value if they are in the same point band. Requiring them to have the exact same number of points is not considered acceptable by the Commission. You have to find a male job class of the same value within the same group of employees. Use the lowest paid male job class as the comparator if there is more than one. If there are none, look in the same establishment for a male job class of the same value and, again, use the lowest if there are two or more. If this fails, you have to look for male job classes of less value and, in such a case, use the highest paid as the male comparator.

The type of comparison outlined above is called job-to-job comparison. If this method fails to produce a male comparator, the Act requires that employers in the broader public sector use the proxy method which involves finding male comparator job classes in other, similar organizations.

Defensible Differences in Job Rates

Having identified differences in job rates between male and female job classes, the employer must determine whether they are defensible. Section 8 of the Act provides five allowable reasons for such differences:

- a formal seniority system;
- a temporary training assignment;
- a merit compensation plan with formal performance appraisals;
- red-circling — when an employee's compensation has been frozen or increases are curtailed because the person is in a job which has been evaluated to a lower salary grade; and
- a skills shortage which causes a temporary increase in compensation because of difficulty in recruiting.

Determine the Required Pay Adjustments

Once you have made the comparisons, you can determine how and when to make the pay adjustments. The Act required that pay increases resulting from job-to-job comparisons had to occur between January 1, 1990 and January 1,

1994. The exact timing depended on the size of the employer (measured by number of employees) and whether it was in the public, broader public or private sector.

Increases to incumbents of female job classes have to be continued until their job rate is equal to those of the male comparator job classes. Private sector employers have to pay out at least 1% of their total Ontario payroll annually until pay equity is achieved.

Post the Pay Equity Plan

A pay equity plan must be posted in the workplace by all broader public and public sector employers and those private sector employers with 100 or more employees. Private sector employers with 10 to 99 employees can choose whether or not to post a plan. The information that must be posted is found in s. 13 of the Act; it includes the identification of male and female job classes, the gender-neutral comparison system used and the results of the comparisons of the job classes. Non-union employees have 90 days from the posting of this plan to object and the employer has seven days in which to make any adjustments and post a notice stating what they were, if there were any. The employees then have 30 days to file any objections with the Commission.

In unionized organizations the pay equity plan is considered approved when the employer and the bargaining agent have agreed and the plan is posted. The pay equity is deemed to be part of the collective agreement.

Involvement of the Employees

The Act requires that the union and the employer negotiate in good faith on the gender-neutral comparison system to be used for a pay equity plan. The employer is not required to negotiate a pay equity plan with non-unionized employees, although the Commission does encourage employers to involve employees in the process of developing a pay equity plan especially with participation on job evaluation committees.

Maintain Pay Equity

Section 7 of the Act requires employers to maintain pay equity after it has been achieved. It specifically prohibits unions and employers from agreeing to compensation programs that would violate pay equity. This may be the most difficult part of the whole pay equity process in Ontario. Problems could arise from any of the following:

- change in the grading of a job;
- revisions to the job evaluation system;
- different rates of increases in the compensation of other pay equity units which include comparator jobs;

- circumstances allowing a permissible difference in compensation change;
- all or part of the employer organization being merged with, or acquired by, another company; and
- benefit packages being revised.

Enforcement

There are two bodies responsible for enforcement of the Act — the Review Services Branch of the Commission and the Pay Equity Hearings Tribunal. Employers are not required to submit their pay equity plans to the Commission but there are two avenues of enforcement. Employees can file a complaint with the Review Services Branch; the branch can conduct random audits of employers to ensure compliance. Review officers can enter an employer's premises and request relevant documentation at any reasonable time.

A review officer will attempt to arrange settlement of a complaint but, if considered necessary, may refer the matter to the Pay Equity Hearings Tribunal, which is a quasi-judicial body with the authority to make final decisions on all matters arising under the Act. Decisions are final and binding on all parties and can only be appealed to the Ontario courts if the Tribunal exceeded its authority.

PAY EQUITY IN QUEBEC

Introduction

Quebec's pay equity legislation, the *Pay Equity Act*[7] (the "Quebec Act"), became effective November 21, 1997, and the Pay Equity Commission was established as a department of the Ministry of Labour. It is a proactive piece of legislation and replaces the former complaint-based model in s. 19 of the Quebec *Charter of Human Rights and Freedoms*.[8]

As of November 21, 1997, all provincially regulated employers with ten or more employees operating in the Province of Quebec had to comply with the new pay equity legislation. As in Ontario, the purpose of the legislation is to eliminate the systemic salary gap between female and male job classes of equal value.

The Pay Equity Commission's function is to hear and resolve any questions regarding the legislation. The legislation requires that the employer initiate the compliance process, post the completed plan and report to the Commission by specified dates. While the legislation relates specifically to employers with ten or more employees, the Commission will investigate complaints under s. 19 of

---

[7] R.S.Q., c. E-12.001.

[8] R.S.Q., c. C-12.

the Quebec Charter filed by an employee of an organization employing fewer than ten employees, alleging discrimination in compensation between a predominantly female job class and a predominantly male job class.

Specified Deadlines

Unlike Ontario, where deadlines are different for different sizes of employer (by number of employees), all employers in Quebec should have completed a pay equity plan *or* have determined what salary adjustments will be required as of November 21, 2001. By November 21, 2005, employers must have corrected all salary gaps. The Commission may authorize a three-year delay in exceptional circumstances.

Pay Equity Plans and Employee Committees

Depending on the size of the organization, some employers are required to develop a pay equity plan and/or establish an employee committee. The following table provides the details:

SIZE OF EMPLOYER	PLAN REQUIRED	COMMITTEE REQUIRED
100 or more employees	Yes	Yes
50 to 99 employees	Yes	Optional
10 to 49 employees	Optional	Optional
less than 10 employees	Not applicable	

Development of a Pay Equity Plan

This is the process that should be followed in developing a pay equity plan:

- *Identify your employees* — An employee is defined in s. 8 of the Quebec Act as "any natural person who undertakes to do work for remuneration under the direction or control of an employer". The following groups are excluded from this definition:
  - students;
  - trainees;
  - senior management officers (the Commission provides a "guideline" for determining who is in this group — it includes a very senior position, a job with autonomy and significant decision-making and true participation in the articulation of the policies and objectives of the organization);
  - persons eligible for certain professional integration measures (social assistance and persons with disabilities under income security legislation);

- independent operators; and
- police officers and fire-fighters.
- *Identify the number of employees* — The number of salaried employees corresponds to the average number of employees on the organization's payroll per pay period during the reference period. For organizations established *prior* to November 21, 1996, the reference period is November 21, 1996 to November 21, 1997. For organizations established *after* November 21, 1996, the reference period is 12 months after the date the first employee began work with the employer.
- *Identify the number of pay equity plans required* — Generally speaking there will be one pay equity plan for each organization. The Commission may approve multiple plans for employers with multiple locations and those with union and non-union employees.
- *Set up the pay equity committee* — Where required, an employee committee must consist of a minimum of three representatives; one-third of them must be employer representatives and two-thirds must be representatives of the employees. Further, one-half of these must be women. The employer representatives, and the employee representatives, each acting as a group, have a single vote. Where the employee representatives cannot agree in order to vote, the employer vote shall prevail.
- *Identify female and male job classes* — Employees with similar duties and responsibilities, qualifications, job rates and/or compensation scales may be grouped together in a single job class. A job class can consist of only one position. Where employees are grouped together, the job rate for purposes of pay equity is the highest rate of compensation or maximum in the compensation scale applicable to the positions within the class. Here are the factors to consider in determining the gender of a job class:
  - the percentage of incumbents — a male job class has 60% male incumbents and a female job class has 60% female incumbents (a neutral job class has less than 60% of either gender);
  - the historical incumbency of the job class within the enterprise;
  - gender stereotypes;
  - significant difference in the rate of representation of gender compared with the total workforce; and
  - the pay equity committee (or the employer if there is no committee) identifies job classes.
- *Select a job evaluation method* — The gender-neutral job evaluation system must measure the following characteristics of job content (as in the Ontario *Pay Equity Act* these factors are not defined):
  - required qualifications;
  - responsibilities;
  - effort; and
  - working conditions.

- *Evaluate job classes* — The gender-neutral job evaluation system selected must be used to evaluate all male and female job classes. Use the characteristics of the job class and not those of incumbents The pay equity committee (or the employer where there is no committee) will evaluate job classes using one of the following two methods:
  - job-to-job method of comparison for valuation of job classes on an individual basis; or
  - proportional method of comparison where the job-to-job method of comparison cannot be applied to a predominantly female job class.
- *Calculate salary gaps* — Compare the compensation of female job classes to that of male job classes. You must calculate the value of benefits when those having a specific value are not equally available to all the job classes involved. For pay equity purposes total compensation includes:
  - base pay;
  - flexible pay — merit, performance, gainsharing income;
  - benefits — sick leave, family leave, vacation, holidays, non-salary benefits (clothing, tools), allowances, tuition; and
  - wage protection plans including pension, health and disability insurance.
- *Identify permissible reasons for differences in compensation* — The Quebec Act allows differences in total compensation for any of the following reasons:
  - seniority;
  - assignments of fixed duration;
  - regional differences in pay (unless accommodated by multiple pay equity plans);
  - skills shortages;
  - "red circling"; and
  - non-receipt of benefits with monetary value in a temporary or casual job.
- *Post the pay equity plan* — The final results of the pay equity plan must be posted in a visible and easily accessible place. The plan must include:
  - the male and female job classes within the enterprise;
  - the gender-neutral method used to determine the value of job classes;
  - the value (results of job evaluation) of the male and female gender job classes, value comparisons and required adjustments;
  - the terms and conditions of payment of pay equity adjustments; and
  - employee rights and remedies provided under the Quebec Act (for example, the right to additional information from the pay equity committee).
- *Make pay adjustments where required* — All employers subject to the legislation must begin adjustments by November 21, 2001, and have achieved pay equity by November 21, 2005. The legislation does not specify the timing and amount of increases except for the final compliance date. The Commission may authorize an employer, who demonstrates an inability to

pay the adjustments in compensation, to extend by a maximum of three years the period over which the adjustments are spread. Where the Commission has reasonable grounds to believe that the financial situation of the employer has improved, it may order payment of the adjustments or determine new terms and conditions, including requiring the employer to obtain a loan from a financial institution to make adjustments.

- *Maintain pay equity* — The employer (and bargaining agents where applicable) is obliged to maintain pay equity, taking into consideration the following organizational changes:
  - creation of new positions;
  - creation of new job classes;
  - modification of existing positions; and
  - negotiation or renewal of collective agreements.

CONCLUSION

Some employers, consultants in the field and pay equity officials treat pay equity as an issue that is separate from other compensation issues. They develop a "pay equity plan" which appears to meet the requirements of the applicable legislation and then let it sit on a shelf. At the same time they continue to administer compensation programs without regard to the pay equity plan.

In my opinion, this is wrong from both a technical and philosophical perspective. Technically, it is wrong because all compensation that you offer employees is part of the total rewards package. You cannot operate pay plans independently of each other, especially when they apply to the same component of the compensation package, such as salaries.

Philosophically, or even ethically, I cannot understand how an employer can have one part of a compensation program that officially supports "equity" and another that does not do so. The professionals call this "cognitive dissonance" and I get it in a big way when I see this approach.

However, in the final analysis, it is your company or organization and it is up to you how "technically" or "ethically" correct you choose to be. Remember that I said earlier in this book that any compensation program reflects the "values" and culture of the organization. There are very few absolute rules. It is up to you.

18

Work/Life Balance

INTRODUCTION

In the early years of the 21st century employers are finding that prospective employees are difficult to attract to the company using only the traditional mix of salaries, bonuses, stock options and benefits. For a variety of reasons, including downsizing, advances in technology, demographics and changes in lifestyle, employees are finding that it is increasingly difficult to "have a life" and a successful career or job at the same time. This has led to the development of "work/life balance" and the concept of "total rewards", as advanced by WorldatWork.[1] Total rewards are now defined as compensation (primarily cash or near cash), benefits and "the work experience".

This chapter will look at various aspects of this new concept of work/life balance. It discusses the following:

- why there is a need for work/life balance in your compensation program;
- the benefits of having a work/life balance program;
- general principles for selecting a work/life benefit or program;
- responsibility for work/life programs; and
- specific components that can be included in a work/life balance program.

---

[1] Formerly the American/Canadian Compensation Associations.

WHY WORK/LIFE BALANCE?

Several recent studies of Canadian workers show that they are having severe difficulty balancing work and family life and that the degree of difficulty has increased over the past decade or so. One report, "Work-Life Balance in the New Millenium: Where are we? Where do we need to go?", was sponsored by the Canadian Policy Research Networks. It found that:[2]

- All workers at all levels reported an increase in conflict between work and family compared with ten years before.
- Fifty-five per cent of workers reported high levels of stress compared with 47% in a similar study in 1991.
- The number of employees taking work home jumped from 31% to 52%.
- The number of respondents reporting elder care responsibilities jumped from 6% to 25%.

A similar study of employees by the Family and Work Institute based in New York City produced the following results in 1998:[3]

- nearly 25% of employees felt nervous or stressed often or very often;
- 13% often or very often had difficulty coping with everyday life;
- 26% often or very often felt emotionally drained by their work;
- 28% often or very often did not have the energy to do things with their family; and
- 36% often or very often felt used up at the end of the workday.

REASONS FOR DEVELOPING A WORK/LIFE BALANCE PROGRAM

Surveys have shown that highly talented people, who can work almost anywhere, want flexibility and choice so that they can integrate their lifestyle and their occupation. Employers are also under huge pressures to increase productivity and get more work out of fewer people. Leading-edge employers are coming up with ways to improve life on the job and allow the employee more time and flexibility to deal with personal and family needs away from the workplace.

Many compensation practitioners believe that the benefits of these programs are not measurable but are based more on attitude than fact. However, one study at First Tennessee Bank found significant measurable results after revamping

---

[2] E. Church, "Work-life Stresses Mount for Canadians", *The Globe and Mail* (October 23, 2001), p. B6.

[3] A. Vincola, "Helping Employees Balance Work/Life Issues" (06/01) *Workspan*, at p. 30.

their work procedures and schedules to be more in accordance with the work and family needs of the employees. These results included:[4]

- Customer account reconciliation time was reduced to four days from ten.
- Overall revenue growth was 11% compared to the industry average of 6% to 7%.
- Business units with managers considered most supportive of these initiatives had 7% higher customer-retention rates than other units.

At Statistics Canada, similar programs resulted in turnover rates that are 50% of those in other government agencies and the lowest rate of grievances in any department of the government.[5]

GENERAL PRINCIPLES FOR SELECTING A WORK/LIFE BENEFIT

If you have decided that you wish to provide some sort of work/life balance program for your employees, there are some general principles that you can use to select those most appropriate to your situation. They are not significantly different from those you should use when choosing any new component of your rewards package but there are some differences which I will emphasize. Here are the principles:

- The feature must be of interest or appeal to your staff. Consider their demographics. If they are all single males in their twenties they will not be as interested in day care as will young women with small children. On the other hand, employees whose children have grown up and left home may find the idea of paid sabbaticals more appealing than younger staff with children, simply because they have the time.
- The cost of the feature is also important. Some of the most appealing may appear to have little or no cost, such as sabbaticals. You simply let the employee go away for six months and the other employees pick up the slack. However, one company found that, at one point, three-quarters of one department became eligible to go on sabbatical at the same time. Aside from the problem of replacement costs, there were additional concerns about equitably scheduling the time off. It may also be very difficult to precisely calculate the cost, or the value, of a work/life component, unlike insured benefits which are easy; just ask your carrier for a quote. Value is in the eye of the beholder, the employee or prospective employee, and this can be difficult to assess.

---

[4] S. Burud, "Measuring the Impact of Work/Life Initiatives with Metrics" (Winter, 1998) *ACA Journal*, at p. 87.
[5] "Strategic Approaches to Work/life Balance" (2000), 13:1 *Worklife*, at p. 8.

- Obviously, you should try to provide work/life features that your competitors for employees will find difficult to match. A very large company like IBM Canada in Markham, Ontario, can provide a day care and fitness centre that other, smaller employers in the information technology industry cannot hope to provide.
- If possible, offer a work/life feature to the employees that they cannot obtain if you simply paid them more cash and let them purchase the product or service on their own. Providing them with the opportunity to telecommute, or operate from a home office, which you equip, is an example of this sort of feature.

RESPONSIBILITY FOR WORK/LIFE BALANCE

In looking at this issue of work/life balance, one can take a very narrow or very broad approach. The narrow approach simply looks at this as additions to the "benefits" package offered to employees, with no change in the nature of work or the demands of the workplace on the individual. The broadest approach calls for a fundamental rethinking of the relative roles of work and family life and how they are integrated. For example, it calls for a new look at the definition of career success and the involvement of a variety of key participants, including employers, unions, governments, family advocates, professional associations and community groups.

However, at the company level, there is still the practical question of which individual function or person should be given this responsibility. In my opinion, the person who is responsible for the compensation function is the natural answer. This assumes, of course, that you have accepted my initial premise that the employer has to take a total rewards approach to compensation and not just consider salaries, wages, bonuses and benefits.

COMPONENTS OF A WORK/LIFE BALANCE PROGRAM

Here are some of the major components of a work/life balance program that are starting to appear in Canadian and American companies. Remember, however, that they do not occur in large numbers of companies and that this concept is rapidly evolving. It is quite possible that this chapter will be out of date before it gets to the printer. However, we have to start somewhere. These programs can be grouped into four broad categories:

- organization of work time;
- family-related leave;
- child and dependent care services; and
- employee benefits.

Organization of Work Time

Work Design

The design of jobs is the primary cause of many of the problems connected with integrating work and family life. Employers should look at how to design work in such a way that it results both in high performance work and a satisfactory life outside of work.

Flexible Work Arrangements

There are a variety of approaches, including part-time employment, flex-time, job sharing, compressed work weeks, telecommuting and virtual officing. One employer has established a formal flex-time policy that allows employees to design a five-day work schedule with flexible starting and ending times, as long as they are working during the core set hours of 9:00 a.m. to 3:30 p.m. Employees select and work their preferred work schedule with management approval.

Other policies that support work and family include overtime polices that permit refusal of overtime work and time off in lieu of payment for such work. Giving employees a choice in the scheduling of their work also helps. One employer, Casino Windsor, in Windsor, Ontario, has a clause in its collective agreement that recognizes the right of employees to a family life:[6] "The parties acknowledge the employer's right to schedule employees to meet the demands of the business. The parties also acknowledge the right of employees to maintain a family life."

Family-Related Leave

Maternity Leave

There are legislated minimums for maternity leave in all Canadian jurisdictions. However, some employers are enacting formal polices that go beyond the legislation and provide for: employee choice in the starting and ending dates for maternity leave; the length thereof; benefits during the leave; and seniority and return to work protection. Leave policies are also being provided to new fathers and couples who are adopting.

Other Leaves Related to Family

Employees are being allowed to use their own sick leave credits to take care of family members, including parents, children and other family members for whom they have responsibility. Leave can also be granted for family

---

[6] V. Galt, "Life and Profit on the Table in 'Family-friendly' Contracts", *The Globe and Mail* (July 16, 2001), pp. A1 and A6.

appointments, such as counselling and cases of violence in the family or appearance in court.

Child and Dependent Care Services

Dependent Care Resource and Referral

Employers are providing assistance to employees in locating and/or arranging for day care or elder care for children or parents.

Day Care

Some employers are providing on-site day care for children of employees. Others provide the same services but away from the workplace. On-site day care can be especially useful to employees when there are multi-shifts and/or extensive, unpredictable overtime involved. Other employers are providing subsidies for day care or reimbursement of child care expenses under specific circumstances.

Special Leaves for Personal Business

Many companies offer some form of special leave for family-related events, such as taking a parent to a doctor's appointment. One company specified that such leaves had to be early in the morning or late in the afternoon.

Expenses for Dependent Care

Some employers reimburse employees for dependent care travel-related expenses incurred outside normal work hours.

Employee Benefits

Employee Assistance Program

The employee assistance program ("EAP") is one of the earliest versions of this type of benefit. An EAP provider is selected and employees are given a telephone number which they can call at any time and receive referrals to various types of professional help, such as psychiatrists, psychologists, family and marriage counsellors, paramedical and nursing services, substance abuse, stop smoking or weight loss programs.

Flexible Spending Accounts

Under such accounts, money is set aside on a pre-tax basis for both health care and child care.

Financial Planning

A "Future Saver" software program is available via the Intranet site. This helps employees develop a personal savings and investment strategy.

Fitness Centre

Some employers now provide a centre equipped with free weights as well as Nautilus-type equipment; various aerobics, step and stretching classes are also offered to employees. A corporate-sponsored health club membership provides employees with corporate-sponsored membership in a nearby fitness facility.

Volunteerism

Employers are now recognizing that volunteer work by employees benefits both the company and the employee. Some have established formal programs to encourage and assist employees in finding volunteer work that matches their interests and supports corporate values.

CONCLUSION

Work/life balance, or work and family programs, are a new and rapidly evolving part of the "total rewards" that you, as an employer, can offer your employees. Since this subject is so new it may be one where you can gain a competitive advantage in the attraction and retention of key employees, in some cases at relatively low cost. Use your imagination and consult your employees.

19

Communication of Pay Programs

INTRODUCTION

All the work you have done so far in developing your rewards program will be wasted unless you tell your employees about it. I can actually make this a very short chapter by telling you to disclose everything to your staff. I believe it is impossible to communicate too much. If you don't tell them something, you can be sure that they will fill in the gaps. They do this by making stuff up, and they usually get it wrong. One study showed that employees consistently underestimate the income of those below them in the hierarchy and over-estimate the income of those above them.

Another recent study by WorldatWork[1] and the Leblanc Group showed that:[2]

- less than one-half of the employees in the survey knew the average base pay increase given in their company;
- only 41% understood how their base pay increase was calculated; and
- 36% understood how their salary range was constructed.

The manager of the survey said that "the key finding in this project is that the more employees know about the process of determining compensation, the happier they are with their level of pay and their employer. The key to employee satisfaction, when it comes to pay, is in providing them the knowledge to understand its basis".[3]

---

[1] Formerly the Canadian/American Compensation Association.
[2] J. Handel, "Does It Matter What Employees Know About Pay?" (2002), 10:2 *Canadian News – A WorldatWork Publication* 15 (formerly *Canadian News*).
[3] *Ibid.*

This chapter will discuss the following aspects of communicating rewards:

- what to communicate;
- communications during the design process;
- communications after implementation of a new program; and
- methods of communicating.

WHAT TO COMMUNICATE

Communication of rewards can really be grouped into four broad categories: working conditions; base salaries; incentive plans; and benefits. Here is a list of the items that can be included in each category. Whatever the form, paper or electronic (either or both), these are the major compensation items that should be included:

- *Working conditions —*
  - hours of work;
  - overtime rates;
  - shift and weekend premiums;
  - vacations;
  - holidays;
  - shift schedule;
  - lunch periods;
  - call-in pay;
  - rest periods;
  - standby pay;
  - lead-hand premiums;
  - bereavement leave;
  - jury duty; and
  - report to work provisions.
- *Benefits —*
  - government-provided retirement plans;
  - company retirement plans;
  - life insurance;
  - accidental death and dismemberment insurance;
  - health insurance;
  - long-term disability insurance;
  - short-term disability insurance;
  - dental insurance;
  - major medical insurance; and
  - cost sharing.
- *Base Salaries —*
  - the use of the job description questionnaire;
  - access to job descriptions;

- job evaluation —
    - type of plan;
    - factors used;
    - difference between job evaluation and performance appraisal;
    - point bands;
    - appeals;
- salary grades —
    - how ranges are established;
    - step-rate or 3M system;
    - progression through ranges;
    - pay equity;
- policy line re salaries —
    - use of surveys;
    - competition for labour;
    - labour market adjustments;
- changes in jobs —
    - current job;
    - demotions;
    - promotions.
- *Incentive plans* —
    - membership;
    - allocation formula;
    - establishing pool of funds for distribution;
    - timing of payments; and
    - tax implications (if a deferred plan).

COMMUNICATION DURING DESIGN

While you are designing a new compensation program, or any component thereof, you have a golden opportunity for communications. In Chapter 1, "Assessing Your Situation", I discussed the merits of employee involvement in plan design.

Employee involvement may be more useful as a communications tool than any other function. It has the unique advantage of being a two-way communications device. Information flows from the company to the employees and from them to the company. This is in stark contrast with most corporate communication programs which tend to be totally one way — from the top down. You cannot have an effective compensation program without feedback and data from your employees. You cannot possibly design something that will interest or motivate them if you do not know what they are thinking.

There are really three points during the design phase when significant communication can take place. The first is at the commencement of the project, when the chief executive, or some other very senior person, should make an announcement, in writing, which will include:

- the decision to develop a plan;
- reasons for the decision;
- objectives of the plan; and
- who will be involved.

During the design phase, periodic progress reports should also be made. The magic of employee involvement is that they will provide continuous progress reports without very much effort on your part. The final opportunity is of course when the program has been finalized, as it is being implemented.

COMMUNICATION AFTER IMPLEMENTATION OF A NEW PROGRAM

Once you have implemented a new program, you must ensure that regular communication becomes a routine part of your operations. There are specific times when you can communicate about the compensation plan. These times include:

- external recruiting;
- internal job postings;
- orientation of new employees;
- supervisory training;
- when employees join a particular incentive plan, *e.g.*, profit sharing;
- employee meetings;
- paydays;
- payment of bonuses;
- retirement planning;
- salary increase time; and
- introduction of new salary schedule.

External Recruiting

One of the major purposes of any rewards program is to attract the best candidates that the labour market has to offer. An outstanding rewards program should be part of the sales pitch. Use it during interviews. Since your recruiters or line mangers are not usually part of the compensation department, make sure that they understand it. Mention it in your recruitment advertising and tell employment agencies about it.

The rise of the Internet has produced a golden opportunity for employers to brag about the new and leading-edge compensation programs they will introduce as a result of reading and using this book. Employers are increasingly putting a section on their corporate website which I will call "the employment section". Here they provide information about employment opportunities at their organization. The amount of information varies widely. It can be just basic contact information, such as e-mail or regular address and fax or telephone number, so a prospective applicant can send in their resumé. Some list current job openings with actual, brief job descriptions.

However, very few provide any information about their total rewards package. Almost none provide any "benefits" data. In my opinion, this is a major mistake. In one recent survey, 82% of applicants looking at corporate websites when conducting a job search said they wanted to find benefit information on the site.[4]

This book is not concerned with the merits of including employment information on your website. Take it as given that I believe it is important, but that is up to you to decide. If you do go this route, the issue then becomes how far you go beyond providing just general contact information and current job openings, specifically with regards to your rewards package. Although I generally believe that "more is better", in the case of your website I recommend some restraint. Here are some of the items that I think should be mentioned:

- If you have a very specific policy line, state it explicitly. For example, one company had a policy that it would pay hourly and clerical employees at the 90th percentile in the city in which it was located. *Do not* say that you pay "competitive wages and salaries". Virtually all advertisements say this and the phrase has become totally meaningless.
- Actual salary ranges (or at least the range within which you are prepared to hire) for jobs listed on the website.
- Any incentive plans that provide a significant portion of the total cash package, such as profit sharing, gainsharing or an ESOP.
- The major components of the benefits package.
- Any working conditions policies that are significantly better than the competition, such as vacations.
- Any particular offerings that fall in the area of work/life balance, such as day care centres or on-site fitness facilities.
- The costs, if any, to employees for the benefits and work/life features of your package.

Internal Job Postings

Many employers "post" jobs on their bulletin boards or in employee newsletters so that current employees have a chance to apply. In my experience most of these postings do not include the salary grade or range of the job being posted. The usual rationale was that this was confidential and the employees

---

[4] D. Brown, "Who's Looking Online? Most Firms Don't Know" (August 13, 2001), Can. H.R. Rep., p. 2.

could be told what sort of increase they could expect if they applied for, and got, the job. I think this rationale is nonsense. Of course, if you are in the position that such data does not exist and you are willing to pay whatever an acceptable candidate will accept, there is no point. However, if you have followed the prescriptions laid out in this book, especially in Chapters 3 to 7, you will have this information. Therefore, put it in the job posting. It will enable those employees who are considering applying for the job to make a better and more informed decision. It also promotes the fact that your salary ranges are constructed in a logical fashion and are competitive with the rest of the world.

Orientation

Many companies do not have a formal orientation program. Nevertheless, new employees have to be put on the payroll and enrolled in your benefit programs. Forms for group life insurance, pension plans and income tax have to be filled out. This means that you have their attention, at least for a while. Take this opportunity to review your compensation program with the new employee. If you have prepared written or other material, provide it at this point.

Supervisory Training

Your front-line managers and supervisors are vital links in the communications program. This is even more so if you have a merit increase component of the program. Supervisors and managers are usually the first persons an employee with questions about pay will approach. They must be thoroughly grounded in all aspects of the compensation program. This is especially true if you use a performance appraisal mechanism[5] to determine any part of an employee's compensation.

Joining a Group Incentive Plan

Group incentive plans, like profit sharing, often have a length of service requirement that must be completed before an employee can "become a member" of the plan. For example, Valley City Manufacturing of Dundas, Ontario, requires that employees have one year of service before they join the profit-sharing plan.

This is an opportunity to make sure that the employee, or new member, is aware that he or she has joined that special group and appreciates the significance of it. It is also an excellent opportunity to explain the operation of the incentive plan with regard to four critical aspects:

- membership;
- how the bonus pool is determined;

---

[5] See Chapter 16, "Performance Management and Rewards".

- how the pool is divided amongst the members; and
- how the employee can affect the results.

Employee Meetings

Meetings between large groups of employees and management representatives responsible for compensation programs can be very effective methods of communicating. Such meetings can be held for a variety of reasons, such as:

- introduction of a new program;
- release of periodic (annually or quarterly) financial or operating results; and
- introduction of a new product or line of business that could affect the rewards package.

In companies with more than one location, it may be necessary to have more than one meeting on the same subject. Even monthly meetings are useful if there is an actual agenda, *i.e.*, something to talk about. Many companies often hold an annual meeting to announce the results of their group incentive plan, such as profit sharing, and hand out the cheques. The disadvantage of annual meetings is that you are communicating the results of their actions to the employees long after they are able to do anything about performance that is not up to expectations. Meetings with groups of employees are most effective when there is dialogue. The employees need to be able to ask questions and obtain reasonably coherent answers.

Cheques

There are two possible chances for communicating compensation in the distribution of cheques, at least if you have a component of your compensation program that is over and above base salary.

If you do, the distribution of the annual (or quarterly or monthly) bonus cheques is a glorious opportunity to promote your compensation program, or at least the bonus part of it. Obviously, the frequency of your bonus calculation affects the frequency and timing of distribution of payments. As you have seen in the chapters on profit sharing and productivity gainsharing, they can have quite different payment schedules.

Nevertheless, whatever the schedule, use this opportunity. Even if your company has direct bank deposit of regular pay cheques, consider handing out the bonus cheques directly. If the company is small enough, the owner/manager can do this in person. Companies that are too large for the chief executive officer to do this personally with each employee can delegate this function to other executives, such as vice-presidents or directors. Having a senior person deliver the cheque sends the double message that the company considers the program important to their overall operations and that the employee is an important part of that program.

The other opportunity for communication revolves around regular pay cheques. Legislation requires that you provide employees with a statement of earnings, whether or not you use direct deposit. A lot of information can be placed in the same envelope as the earnings statement. This information could include the traditional payroll stuffers and other items, such as corporate financial statements, investment results of deferred plans, and performance of company stock when you have an ESOP.

Pay envelopes have two advantages. First, you can be sure that the employee, and often his family, will receive the material. You can't control whether or not he reads it, so don't worry about it. The second advantage is that payrolls are done relatively frequently and you have a lot of opportunities to "communicate."

Pre-retirement Planning

If you have employees who are retiring from your organization, you will probably be providing some sort of financial and other planning (*e.g.*, housing) for them in the last few years of employment. This may be the time when communications about compensation can be of most benefit to the employee. In my opinion, the employer has a moral obligation to ensure that the employee understands the options regarding pension income and the other benefits, such as life insurance, that may be provided post-retirement.

The employee will need to be advised on the options available under your pension plan (*e.g.*, life annuity) and probably under government plans, such as the Canada and Quebec Pension Plans and Old Age Security. The spouse should also be included in this particular part of the compensation communications program. It is not unusual to begin this process ten years before the scheduled retirement date. Sometimes, the planned date gets moved up because of health or other considerations.

Often, deferred profit-sharing plans and group registered retirement saving plans allow employees choices about how their funds are invested.[6] In such a case, it may be useful to start retirement planning even earlier as changes in investment strategy, such as switching from an equity fund to fixed income, can take years to pay off.

COMMUNICATIONS MEDIA

The last item regarding communications is the need for a document(s) that the employee can review at his or her leisure. Actually, the term document is

---

[6]   See Chapter 12, "Team-Based Incentives".

somewhat lacking in this era of computers and the Internet. The "document" no longer has to be words, reproduced in ink, on paper. It can be in electronic form. You can use the Internet or your company intranet as the repository of the information that traditionally has been made available in the form of the "employee handbook".

Many larger companies are setting up "portals" whereby employees can sign up for benefits, change their beneficiaries or coverage, submit expenses and generally obtain information about the benefits package.

Obviously, it may be more appropriate to provide the information in more than one booklet or vehicle.

CONCLUSION

Communications may be the most important aspect of your rewards program. Many companies have technically outstanding programs. However, when they communicate them badly, or not at all, they essentially waste their money. I do not mean just the money they spent on designing, implementing and administering the program. I also mean the money they pay out. Many incentive plans become nothing more than a different mechanism to deliver base pay because of poor communications. Let's take another look at the description of expectancy theory.

Expectancy theory maintains that employees will be motivated by certain rewards if they:

- know what they are;
- believe they can achieve the desired results or behaviour; and
- believe that the company will actually deliver the rewards.

Secrecy about the size and reasons for salary increase in so-called merit-pay programs ensures that none of these expectations will be met. That's why most of them fail.

One final word on communications from an experienced human resources manager that I worked for long ago. He said, and I paraphrase, "if it makes sense and it is logical and defensible, tell them; if not, don't tell them". This is an extremely sound basis for a communications plan.

20

Putting it All Together — The Design Process

INTRODUCTION

This chapter will allow you to bring together most of the "mechanics" involved in the process of designing a comprehensive compensation program. There is a flow chart,[1] in the form of a table, for each of the major processes listed below (use them to track your progress):

- developing a classification structure;
- obtaining salary information from published surveys;
- conducting your own compensation survey;
- developing a step-rate salary administration program;
- developing a 3M salary administration program;
- developing a large group incentive plan;
- developing a benefits, working conditions, work/life balance program; and
- developing a performance appraisal system.

---

[1] This flow chart is also available on the accompanying CD-ROM.

DEVELOPING A CLASSIFICATION STRUCTURE

STEP NUMBER	ACTION	CHAPTER NUMBER/ APPENDIX	NOTES – COMMENTS	DONE ✓
1	Assess the situation	Chapter 1	• use the checklist at the end of the chapter (it can also be printed from the CD-ROM)	
2	Review your objectives in developing and/or modifying your compensation program	Chapter 1		
3	Determine exactly who your employees are	Chapter 1	• be sure to exclude contractors and consultants, although you may wish to include contract employees	
4	Determine how employees will be grouped for pay purposes	Chapter 1	• one compensation system for all employees is highly desirable • take any union groups into account	
5	Decide whether, and how, you will involve employees in the design process	Chapters 1 and 18	• employee involvement is critical	
6	Make sure you know what employment legislation applies to your company	Chapter 1	• federal, provincial and/or territorial law may apply	

STEP NUMBER	ACTION	CHAPTER NUMBER/ APPENDIX	NOTES – COMMENTS	DONE √
7	For each group, set your compensation policy	Chapter 2	• policy line, job or person-based, internal equity, definition of competition, components of the pay package	
8	Set up the compensation function	Chapter 2	• customer or functional basis	
9	Select and train the job evaluation committee	Chapter 3	• assuming you have decided on job-based pay system	
10	Review major types of job evaluation	Chapter 3	• primarily whole-job ranking *or* a point-rating plan *or* market-pricing	
11	Select a job evaluation plan	Chapter 3 Appendix D	• build your own • use or adapt the Tyson-Totten plan • buy from consulting firm	
12	Modify the job evaluation plan	Chapter 3 Appendix F	• change or add factors • change or add degrees	
13	Develop the JDQ	Chapter 4 Appendix E	• you can use the JDQ in Appendix E unchanged, unless you changed the plan in Appendix D	
14	Determine method of distribution for the JDQ	Chapter 4	• this is the basic question: "Who writes the job description?"	

STEP NUMBER	ACTION	CHAPTER NUMBER/ APPENDIX	NOTES – COMMENTS	DONE ✓
15	Have employees complete the JDQ	Chapter 4		
16	Have managers review and approve completed JDQs	Chapter 4		
17	First meeting of the job evaluation committee	Chapter 5		
18	Set rules for running the committee	Chapter 5	• quorum, confidentiality, chair, voting or consensus, evaluation of members' jobs, schedule of meetings	
19	Review rules for evaluating jobs	Chapter 5	• one job at a time, random order, job not person, use documentation	
20	Select benchmark jobs	Chapter 5		
21	Evaluate benchmark jobs	Chapter 5		
22	Assess ratings of benchmarks factor by factor and adjust job evaluation plan as required	Chapter 5 Appendix F		
23	Finalize benchmark ratings	Chapter 5		

STEP NUMBER	ACTION	CHAPTER NUMBER/ APPENDIX	NOTES – COMMENTS	DONE ✓
24	Weight factors	Chapter 5 Appendix G	• use the worksheet on page 76 (it can be printed from the CD-ROM)	
25	Develop point table	Chapter 5 Appendix G	• use the worksheet on page 77 • choose from three formulae on the CD-ROM	
26	Evaluate all other jobs	Chapter 5	• review rules of job evaluation	
27	Calculate point totals	Chapter 5 Appendix G	• if you are using the spreadsheets on the CD-ROM, you will be doing this continuously	
28	Establish point bands	Chapter 5	• go high-tech with coloured crayons	
29	Check the "one-pointers"	Chapter 5	• look at jobs right on the edge of the point band, and any others that don't seem right	
30	Finalize the ratings	Chapter 5	• you have now established the "classification structure" • this is a good point in the process for a senior management review	
31	Do pay equity analysis	Chapter 5 Chapter 17	• only required for private sector employers in Ontario, Quebec or under federal jurisdiction	

OBTAINING SALARY INFORMATION FROM PUBLISHED DATA

STEP NUMBER	ACTION	CHAPTER NUMBER/ APPENDIX	NOTES – COMMENTS	DONE √
1	Review strategy re: definition of "competition for labour"	Chapter 2	• decide which companies, industries or geographical areas you will review for salary data	
2	Obtain information on surveys available that are suitable for this purpose	Chapter 6 Appendix B	• check your local sources for more specialized data	
3	Purchase the selected surveys	Chapter 6 Appendix B	• cost can be significantly lower if you participate in the survey, however, this often requires 6 to 12 months' advance planning	
4	Identify jobs in the surveys that match jobs in your classification structure	Chapter 6	• it is desirable to obtain at least one "survey" job for each salary grade • more is better, but sometimes even one is not possible	
5	Identify all possible survey data that matches your "policy" line for base salary, *e.g.*, median or third quartile	Chapter 2		
		Chapter 6	• use of survey data • record data on spreadsheets on CD-ROM	

STEP NUMBER	ACTION	CHAPTER NUMBER/ APPENDIX	NOTES – COMMENTS	DONE √
6	Eliminate marginal data points	Chapter 6	• consider number of positions and organizations, as well as job match and survey quality	
7	Bring remaining data points to a common date, *i.e.*, "age" the data	Chapter 6	• the common date will usually be the date on which you wish to start your new program	
8	Develop job rates or control points for each salary grade	Chapter 6	• use spreadsheet on CD-ROM	
9	The end result is a salary schedule	Chapter 6	• senior management should be involved at this point for review and approval	

CONDUCTING YOUR OWN COMPENSATION SURVEY

STEP NUMBER	ACTION	CHAPTER NUMBER/ APPENDIX	NOTES – COMMENTS	DONE √
1	Identify jobs to be included in survey	Chapter 6	• select jobs from the classification structure that are common in other organizations	
2	Determine the "components" of the pay package that you wish to survey	Chapters 6, 8, 9, 13, 14 and 15	• base salary, bonuses, stock plans, benefits, working conditions, other incentives	
3	Identify the organizations and/or geographic area for the survey	Chapter 6		
4	Contact survey participants and obtain their agreement to complete the survey	Chapter 6	• prior consent will ensure you have enough data to make the survey worthwhile	
5	Prepare survey questionnaire	Chapter 6		
6	Distribute questionnaire	Chapter 6	• decide on regular mail, e-mail, fax, by telephone or in person	
7	Send out reminder shortly before due date of survey	Chapter 6	• your survey may not be a high priority for some of the participants — often the most valuable ones	

STEP NUMBER	ACTION	CHAPTER NUMBER/ APPENDIX	NOTES – COMMENTS	DONE ✓
8	Collect completed surveys and input data into a spreadsheet	Chapter 6 Appendix G	• you may wish to incorporate this survey data into a review of other surveys • use spreadsheet on CD-ROM	
9	Prepare and distribute participants' report	Chapter 6	• this is critical if you ever plan to repeat the survey; it is also good manners	
10	Incorporate survey results into your salary planning	Chapters 6 and 7	• you may have done a custom survey as part of a new program, or for the purpose of updating your existing salary schedule	

DEVELOPING A STEP-RATE SALARY ADMINISTRATION PROGRAM

STEP NUMBER	ACTION	CHAPTER NUMBER/ APPENDIX	NOTES – COMMENTS	DONE ✓
1	Review your new set of salary range control points or job rates	Chapter 6	• this assumes you have already decided on a step-rate rather than a 3M system	
2	Establish the minimum of the range	Chapter 7		
3	Establish the number of steps	Chapter 7		
4	Review the size of the steps	Chapter 7	• the size of the steps is affected by the combination of the minimum and the number of steps	
5	Determine the timing between steps	Chapter 7	• consider how long an employee takes to learn a job	
6	Establish the reasons for advancing a step	Chapter 7	• there is no partial step; an employee either advances the step or is delayed • progression can be automatic or depend on performance	
7	Incorporate your performance appraisal system if you have decided on a merit component	Chapter 16		

STEP NUMBER	ACTION	CHAPTER NUMBER/ APPENDIX	NOTES – COMMENTS	DONE √
8	Determine whether or not to have "merit" steps above the job rate	Chapters 7 and 16	• if you do decide on this, you will need a performance appraisal mechanism	
9	Document the process	Chapters 7 and 19		
10	Select transition methodology and cost	Chapter 10	• there are two ways to convert to a step-rate system	
11	Obtain senior management approval	Chapter 7	• this is a major policy decision	
12	Communicate the results to employees and management	Chapters 1, 7 and 19	• communication is critical; review section on employee involvement in Chapter 1	

DEVELOPING A 3M SALARY ADMINISTRATION PROGRAM

STEP NUMBER	ACTION	CHAPTER NUMBER/ APPENDIX	NOTES – COMMENTS	DONE √
1	Review your new set of salary range control points or job rates	Chapter 6	• this assumes you have already decided on using ranges rather than a step-rate system	
2	Establish the width of your ranges	Chapter 7	• plus/minus 20% is the most common, although you can vary them • narrower ranges should be at the bottom of your classification structure/salary schedule	
3	Select the number of salary range segments	Chapter 7	• thirds are most common	
4	Determine the number of performance ratings you will have	Chapters 7 and 16	• you need both of these for the next step	
5	Build your salary increase table around X	Chapters 7 and 16	• this table can be used on an ongoing basis as X changes	
6	Decide whether to use anniversary dates or a common date for salary increases	Chapters 1, 7 and 16	• review expectancy theory • use anniversary dates; a common date negates the whole concept of pay for performance	

STEP NUMBER	ACTION	CHAPTER NUMBER/ APPENDIX	NOTES – COMMENTS	DONE √
7	Determine the length of time between possible increases	Chapter 7	• for employees in the middle third, the most common is 12 months • consider having shorter periods for those lower in the range and/or with above satisfactory performance ratings	
8	Detail procedure for initiation and approval of salary increases	Chapter 7		
9	Decide on transition methodology and cost new system	Chapters 7 and 10 Appendix G	• use the spreadsheets on the CD-ROM	
10	Obtain senior management approval	Chapter 7		
11	Communicate the results to employees and management	Chapters 1, 7 and 19	• communication is critical • review section on employee involvement in Chapter 1	

DEVELOPING A GROUP INCENTIVE PLAN

STEP NUMBER	ACTION	CHAPTER/ APPENDIX NUMBER	NOTES – COMMENTS	DONE √
1	Decide on type of plan	Chapters 11, 12, 13, 14 and 15	• choices are team plans, profit sharing, productivity gainsharing or ESOPs	
2	Determine amount of funds to be used		• use the 3% to 5% of base pay rule of thumb	
3	Set up employee committee	Chapter 1	• this is an option, but I highly recommend it	
4	First meeting of the committee — review decisions involved in the plan	Chapters 11, 12, 13, 14 and 15	• these vary by the type of plan, but all plans include the allocation formula and membership rules	
5	Committee members meet with their constituencies to obtain input		• allow enough time for this • leave the method of meeting up to the individual committee members	
6	Second meeting of the committee — first part: obtain their feedback, without comment, on each major issue presented in Step 4		• let them report the consensus of their section • record it on flip charts	
7	Second meeting of the committee — second part		• try and reach consensus on the major issues	

STEP NUMBER	ACTION	CHAPTER/ APPENDIX NUMBER	NOTES – COMMENTS	DONE √
8	Develop model plans (2 or 3)		• just do the major features at this time	
9	Review with senior management and agree on one model (or combination)		• set up this model on a spreadsheet	
10	Test the model using historical and projected data for financial or operating performance and revise			
11	Review again with senior management			
12	Review final prototype with committee			
13	Document plan and prepare employee communication	Chapter 19	• as always, timely and clear communication is critical	
14	Pick a date and implement plan			

DEVELOPING A BENEFITS/WORKING CONDITIONS/WORK LIFE BALANCE PROGRAM

STEP NUMBER	ACTION	CHAPTER NUMBER/ APPENDIX	NOTES – COMMENTS	DONE ✓
1	Assess your current program	Chapter 1 Appendix G	• use the checklist on the CD-ROM	
2	Establish employee groups	Chapter 2	• you may decide to have one program for all employees or group them	
3	Identify areas of concern for each group	Chapters 8, 9 and 18	• each group may have different concerns	
4	Acquire surveys and/or conduct your own	Chapter 6	• although Chapter 6 is primarily concerned with salary surveys, the general principles of acquiring and/or conducting surveys are very similar	
5	Identify predominant practices for each of the relevant items	Chapters 8, 9 and 18	• consider your policy position when doing this	
6	Identify changes or additions to your current practices			
7	Cost proposed changes/additions or obtain quotes from insurance carriers			

STEP NUMBER	ACTION	CHAPTER NUMBER/ APPENDIX	NOTES – COMMENTS	DONE √
8	Obtain senior management approval		• costs of changes could vary significantly	
9	Prepare communication materials and sign up employees		• for change in insured benefits, the carriers will often provide written material	

DEVELOPING A PERFORMANCE APPRAISAL SYSTEM

STEP NUMBER	ACTION	CHAPTER NUMBER/ APPENDIX	NOTES – COMMENTS	DONE √
1	Identify the rewards program for which the performance appraisal system will be used	Chapters 7 and 16	• this will probably be one of the two salary administration systems or a group incentive plan	
2	Clarify precisely how the appraisal system will be used	Chapter 16		
3	Decide on the type of appraisal technique	Chapter 16	• this will normally be a rating scale	
4	Select your job-related factors	Chapter 16		
5	Determine the number of rating levels	Chapters 7 and 16	• odd or even numbered, plus the absolute number	
6	Write descriptions of the various levels of performance by factor	Chapter 16	• use short phrases, single word anchors and/or paragraphs	
7	Test the draft rating scale	Chapter 16	• have some supervisors or managers try rating their employees	
8	Revise accordingly		• it will be unusual if you don't make any revisions	

STEP NUMBER	ACTION	CHAPTER NUMBER/ APPENDIX	NOTES – COMMENTS	DONE √
9	Establish procedure for conducting appraisals	Chapter 16	• this may vary a lot, depending on the reward program affected	
10	Document the policy and procedures and prepare training and communication materials			
11	Obtain senior management approval		• make sure they truly support this and are not just paying lip service — a common condition with performance appraisal systems	
12	Train supervisory/managerial staff who will be required to use the system	Chapter 16	• this is vital to the success of the program	
13	Communicate the impact to the employees	Chapters 16 and 19	• the type of reward program chosen in Step 1 may affect this phase	

CONCLUSION

This chapter has brought together virtually all the elements necessary to plan and conduct the development of a new compensation program. I have assumed that you are basically "starting from scratch". This will often not be the case, so you may have to select the point in the steps listed above at which you start your own process. This is a judgment call that is best left up to you.

Appendix A

Human Resources and Related Professional Associations

This appendix includes a list of the major professional and commercial associations of interest to compensation and human resources professionals in Canada.

Employee Involvement Association
525 S.W. 5th Street
Suite A
Des Moines, Iowa
U.S.A. 50309-4501
Telephone: (515) 282-8129
Fax: (515) 282-9117
Website: www.eianet.org

Human Resources Professionals Association of Ontario (HRPAO)
2 Bloor Street West
Suite 1902
Toronto, Ontario
M4W 3E2
Telephone: (416) 923-2324   1-800-387-1311 (Ontario only)
Fax: (416) 923-7624
Website: www.hrpao.org

Human Resources Association of Nova Scotia (HRANS)
P.O. Box 592
Halifax, Nova Scotia
B3J 2R7
Telephone: (902) 860-0877
Fax: (902) 860-1240
Website: www.hrans.org

Ordre des conseillers en resources humaines et en relations industrielles agréés du Québec (ORHRI)
1253 McGill College Avenue
Suite 820
Montreal, Quebec
H2P 1Y6
Telephone: (514) 879-1636
Fax: (514) 879-1722
Website: www.rhri.org

British Columbia Human Resources Management Association (BCHRMA)
704-1130 Pender Street
Vancouver, British Columbia
V6E 4A4
Telephone: (604) 684-7228
Fax: (604) 684-3225
Website: www.bchrma.org

Saskatchewan Council of Human Resource Association (SCHRA)
P.O. Box 4583
Regina, Saskatchewan
S4P 3Y3
Telephone: (306) 525-2377
Fax: (306) 347-2303
Website: www.schra.ca

Human Resources Institute of Alberta (HRIA)
Glenora P.O. Box 53063
Edmonton, Alberta
T5N 4A8
Telephone: 1-800-668-6125
Fax: (403) 443-1956
Website: www.hria.ab.ca

Human Resources Management Association of Manitoba (HRMAM)
385 St. Mary Avenue
Winnipeg, Manitoba
R3C 0N1
Telephone: (204) 943-2836
Fax: (204) 943-1109
Website: www.hrmam.org

WorldatWork
(formerly American/Canadian Compensation Associations)
P.O. Box 9455
Postal Station A
Toronto, Ontario
M5W 4E1
Telephone: (877) 951-9191 (toll free)
Fax: (480) 488-8352
Website: www.worldatwork.org

Profit Sharing/401(k) Council of America
10 South Riverside Plaza
Suite 1460
Chicago, Illinois
U.S.A. 60606-3802
Telephone: (312) 441-8550
Fax: (312) 441-8559
Website: www.psca.org

ESOP Association Canada
390 Bay Street
Suite 2000
Toronto, Ontario
M5H 2Y2
Telephone: (416) 862-2345
Fax: (416) 694-9263
Website: www.esop-canada.com

Canadian Council of Human Resources Associations
Website: www.cchra-ccrha.ca

Appendix **B**

Sources of Labour Market Information

This appendix lists a variety of sources of information about labour market compensation in Canada. It has three sections:

- publicly available surveys;
- websites; and
- publications.

PUBLICLY AVAILABLE SURVEYS IN CANADA

The following table lists a variety of organizations which conduct Canadian compensation surveys. Such surveys may include salaries, wages, benefits, working conditions or other components of the total rewards package. Although I have tried rigorously to make this list as comprehensive and current as is reasonably possible, it is important to recognize that new surveys frequently appear in the marketplace.

These surveys are conducted by a variety of consulting and/or accounting firms, boards of trade, chambers of commerce, professional associations, industry associations and government departments. Some surveys are only available to participants or to members of the sponsoring organization.

You can readily see from the following table that these surveys vary widely in geography, occupations, companies and industries. Timing, both with regard to the conduct of the survey and when the data is available, also varies considerably. It is important for you to take some time reviewing your needs and the descriptions provided before purchasing or agreeing to participate in any of them. Prices vary considerably. The cost is usually significantly lower for those organizations that participate in the survey than for those who just purchase the finished report.

Survey Organization	Occupational Groups Included	Geographic Area	Type of Compensation Data	Telephone
Alliance of Manufacturers and Exporters of Canada	• Non-executive salaried employees • Hourly employees • Middle management	Each province	Salaries and benefits	(416) 798-8000
Aon Consulting	Executive, middle management and professional	Canada	Cash compensation plus short/long-term incentives, perquisites	(416) 542-5500
Professional Engineers of Ontario	Engineers	Ontario	Salaries	(416) 224-1100
Canadian Advanced Technology Association	Employees in advanced technology industries	Canada	Compensation and benefits	(613) 236-6550
Central Ontario Industrial Relations Institute	• Salaried employees • Hourly employees	Ontario and/or geographic region	Salaries, benefits and working conditions	(905) 709-2364
Watson Wyatt Data Services	• Executive, middle management and sales • Office, professional and production employees	Canada, province, key regions and cities if enough data	Salaries and human resource policies	(416) 283-3145
Grand Valley Human Resources Professionals Association	All employees except executives	Guelph, Kitchener, Waterloo, Fergus, Cambridge, Stratford, Brantford	Compensation and benefits	(519) 744-6541
Hewitt Associates	All employees	Canada	Salary increase forecasts	(416) 225-5001

Survey Organization	Occupational Groups Included	Geographic Area	Type of Compensation Data	Telephone
Institut de Recherche et d'information sur la Remuneration	All except executives	Quebec	Salaries, benefits and working conditions	(514) 288-1394 (514) 288-3536
KPMG	All employees	Canada	Benefits costs	(416) 777-8500
London Chamber of Commerce	35 salaried, hourly, supervisory and sales	London and area	Compensation and benefits	(519) 432-7551
Toronto Board of Trade	• Administrative and support • Executive • Management • Information technology • Professional, supervisory and sales	Greater Toronto Area	Cash compensation	(416) 366-6811 fax (416) 366-4906
Toronto Board of Trade	All employees	Greater Toronto Area	Benefits and employment practices	(416) 366-6811 fax (416) 366-4906
Tyson & Associates Limited	All employees	Canada	Profit-sharing	(416) 966-1379 fax (416) 966-8715
Vancouver Board of Trade (Western Compensation and Benefits Consultants)	• Clerical • Information processing • Middle management • Marketing and sales	Greater Vancouver Area	Salaries	(604) 683-9155 (604) 687-2315
Vancouver Board of Trade (Western Compensation and Benefits Consultants)	All employees	Greater Vancouver Area	Employment practices and benefits	(604) 681-2111

Survey Organization	Occupational Groups Included	Geographic Area	Type of Compensation Data	Telephone
William M. Mercer	• Executive, management and professional • Information technology	Canada/province/region, Toronto, Montreal	Salaries, benefits and human resource policies	1-800-631-9628
WorldatWork (formerly Canadian/American Compensation Associations)	All employees	National	Salary increase forecasts	(480) 951-9191

COMPENSATION AND RELATED HUMAN RESOURCES WEBSITES

Organization	Website – www.	Type of Data	Comments
Tyson & Associates Limited	compensationcanada.com	Profit sharing	
Canadian Payroll Association	payroll.ca	Payroll-related data	
Centre for Industrial Relations, University of Toronto	chass.utoronto.ca/cir	All aspects of human resources and industrial relations	This branch of the university includes all research and teaching in this field
ESOP Association Canada	esop-canada.com	Employee share ownership plans	
Government of Canada	labourmarketinformation.ca	Occupational profiles include wage rates and job descriptions	
Government of Canada	hrmanagement.ca	General human resources	Directed towards small/medium-sized companies

Organization	Website — www.	Type of Data	Comments
Hay Group	haygroup.com	Workplace, change in the workplace, rewards, sales management, and assessment and retention	Major consulting firm with the best-known job evaluation system
Hewitt Associates	hewitt.com	Compensation	Major consulting firm
Mercer Human Resources	mercerhr.com	All forms of compensation	
National Center for Employee Ownership	nceo.org	U.S. data on employee ownership	
Profit Sharing/401(k) Council of America	psca.org	Profit sharing in America	Members are companies with profit-sharing plans
Society for Human Resource Management	shrm.org	All aspects of HR directed towards U.S. membership	
Towers Perrin	towers.com	General human resources	Major consulting firm
Watson Wyatt Worldwide	watsonwyatt.com	General compensation plus Human Capital Index®	Includes Strategy@work magazine
Worldatwork	worldatwork.org	Compensation, benefits and the work experience	WorldatWork was previously known as Canadian/American Compensation Associations

PUBLICATIONS

This section contains a listing of Canadian and other publications that you might find useful in designing and implementing a total rewards plan.

Canadian

- R.N. Kanungo and M. Mendonca, *Compensation — Effective Reward Management*, 2nd ed. (Toronto: John Wiley & Sons (Canada) Ltd., 1997)
- R.J. Long, *Compensation in Canada: Strategy, Practice, and Issues* (Toronto: ITP Nelson, 1998)
- R.P. Chaykowski and B. Lewis, *Compensation Practices and Outcomes in Canada and the United States* (Kingston: Queen's University Press, Industrial Relations Centre, 1995)
- M. Butteriss, *Help Wanted: The Complete Guide to Human Resources for Canadian Entrepreneurs* (Toronto: John Wiley & Sons (Canada) Ltd., 1999)
- The West Hawk Group, *Gross Income: Disclosing Executive Pay in Canada* (Toronto: McGilligan Books, 1998)
- R. Theriault, *Mercer Compensation Manual: Theory and Practice* (Quebec: Morin, 1992)
- D.E. Tyson, *Profit Sharing in Canada: How to Develop and Implement Plans That Really Work* (Toronto: John Wiley & Sons (Canada) Ltd., 1996)
- P. Phillips, *Employee Share Ownership Plans — How to Design and Implement an ESOP in Canada* (Toronto: John Wiley & Sons (Canada) Ltd., 2001)

Other

- R.B. Sibson, *Compensation*, 5th ed. (American Compensation Association, American Management Association, 1990)
- T. Flannery, D.A. Hofrichter and P.E. Platten, *People, Performance and Pay* (The Hay Group, Free Press, 1996)
- H. Risher and C.E. Randow, *Public Sector Compensation: An Overview of Present Practices and Emerging Trends* (WorldatWork, 1977)
- A. Kohn, *Punished by Rewards — The Trouble with Gold Stars, Incentive Plans, A's, Praise and Other Bribes* (Houghton Mifflin, 1993)
- J.R. Schuster and P.K. Zingheim, *The New Pay — Linking Employee and Organizational Performance* (Jossey-Bass, 1996)
- *Salary Survey Guidebook — Finding and Evaluating Compensation and Benefits Data* (American Compensation Association, American Management Association, 1998)

Appendix C

Glossary

Ageing data. The process of bringing survey data from the date it was collected to a specified, current date.

Alternative rewards. A variety of new, or revitalized, reward programs that emphasize increasing employee participation and productivity, such as gainsharing plans, skill-based pay, cash incentives, tiered pay plans, profit-sharing and team incentives.

Anniversary date. This can be the anniversary of the employee's hiring, last pay increase or appointment to present job. This date is used as the starting point of the time period during which there is a review of the employee's salary.

Base pay. The salary or wage rate paid on a fixed basis for a specified period, such as an hour, a week or a month.

Benchmark job. a) A common and clearly defined job that is used for conducting compensation surveys. This type of benchmark job is likely to be found in other organizations. b) In point-factor job evaluation plans, a benchmark job is any clearly defined job that is used to illustrate a degree level within a factor.

Benefits. Components of the compensation package that are not base pay or other cash payments and provide for income protection and retirement. These can include life insurance, accidental death and dismemberment, short and long-term disability insurance, pensions, drug and medical plans.

Bonus. A cash payment made in addition to base compensation, usually determined by individual and/or company performance. Bonuses often have a large element of management discretion in their timing and amount.

Broadbanding. The reduction of the large number of narrow salary grades into fewer, broader ranges, or "bands".

Certified compensation professional (CCP). A professional designation granted by WorldatWork (formerly the American/Canadian Compensation Associations) indicating successful completion of the Association's certification process in compensation program theory, design and management.

Classification method of job evaluation. A non-qualitative form of job content evaluation that compares jobs to pre-defined class descriptions established for each job grade. Jobs are placed in whichever classification best describes them. It is usually done by job families.

Classification structure. A listing of job titles within salary grades. This is the end result of the process of job evaluation.

Commission. A formula that provides monetary compensation to a salesperson based on sales volume.

Compa-ratio. The ratio of the actual, current pay of employees with the control points of their respective salary ranges.

Compensable factors. General components of jobs that are used to determine the value or worth of a job in a job evaluation plan.

Compressed work week. A work schedule in which the normal weekly hours are compressed into fewer days. For example, a five-day, 40-hour week can be done in four days of ten hours each.

Compression. Exists when pay differentials are considered inequitable because they are too small. Compression between subordinates and supervisors can result when overtime or incentive pay (such as commissions or productivity gainsharing) paid to subordinates results in annual, monthly or weekly earnings that are greater for them than for their supervisors, who are not eligible for such payments. Compression can also occur between adjacent salary grades.

Consumer Price Index (CPI). A measurement of changes in the cost of living calculated for a fixed "market basket" of goods and services purchased by a hypothetical average Canadian family. It is published by Statistics Canada on a national, regional and local basis.

Control point. The point in a salary range which represents the dollar value that should be paid to employees who are performing satisfactorily after a reasonable length of time on the job.

Cost-of-living adjustment (COLA). An increase in one or more of the components of the compensation package designed to keep up with increases in the cost of living. COLAs are usually triggered by changes in the Consumer Price Index.

CPI. *See* Consumer Price Index.

Critical success factor (CSF). These are the major factors that are used to set goals in a goal sharing plan. They normally have a financial component, expressed in terms of profits, earnings, costs, earnings per share, return on equity, return on assets, etc.

Custom survey. A survey of the compensation paid to various jobs employed at selected companies and/or competitors.

Deferred compensation. Any reward that employees do not receive at the time they earn it or that they give up the right to receive at that time. This is usually done to reduce taxes.

Deferred profit-sharing plan (DPSP). A profit-sharing plan governed primarily by s. 147 of the *Income Tax Act*. A portion of the company's profits is placed in a trust on behalf of the employee/member. These funds are deductible (up to certain limits) by the employer but not taxable to the employee until they are withdrawn.

Defined benefit pension plan. A pension plan that provides a pension that is generally calculated on the basis of final average or best average earnings and years of service. The amount of defined benefit pension that can be provided under a plan registered under the *Income Tax Act* is limited, in general terms, to the lesser of 2% of the employee's best average earnings and $1,722 per year of service. The $1,722 limit will be indexed to increases in the average wage starting in 2005.

Defined contribution pension plan. A pension plan that provides whatever pension income the accumulated contributions and return on investment in the plan will buy at retirement. Total annual contributions are limited to 18% of earnings up to a maximum of $13,500.

Demotion. The employee is moved from one job to a job in a lower salary grade.

Discretionary plan. An incentive plan in which the total funds allocated to the plan are determined by an assessment of organizational or participant performance, usually by the CEO or the Board of Directors.

DPSP. *See* Deferred profit-sharing plan.

Employee stock ownership plan (ESOP). A plan that allows employees to acquire, by various methods, shares of the employer company.

Employee profit-sharing plan (EPSP). A profit-sharing plan established by s. 144 of the *Income Tax Act*. A share of profits is placed in a trust for the employee. These funds are deductible to the corporation but taxable to the employee. Capital gains and interest income are also taxable to the employee.

EPSP. *See* Employee's profit-sharing plan.

ESOP. *See* Employee stock ownership plan.

Exempt employee. An American term which means employees who are exempt from the overtime provisions of the *Fair Labor Standards Act*. Groups that are exempt include outside sales representatives, administrative, professional and executive employees.

Extrinsic rewards. Work-related rewards that have monetary or physical value, as opposed to intrinsic rewards, which have non-monetary value, such as recognition for good job performance.

Factor comparison plan. A job evaluation plan that utilizes existing pay rates and/or market data to determine the relative weight of factors used to compare jobs.

Fiscal year cost. The cost to the employer of a pay increase within the current fiscal year. For example, if an employee received a salary increase of $2,000 annually, nine months into the fiscal year, there would be a fiscal year cost of $500. This is frequently called first-year cost.

Flex-time. Employees are given some latitude in when they start and/or finish their work day and when they take lunch and other breaks. They are usually required to be at work for certain core hours.

Gainsharing. A type of incentive plan (also know as productivity gainsharing) that rewards eligible employees in a business unit for improving the unit's productivity. The best known are called Scanlon, Rucker and Improshare.™

Goal sharing. A variation of gainsharing, in which an employee's performance is compared with future goals, instead of past performance.

Golden parachute. A contract of employment that ensures payments to key executives in the event that their position is altered if the company is sold, dissolved or restructured, or if there is a change of control.

Housing allowance. An extra payment made to employees that equals (or approximates) the difference between the cost of housing at their home location and some remote location, such as northern Canada, where housing is prohibitively expensive.

Human resource information system (HRIS). A computer software or data base of information that is used in human resources management.

Independent contractor. A person working for the employer who is not an employee. This person invoices the employer and is paid like any other supplier of goods or services. He or she is not included in the employer's benefits plans or covered by employment standards legislation.

Indirect compensation. Any form of compensation that is not cash.

Intrinsic rewards. Rewards with non-monetary or physical value that result from an employee's personal aspirations, such as the opportunity to learn new skills that will advance his or her career.

Job. A collection of tasks, duties and responsibilities which can be performed by one person.

Job analysis. The systematic process of obtaining data about jobs. Job analysis provides the information needed to conduct job evaluation.

Job content. The actual components of a job, including tasks, task elements, duties, responsibilities, etc.

Job-content evaluation. Job evaluation methods that measure the worth of jobs on the basis of their content, as opposed to market data.

Job description. A formal document that identifies the important functions of a specific job in a standard format. The length and content will vary depending on the specific purpose thereof.

Job evaluation. The process of determining the relative value of jobs within an organization.

Job family. A group of jobs in the same general field of work. Within a family of jobs there are different levels of skill, effort or responsibility (*e.g.*, junior, intermediate and senior systems analyst).

Job sharing. Two or more employees share the responsibility for one full-time job.

Job specifications. The minimum required qualifications and characteristics (*i.e.*, the knowledge, skills and abilities) an individual must possess to perform a job satisfactorily.

Job-worth hierarchy. The result of a formal job evaluation process; a ranking of an organization's jobs according to their relative worth.

Knowledge-based pay. *See* Skill-based pay.

Lateral transfer. The movement of an employee from one job to another in the same salary grade, as established by the job evaluation system.

Long-term incentive. Any compensation component (*e.g.*, stock option, stock grants or cash bonuses) that is given to an employee for sustained performance over a long period, usually more than one year.

Lump-sum increase. A pay increase that an employee receives as a single cash payment, instead of an increase in base salary.

Market-based evaluation. A job evaluation methodology that constructs a job-worth hierarchy using pay rates for similar jobs in the marketplace.

Market pricing. The process of identifying pay levels for specific jobs in the external market. This is usually done through the use of salary surveys or the conduct of a customized survey.

Merit increase. An increase in base salary given to an employee which varies according to some measurement of individual job performance.

Midpoint. The salary level that is midway between the minimum and maximum pay rates of a 3M type salary range. *See also* Control point.

Ontario Pay Equity Act. The most proactive pay equity legislation in Canada, it requires Ontario employers to establish and maintain pay equity in their establishments.

Option price. The price to be paid by an employee to purchase shares under a stock option plan.

Overtime. Time worked in excess of normal working hours as defined by provincial and federal labour legislation. Employment standards legislation may be exceeded by company policy or a collective agreement.

Pay equity. The concept of equal pay for work of equal value within an organization.

Performance appraisal. The process of evaluating the performance of an employee, or the end result of such a process. Performance appraisals are often used to determine the size and/or timing of a merit increase or other payment of a reward.

Performance management. The overall process by which employees receive direction, feedback and reinforcement for their performance. Its components are objectives, measurements, performance appraisal, coaching, feedback, reinforcement and rewards.

Perquisites (perks). Unique non-cash compensation components which are normally only available to senior executives. Typical perquisites include executive dining rooms, first-class air travel, financial counselling, luxury cars and club memberships.

Phantom stock plan. An executive incentive plan. "Phantom" or notional shares are granted to the employee. After a defined period, the executive receives a cash payment equal to the appreciation in the price of actual stock over the same period of time.

Point band. A range of points with a minimum and a maximum within which all jobs are considered equal in value. When a point band is given a number it is called a salary grade.

Point-factor plan. Also known as a point-rating plan. The most prevalent form of job evaluation. Such a plan includes specific compensable factors, such as skill, effort, responsibility and working conditions, and divides these into degree levels. Jobs are compared with these degree definitions and assigned points for each. Point totals determine the salary grade of the job.

Premium pay. A general term which includes any addition to the regular rate of pay for employees who work overtime hours, holidays or shifts other than the normal day shift.

Promotion. The move of an employee to a job in a higher job classification or pay grade than the current job.

Published salary survey. A salary survey produced by organizations such as boards of trade, chambers of commerce, industry associations, the government or consulting firms.

Ranking plan. A job evaluation plan in which each job in the organization is compared, as a whole, with every other job in the organization.

Reclassification. A change to the salary grade of a job because of a reassessment using the job evaluation plan.

Recognition programs. Programs by which the employer acknowledges employees' accomplishments for long service, outstanding job performance, attendance, cost improvement suggestions, quality, safety and productivity.

Red-circling. The practice of curtailing or freezing increases in an employee's salary when it exceeds some point in the salary range (usually the control point) until the control point is increased above the employee's salary.

Return on equity (ROE). The ratio of a company's financial return to its shareholders' equity.

Sabbatical. Paid time off from work during which employees can pursue personal and/or professional growth or perform community service.

Salary grade. A level within the salary schedule in which there are one or more jobs all of which are considered equal in value and will have the same salary range.

Salary structure. A complete set of ranges applied to a classification structure. This will include control points (which can be midpoints or maximums) and all other points in the ranges that will be used for salary administration purposes. Salaries can be expressed as any or all of annual, monthly, weekly or hourly rates.

Salary range. The dollar value at all ponts, including the minimum and maximum, that comprise a pay or salary grade.

Salary survey. A published or custom survey that reports the salary levels of specific jobs within participating organizations.

Self-directed work team. An employee group that is responsible for an entire product or process. The team both plans and performs the work. It also has some support, administration and co-ordination functions.

Seniority. The length of service an employee has with the organization.

Severance pay. Payment to an employee due to the termination of employment.

Single-rate system. A system of salary administration in which there is only one monetary value for a salary grade or job level. All employees in that level/grade receive the same rate of pay regardless of length of service or performance.

Skill. Any developed or acquired ability required to perform a specific job.

Skill-based pay. Increases in base pay are earned when the employee masters various tasks or jobs, or acquires specific skills, rather than the overall job performance of the employee. Often called pay-for-knowledge.

Skill block. A specific group of skills to be acquired in a block before a pay increase will be granted.

Slotting. A variation on job evaluation whereby jobs are placed (slotted) into an existing job-worth hierarchy (classification structure) based on their perceived relationship to other jobs in that hierarchy. Slotting is normally used for new or revised jobs when the primary job evaluation system is market-pricing or whole-job ranking.

Step-rate increase. Salary increase based on the employee's time on the job.

Stock option. The right to purchase shares of the employer company at a fixed price during a specified period.

Stock purchase plan. A plan that allows employees to buy company stock, with the company contributing a specified amount for each unit of employee contributions, or with the stock offered at a fixed below-market price and paid for in full by the employees.

Top-hat plan. Any compensation plan that provides benefits only to executives and other highly paid employees.

Total compensation. The complete rewards package of direct and indirect compensation, including all forms of cash, benefits and working conditions.

Underwater. A stock option that is underwater is not worth exercising because the option price is higher than the market value of the stock.

Variable pay. Any form of pay that varies with an employee's performance. It is not part of base pay.

Vesting. When a compensation or benefits element becomes non-forfeitable, it is considered vested.

Whole-job ranking. The job evaluation process that compares each whole job with all other whole jobs and groups them into a structure according to their relative worth to the organization. This process does not use compensable factors.

Working conditions. The physical environment in which a job is performed, including temperature, weather, location, dust, fumes, smell and danger.

Work/life balance program. A program set up by progressive companies to provide services, terms of employment or other benefits that enable the employee to effectively balance the demands of work and family life.

Appendix **D**

Tyson-Totten Job Evaluation Plan

INTRODUCTION

This appendix contains the Tyson-Totten Job Evaluation Plan. This plan was designed so that it:

- allows for the addition/deletion of, or changes to, any of the factor and degree definitions;
- permits each organization to determine factor weightings that reflect its own values;
- can be used to comply with pay equity legislation; and
- is useable for organizations with 300 or fewer jobs.

The Plan is a classic point-rating (or point-factor) job evaluation plan and includes the following ten factors:

- Factor 1 — Communications/Contacts
- Factor 2 — Complexity
- Factor 3 — Mental Effort
- Factor 4 — Physical Effort
- Factor 5 — Accountability
- Factor 6 — Independent Action/Initiative
- Factor 7 — Working Conditions
- Factor 8 — Supervision
- Factor 9 — Education
- Factor 10 — Experience

The appendix is organized like a job evaluation manual with each factor on a separate page. It is also available on the CD-ROM that accompanies this book.

307

FACTOR 1 — COMMUNICATIONS/CONTACTS

Factor Definition

This factor refers to the requirements of the job to interact with people, inside and outside the company, for the purpose of exchanging information, providing explanations, reaching agreement with others or influencing their actions. It considers the nature, the frequency of the contact and the level of persons contacted.

Rules of Application

1. No credit is to be given for supervisory contacts recognized under the Supervision factor.

Degree Levels

1. Contacts with immediate associates only. Contacts are for the purpose of giving, obtaining and/or exchanging information of a routine nature.
2. Some contacts outside immediate area of work or outside organization. Contacts are for the same purpose as Degree 1 and may require the employee to integrate work effort with that of others.
3. Many contacts outside immediate area of work or outside organization. Contacts require judgment, tact and diplomacy in order to obtain co-operation and/or approval of action.
4. Regular contacts outside immediate area of work or outside organization. Contacts are of a demanding nature and require judgment, tact and diplomacy to obtain co-operation, agreement or approval of action in many different situations.
5. Extensive contacts outside immediate area of work or outside organization. Contacts involve working with or influencing others in potentially controversial or sensitive situations.

FACTOR 2 — COMPLEXITY

Factor Definition

This factor measures the difficulty of work problems and considers the following: difficulty of solutions, decision-making, diversity, analysis, availability of policies and procedures, gathering and application of general principles.

Rules of Application

1.   When determining the amount of judgment required, consider controls imposed on the job. These controls or procedures may be written, established by precedent or oral instructions from a supervisor.

Degree Levels

1.   Work is routine and requires little, if any, analysis or problem-solving. Decisions are made on the basis of clearly established rules or precedents and there is seldom any decision-making.
2.   Work is generally standardized and well-defined and duties of the job involve some analysis. Decisions are required and are usually governed by clearly established rules or precedents.
3.   Work is somewhat diversified and most job duties involve a moderate degree of analysis. Decision-making is based on exceptions to accepted or established rules or precedents.
4.   Work is routinely diverse in nature and regular analysis is involved in many of the job's duties. Decision-making is often outside established rules or precedents.
5.   Work is relatively complicated on an ongoing basis with an extensive variety of tasks. Decisions involve a considerable degree of analysis as there are seldom policies or procedures to follow. Job is performed within a framework of changing conditions.
6.   Work is complex and diverse with extensive analysis required on a continuous basis. Decisions serve as guides and directives to the organization on broad policies and long-term programs. Frequent development of new techniques is required.

FACTOR 3 — MENTAL EFFORT

Factor Definition

This factor considers the amount of mental or intellectual effort which must be exerted to perform the job, taking into account results or activities such as: mental fatigue, accuracy required, deadlines, volume, concentration on detail, interruptions, frequency and duration of activity.

Rules of Application

1.   Pressure means deadlines or volume requirements applied to an individual by external sources.

Degree Level

1.   Minimal mental effort required. Performs work involving little variety or pressure.
2.   Medium mental effort. Performs work where there is some variety in tasks but changes are infrequent. Duties occasionally require close attention. Character of work causes minimal and infrequent pressure.
3.   Considerable mental demand. Performs tasks requiring frequent close attention or work where frequent changes in tasks occur. Character of work causes intermittent pressure.
4.   Heavy mental demand. Performs tasks requiring close concentration most of the time or where character of work leads to frequent pressure situations.
5.   Very heavy mental demand. Performs tasks requiring steady, close concentration or where character of work involves constant pressure.

FACTOR 4 — PHYSICAL EFFORT

Factor Definition

This factor considers the degree of physical demand required to perform the job, taking into account the following: eyestrain, endurance, sitting, standing, lifting, carrying and climbing.

Rules of Application

1. Consider the frequency and amount of activity.

Degree Levels

1. Minimum physical demand. Performs tasks requiring minimum physical exertion in a variety of normal positions, such as intermittent sitting, standing, walking, ordinary office tasks.
2. Light physical demand. Performs tasks requiring light physical exertion, such as intermittent standing, sitting, walking or climbing stairs, using light tools, handling lightweight materials or documents or occasional visual concentration.
3. Moderate physical demand. Performs tasks requiring moderate physical exertion, such as frequent climbing or working from ladders, using medium-sized tools and machines and/or medium weight materials or regular visual concentration.
4. Heavy physical demand. Performs tasks requiring heavy physical exertion, difficult work positions.

FACTOR 5 — ACCOUNTABILITY

Factor Definition

This factor represents the impact of job duties upon the organization in terms of its consequences such as: financial results, public relations, client/user relations, confidentiality, employee relations, safety of others, usage of physical resources.

Rules of Application

1. Consider the breadth of impact on the decisions taken, especially outside the job's immediate sphere of influence.
2. "Areas" can be used to describe an individual's immediate work site, department or branch in which the work is performed. (Consider the section of the company for which the job is responsible.)

Degree Levels

1. Job duties have minor effect on the area with impact limited to the particular job only. Tasks performed are not related to others in the area or elsewhere and any errors are easily detected and corrected.
2. Job duties have moderate effect on the area. Tasks performed are related mostly to others in the area and errors may affect the work of others in the area.
3. Job duties have significant effect on the area and/or a minor effect on other areas. Tasks performed may relate to other areas and errors may be somewhat difficult to detect, resulting in delays or inconvenience to other areas.
4. Job duties routinely have a moderate effect on other areas. Tasks performed regularly relate to other areas and errors, which may be difficult to detect, can cause substantial delays or inconvenience and may be difficult to resolve.
5. Job duties have significant effect on other areas. Tasks performed relate to most areas of the company. Errors can cause serious breakdowns in operational control as well as considerable delay.
6. Job duties have a major overall effect on most company activities. Tasks performed relate to company policy and procedural matters of a long-term nature. Errors may not always be readily apparent and may not be reversible.

FACTOR 6 — INDEPENDENT ACTION/INITIATIVE

Factor Definition

This factor considers the extent to which the work of the employee is supervised or directed, with that supervision or direction broken down into three areas: initial instruction, direction or advice received; the point at which direction etc. is to be sought from the supervisor once work has commenced; the frequency of checks on the progress and quality of work.

This factor refers to the requirements of the job for creativity, planning the work, applying procedures and carrying out assignments.

Degree Levels

1.　Work assigned has a set procedure or is accompanied by specific and detailed instructions. Frequent progress checks for quality and accuracy provided by the supervisor or by other routine procedures.
2.　Tasks normally accompanied by instructions while some details are left to the employee's discretion. Doubtful questions related to instructions must be referred to the supervisor. Progress and quality checks are provided at various stages of the work process. Some creativity may be required from time to time.
3.　Tasks are normally accompanied or covered by general instructions or discussion, or advice on special aspects only, with most details left to the discretion of the employee. Unusual problems and relatively important matters are referred to the supervisor. Periodic progress and quality checks are provided only at significant stages of the work process. Creativity is required regularly in various aspects of the job.
4.　Little advice or instruction are provided except on important points. Infrequent reference to the supervisor for instructions and then only on important matters or for objective clarification, interpretation and/or integration with departmental or institutional policies, practices, procedures or priorities. Only occasional checks are provided and these are on the general performance of the work. There can be a significant amount of creativity necessary on a constant basis.

FACTOR 7 — WORKING CONDITIONS

Factor Definition

This factor measures the environmental conditions surrounding a job, such as: dust, dirt, fumes, heat and cold, noise, vibration, inclement weather and equipment utilized. It also considers the health and safety hazards inherent in the job.

Rules of Application

1.   Consider the amount of disagreeability of the above conditions.
2.   Consider the amount and frequency of the condition.

Degree Levels

1.   Job requires practically no exposure to undesirable or disagreeable conditions.
2.   Job requires occasional exposure to minor undesirable or disagreeable conditions.
3.   Job requires frequent exposure to minor undesirable or disagreeable conditions, and/or occasional exposure to major undesirable or disagreeable conditions.
4.   Job requires frequent exposure to major undesirable and disagreeable conditions which could have a direct effect upon occupational health and/or safety.

FACTOR 8 — SUPERVISION

Factor Definition

This factor measures the degree of responsibility for supervision and direction of employees (direct and indirect). It considers the level of employees supervised and the number of positions supervised.

It also measures the extent to which the employee is responsible for the supervision and guidance of the work of other employees. Supervisory functions may include: planning, organizing, scheduling and coordinating of work; assigning of work and/or personnel; maintaining quality, accuracy and quantity of work; giving instruction, direction, guidance, discipline and advice; developing work methods, procedures and standards for the work group.

Rules of Application

1. Use only directly reporting positions for the number of positions supervised.
2. a. "Group A" will be understood to mean jobs that require a formal education of secondary school graduation or less.
   b. "Group B" will be understood to mean jobs that require more than secondary school graduation OR "full supervision" of at least a small unit of "Group A" employees.
3. "Full supervision" is defined as the ability to effectively recommend the hiring, firing, discipline and assessment of employees.

Degree Levels

1. Supervisory responsibility is not normally part of the job requirements, but there may be a requirement to show other employees how to perform tasks or duties.
2. The job requires the employee to periodically assume some of the normal supervisory responsibilities over other employees.
3. The job requires that the employee act as a "team leader".* The employee does the same work as the employees that are supervised but, in addition, performs some of the normal supervisory functions.
4. The employee is responsible for "full supervision" of a unit of 1 to 10 Group A employees.
5. The employee is responsible for "full supervision" of a "large" (11+) unit of Group A employees OR a "small" (1 to 10) unit of Group B employees.
6. The employee is responsible for "full supervision" of a "large" (11+) unit of Group B employees.

---

* Other terms are lead hand or working supervisor.

FACTOR 9 — EDUCATION

Factor Definition

This factor measures the minimum amount of formal education and specialized training to perform the job. It will consist of academic and/or technical learning obtained from a recognized educational facility and/or required accreditation.

Rules of Application

1. Specialized training is usually received in a concentrated course of study in a specific field applicable to the work.
2. Journeyman qualification will be considered to consist of Grade 10 plus the number of years of experience and training as specified under the *Apprenticeship and Certification Act, 1998.*[1] Where a period of training for the Journeyman Certificate comprises from 1,800 to 2,000 hours, this will be considered as equal to one year of education.

Degree Levels

1. Grade 10 or less.
2. Grade 12.
3. Grade 12 plus up to one year of further education.
4. Completion of a community college program.
5. Recognized certification, such as PMAC, CPM.
6. University graduation.
7. Graduate degree at a Masters level or a four-year university degree and professional designation such as C.A., P.Eng., C.M.A., C.G.A.
8. Graduate degree at a doctorate level.

---

[1] S.O. 1998, c. 22.

FACTOR 10 — EXPERIENCE

Factor Definition

This factor measures the amount of work experience needed to perform the job. It includes experience in the same and/or related work obtained prior to assuming the duties of the job being evaluated.

Rules of Application

1. This factor deals with job knowledge acquired through previous practical training.
2. Experience is expressed in terms of the minimum amount of time required to qualify for the job.

Degree Levels

1. Less than one year of experience.
2. Minimum of one year but less than two years.
3. Minimum of two years but less than three years.
4. Minimum of three years but less than five years.
5. Minimum of five years but less than eight years.
6. Eight years or more.
7. Eight years or more, but this must include at least five years with the organization *or* at least five years related supervisory/managerial experience.

Appendix E

Job Description Questionnaire

INTRODUCTION

This appendix contains the Job Description Questionnaire ("JDQ") that accompanies the Tyson-Totten Job Evaluation Plan which is provided in Appendix D. It is also available on the CD-ROM that is included with this book.

If you modify the Tyson-Totten Job Evaluation Plan it will usually be necessary to modify this JDQ accordingly. See Appendix F for directions on doing this.

The questionnaire has been set up, both in this appendix and on the CD, to be printed exactly as shown. Please note that page numbers referred to are for this questionnaire, not for this book.

NAME OF ORGANIZATION: _____

The purpose of this questionnaire is to obtain a complete, accurate description of the duties and responsibilities of your job, as well as other data necessary for the evaluation of the job. The questionnaire is not concerned with the characteristics of the person in the job or how well he or she is performing the job.

1. Please read the entire form carefully before completing any of the sections.
2. Describe the job as it currently exists.
3. Add additional sheets if extra space is required.
4. Print or write clearly (or have your answers typed).
5. Forward the completed questionnaire to your supervisor for review and completion of page 8 of this questionnaire.

JOB TITLE: _____

DEPARTMENT: _____

SUPERVISOR (NAME/TITLE): _____

INCUMBENT(S): _____

_____

PREPARED BY:_____   **TELEPHONE:** _____

JOB SUMMARY

Please provide a two or three sentence summary of the overall purpose of the job. It is better to complete this section after the rest of the questionnaire has been filled out.

_____
_____
_____
_____
_____
_____
_____
_____
_____
_____

DUTIES AND RESPONSIBILITIES

List the major duties/responsibilities of your job. Indicate the approximate percentage of time that you spend on each duty over the course of a normal year.

DUTY/RESPONSIBILITY   APPROXIMATE PERCENTAGE
                                              OF TIME

_____

_____
_____
_____
_____
_____
_____
_____
_____
_____
_____
_____
_____
_____
_____
_____
_____
_____
_____
_____
_____
_____
_____
_____
_____
_____
_____
_____
_____
_____
_____
_____
_____
_____
_____
_____
_____

COMMUNICATIONS/CONTACTS

List the people with whom you have job-related contact(s). Provide the title (not the name) and organization, the frequency and nature of the contact. Examples include customers, suppliers, owners, other employees, sales representatives and government officials. Do not list employees in your immediate work area, your subordinates or your immediate supervisor.

TITLE/ORGANIZATION OF CONTACT	FREQUENCY	REASON FOR CONTACT

COMPLEXITY

Keeping in mind the duties described on page 2 of this questionnaire, please give examples of the types of problems you are normally required to solve. Your answer should illustrate the types of decisions you make on your own without reference to your supervisor.

_____
_____
_____
_____

What guidelines, procedures or policies are available to you to assist in performing this job?

_____
_____
_____
_____
_____
_____
_____
_____
_____
_____

MENTAL EFFORT

Consider the mental or intellectual effort required to perform the duties listed previously. Give examples of duties which require mental effort, such as the need for accuracy, volume, concentration, interruptions and similar factors. Describe the frequency as well.

_____
_____
_____
_____
_____
_____
_____
_____
_____
_____
_____
_____
_____
_____

PHYSICAL EFFORT

Please provide a description of the physical effort involved in the job. Such effort may involve endurance, prolonged sitting or standing, lifting, carrying objects or working in awkward positions. Use examples of tasks and indicate how often they are encountered.

_____
_____
_____
_____
_____
_____
_____
_____
_____
_____
_____
_____
_____
_____

ACCOUNTABILITY

Check off the areas below in which the job is expected to achieve results.

( ) Financial Results   ( ) Confidentiality
( ) Public Relations   ( ) Employee Relations
( ) Client/Owner Relations   ( ) Safety of Others
( ) Use of Physical Resources ( ) Other (please detail)

For the items checked above, please give examples and quantities.

_____
_____
_____
_____
_____
_____
_____
_____
_____
_____
_____
_____
_____
_____
_____
_____
_____
_____
_____
_____
_____
_____
_____
_____
_____
_____
_____
_____
_____
_____
_____
_____

INDEPENDENT ACTION/INITIATIVE

Please describe how much freedom to act you are allowed in your job.

_____

_____

_____

_____

_____

_____

_____

_____

List three or four typical problems referred to your supervisor.

_____

_____

_____

_____

_____

_____

_____

_____

WORKING CONDITIONS

Read the list of working conditions below and put a check mark if they impact on your job.

CONDITION	AMOUNT OF EXPOSURE		
	Occasional	Regular	Frequent
Dust, dirt, fumes			
Heat, cold			
Noise			
Vibration			
Inclement weather			
Lighting			

Describe any health or safety hazards related to the job.

_____

_____

_____

SUPERVISION

On the chart below, indicate the title of the position to which you report in the top box, your title in the next box and, in the boxes below yours, the titles of those jobs that you direct or supervise. If there is more than one person in a job reporting to you, write the number of employees in the lower right corner of that box.

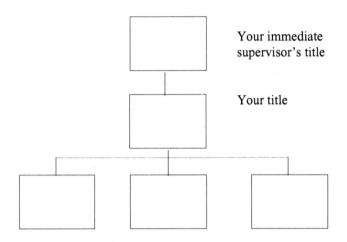

Your immediate
supervisor's title

Your title

Total number of employees supervised/directed by this job is _____.

THIS PAGE SHOULD BE COMPLETED BY THE SUPERVISOR AFTER COMPLETION OF THE PREVIOUS SECTIONS

EDUCATION

What is the minimum formal education required for this job? Do not list the qualifications of the incumbent unless they are identical to those required for the job.

_____

_____

_____

_____

EXPERIENCE

What is the minimum amount of experience (in months or years) required for an employee to perform this job. Include experience in related or lesser jobs. Describe the type of experience. Do not include the amount of experience the incumbent has on the job.

_____

_____

_____

_____

SUPERVISOR'S COMMENTS

Please provide any additional information which you consider relevant or important to a proper evaluation of this job.

_____

_____

_____

_____

SIGNATURES

EMPLOYEE _____ DATE _____

IMMEDIATE SUPERVISOR _____ DATE _____

NEXT LEVEL OF MANAGEMENT _____ DATE _____

Appendix F

Adapting the Tyson-Totten Job Evaluation Plan

INTRODUCTION

This appendix will take you through the steps you need to carry out in order to use and/or modify the Tyson-Totten Job Evaluation Plan provided in Appendix D. It will review the following:

- selecting factors for the plan;
- defining the factors;
- selecting/describing the degree definitions; and
- modifying the job description questionnaire.

SELECTING FACTORS FOR THE PLAN

The Tyson-Totten Plan has the following ten factors:

- Communications/Contacts;
- Complexity;
- Mental Effort;
- Physical Effort;
- Accountability;
- Independent Action/Initiative;
- Working Conditions;
- Supervision;
- Education; and
- Experience.

Virtually all point-rating plans have these ten factors (or variations thereof). For purposes of pay equity (all known legislation) these ten factors can be grouped as follows:

Tyson-Totten Plan Factor	Pay Equity Factor
Communications/Contacts	Responsibility
Complexity	Responsibility
Mental Effort	Effort
Physical Effort	Effort
Accountability	Responsibility
Independent Action/Initiative	Responsibility
Working Conditions	Working Conditions
Supervision	Responsibility
Education	Skill
Experience	Skill

In order to consider whether *or not* these factors are appropriate, we need to talk about "compensable factors" and their characteristics. The factors listed above are compensable factors. They are the foundation of every point-factor plan. Essentially, compensable factors are the characteristics of jobs that you use to determine the relative pay of those jobs. They have the following characteristics:

- observable or measurable in all jobs;
- characteristics of jobs, not people;
- not gender biased;
- do not overlap;
- vary among jobs, not constant among all jobs (*e.g.*, honesty);
- represent the values of the employer organization; and
- can be simply and clearly defined.

The following list consists of compensable factors, other than those in the Tyson-Totten Plan, that have been used in other point-rating plans. They are grouped according to the major pay equity factors.

- **Skill:**
    - training;
    - interpersonal skills;
    - manual dexterity;
    - time required to learn the job;
    - creativity;

- knowledge of equipment;
- experience with the employer organization;
- experience outside the employer organization;
- knowledge of languages — written or oral.
- **Effort:**
    - volume of work;
    - monotony;
    - requirement to concentrate;
    - pressure of work;
    - small repetitive movements;
    - requirement to lift objects.
- **Responsibility:**
    - responsibility for assets, such as cash, equipment, property;
    - safety of others;
    - quality of work;
    - accuracy of work;
    - judgment.
- **Working conditions:**
    - requirement to travel;
    - exposure to dangerous animals;
    - exposure to toxic substances.

Start with the factors in the Tyson-Totten Plan. You have to determine whether they are the factors that your organization wishes to use to differentiate between jobs for the purpose of paying them. It is critical to recognize that the selection of factors for your job evaluation plan is an exercise in setting values. The factors must be (in addition to meeting any legal requirements) a reflection of what you, the employer, want to pay for.

Most organizations will find that the factors in the Tyson-Totten Plan are adequate. They can never be perfect but they will do the job. Some will find that they want to add or delete factors. Here are illustrations of possible scenarios.

One organization sold agricultural products out of their headquarters in Guelph, Ontario, all over the world except the United States. They did not make the products but rather sold them on behalf of the producers. The general manager had five marketing directors reporting to him and each of them had an administrative assistant. Many of the jobs in the company required the ability to speak and write one or more languages. For example, one territory (sales) of one marketing director included all of Africa and South America. This meant that he and any of his staff who dealt with the customers (like the administrative assistant) were required to speak the languages of the area which included Spanish, Portuguese and French. The job evaluation committee decided that their organization needed a Language Skills factor, since languages were obviously a critical job skill. They therefore added an eleventh factor with four degree levels. They considered adding a factor that measured the amount of travel involved (the marketing director in question had been out of town about 200 days in the previous year) but decided that travel could be considered under the Working Conditions factor.

A situation in which you would delete a factor from the Tyson-Totten Plan could be where the selection of the occupational groups to be included renders one of the factors irrelevant. For example, you may have determined that you will use the plan for all management employees. All of these employees have private offices although some are larger and better furnished than others. Nevertheless, there is not enough difference between the offices to justify any differences in pay. This situation makes the Working Conditions factor ineffective for establishing differences between jobs. (This example will not be applicable in jurisdictions with pay equity legislation.) In a situation like this, you can just take out the Working Conditions factor and work with the other nine factors.

DEFINING THE FACTORS

By now you will have selected the factors you want to use. Doing so will probably take less time than reading the preceding section. You now have to review the factor definitions from the Tyson-Totten Plan and, if you have added any, define them clearly.

Let's work with one of the definitions from the Tyson-Totten Plan: Supervision. Here is the definition from Appendix D:

FACTOR 8 — SUPERVISION

Factor Definition

This factor measures the degree of responsibility for supervision and direction of employees (direct and indirect). It considers the level of employees supervised and the number of positions supervised.

It also measures the extent to which the employee is responsible for the supervision and guidance of the work of other employees. Supervisory functions may include: planning, organizing, scheduling and coordinating of work; assigning of work and/or personnel; maintaining quality, accuracy and quantity of work; giving instruction, direction, guidance, discipline and advice; developing work methods, procedures and standards for the work group.

Rules of Application

1. Use only directly reporting positions for the number of positions supervised.
2. a. "Group A" will be understood to mean jobs that require a formal education of secondary school graduation or less.
    b. "Group B" will be understood to mean jobs that require more than secondary school graduation OR "full supervision" of at least a small unit of "Group A" employees.
3. "Full Supervision" is defined as the ability to effectively recommend the hiring, firing, discipline and assessment of employees.

The Rules of Application are also included in this example because they form an integral part of the definition. The factor does not work without the Rules of Application.

Here is a table that shows some elements of a Supervision factor that can be included or excluded. The second column shows whether or not the element is included in the Tyson-Totten Job Evaluation Plan.

Element	Included/Excluded
Number of direct reports	Included
Number of indirect reports	Excluded
Education level of direct reports	Included
Education level of indirect reports	Included
Full supervision of direct reports	Included
Supervisory responsibilities other than "full supervision"	Included

It does not matter whether or not an element is included in the definition in the Tyson-Totten Plan. It is correct if it suits your values and the culture of your organization. The definition in the Tyson-Totten Plan is merely a starting point.

SELECTING AND DEFINING DEGREE DEFINITIONS

There are two aspects to the process of setting your degree levels: the number of levels you need and the exact definitions thereof. Simply put, degrees are amounts of the factor, and range from the lowest possible to the highest. In my experience, Degree 1 is always the least amount of the factor that can be present in a job in the organization in which the job evaluation plan is being implemented. You should also recognize that it is not always possible to finalize the number and definitions of degrees until you have actually evaluated a number of jobs. This process is usually finished when you have completed the evaluation of benchmark jobs. Here are the steps to follow to set your degree levels. For purposes of discussion, I will use the factor Education from the Tyson-Totten Plan. Here is the complete factor:

FACTOR 9 — EDUCATION

Factor Definition

This factor measures the minimum amount of formal education and specialized training to perform the job. It will consist of academic and/or technical learning obtained from a recognized educational facility and/or required accreditation.

Rules of Application

1. Specialized training is usually received in a concentrated course of study in a specific field applicable to the work.
2. Journeyman qualification will be considered to consist of Grade 10 plus the number of years of experience and training as specified under the *Apprenticeship and Certification Act, 1998.*[1] Where a period of training for the Journeyman Certificate comprises from 1,800 to 2,000 hours, this will be considered as equal to one year of education.

Degree Levels

1. Grade 10 or less.
2. Grade 12.
3. Grade 12 plus up to one year of further education.
4. Completion of a community college program.
5. Recognized certification, such as PMAC or CPM.
6. University graduation.
7. Graduate degree at a Masters level or a four-year university degree and professional designation, such as C.A., P.Eng., C.G.A. or C.M.A.
8. Graduate degree at a doctorate level.

---

[1] S.O. 1998, c. 22.

First, eliminate the obvious. Take out the levels that you do not need. Most organizations do not have jobs that require a doctorate degree so take out Degree 8. Many do not have jobs that necessitate a Master's degree, so you can take Degree 7 out as well if this applies to your organization. Take a look at the lowest degree. In these days where the knowledge worker is king/queen, it is entirely possible that there will not be any jobs with such a low education requirement in your company.

Next, try and imagine a job in your company that fulfils the definition in each of the remaining degrees. (I know that it is difficult without job descriptions as I mentioned repeatedly earlier in the book but give it a shot anyway.)

In carrying out the above two steps it may also become evident that you need to split one of the degrees. A common practice is to distinguish between the technician and technologist level in community college. Generally speaking, a technician diploma requires two years of study and the technologist needs three years. If you have both types of jobs in your company, or feel that the distinction is useful or meaningful in setting pay levels, divide this degree into two parts as follows:

- completion of a two-year community college program;
- completion of a three-year community college program.

Finally, renumber the degrees, starting with one for the lowest level.

MODIFYING THE JOB DESCRIPTION QUESTIONNAIRE

The job description questionnaire ("JDQ") that accompanies the Tyson-Totten Job Evaluation Plan is included in Appendix E. If you do not alter the job evaluation plan, there is no need to adjust the JDQ. However, if you have modified the plan you will have to make corresponding adjustments to the JDQ.

In any point-rating plan with a JDQ, there is a least one question related to each factor. In the Tyson-Totten Plan the questions have been carefully designed to obtain information related to the specific definition of the factor. There are two reasons that you might have to modify the questionnaire: (i) if you changed the definition of a factor; or (ii) if you added a factor. A third, completely obvious one, is if you took out a factor completely.

In the first case, if you changed the factor definition, you have to make sure the question still asks for relevant information. It is hard to generalize about this but I will give you an example that will hopefully illustrate my point.

Look at the factor Working Conditions. Some organizations like to change the definition to include any requirements to travel away from home. The relevant questions would have to be changed to ask: How much time is spent travelling and by what means (car, air, etc.)?

If you add a factor, simply make sure there are questions about it. Remember to make sure that the questions are open-ended. It is often useful to test new questions (or even the whole JDQ) on a few employees to make sure that you are obtaining the data that you want.

CONCLUSION

In this appendix, I have shown you how to adapt the Tyson-Totten Job Evaluation Plan to meet any unique characteristics of your organization, the jobs to be evaluated and your corporate culture. Having done this, you can proceed to print and distribute the JDQ following the procedure described in Chapter 4, "Obtaining Information About Jobs".

Appendix **G**

Contents of the CD-ROM

INTRODUCTION

The CD-ROM accompanying this book includes both text and spreadsheets. The text material is either included in the body of the book or is additional material not necessary to the main message, but which could be useful to you as you work through the process of designing and implementing your compensation program. It can be printed directly from the CD-ROM or downloaded onto your computer and modified to suit your particular situation. The text material is provided in Word 97.

The spreadsheet material is provided in two forms: Quattro Pro 9™ and Microsoft Excel 97.™ The letter Q in the title indicates a Quattro Pro 9 file and the letter X indicates an Excel file. The actual spreadsheets are on the CD-ROM and can be simply downloaded onto your computer or used directly from the compact disc. Some of the spreadsheets contain fictitious names or numbers to illustrate the use of the column. They can simply be typed over.

CONTENTS

The text and spreadsheets included on the CD-ROM are described by chapter below.

- **Chapter 1 — Assessing Your Situation**
  Assessment Checklist
- **Chapter 2 — Strategy**
  Worksheet for Strategic Compensation Planning

- **Chapter 3 — Selecting a Job Evaluation Plan**
  Paired Comparison Worksheet
- **Chapter 5 — Conducting Job Evaluation**
  Factor Weighting Worksheet
  Worksheet for Developing a Point Table
  Spreadsheet 5 - 1 (Q/X), Method A
  Spreadsheet 5 - 2 (Q/X), Method B
  Spreadsheet 5 - 3 (Q/X), Method C
- **Chapter 6 — Salary Surveys**
  Spreadsheet 6 - 1 (Q/X), Consolidating Salary Surveys
  Spreadsheet 6 - 2 (Q/X), Control Point Calculator
- **Chapter 7 — Putting it All Together — Basic Salary Administration**
  Spreadsheet 7 - 1 (Q/X), 3M Salary Increase Table Design
  Salary Increase Authorization Form
- **Chapter 10 — Implementing and Costing Your New Salary Program**
  Spreadsheet 10 - A (Q/X), Implementing a Step-rate System
  Spreadsheet 10 - B (Q/X), Implementing a 3M System
  Spreadsheet 10 - C (Q/X), Compa-ratio
- **Chapter 16 — Performance Management and Rewards**
  Executive Assessment Form
  Performance Appraisal Form — Design Sheet
- **Chapter 20 — Putting it All Together — The Design Process**
  Developing a Classification Structure
  Obtaining Salary Information from Published Data
  Conducting Your Own Compensation Survey
  Developing a Step-rate Salary Administration Program
  Developing a 3M Salary Administration Program
  Developing a Group Incentive Plan
  Developing a Benefits/Working Conditions/Work-Life Balance Program
  Developing a Performance Appraisal System
- **Appendix D — Tyson-Totten Job Evaluation Plan**
- **Appendix E — Job Description Questionnaire**

Index

Accidental Death and Dismemberment Insurance, 146
Administration, 34 (*See also* Salary Administration)
Ageing Survey Data, 97
Allocation Formula, 179
    attendance, 182, 200
    choosing a formula, 183, 202
    combinations, 183, 201
    earnings, 180, 200
    equal distribution, 181
    job levels, 182
    length of service/earnings, 183
    merit ratings, 182, 201
    seniority/length of service, 180
Analysis of Current Situation, 1
Anchors. *See* Performance Appraisal
Annual or Hourly Costs, 141, 153, 164
    benefits, 165
    new salary program, 163, 166
        step-rate, 166
        3M system, 168
    work-related pay, 165
Assessment Checklist, 21
Associations, human resource, 239
Benefits
    accidental death and dismemberment, 146
    checklist, 270

Benefits — *continued*
    competition in the labour market, 33
    costing, 141, 153
    definition, 142
    dental, 147
    disability insurance —
        long-term, 146
        short-term, 146
    holidays, 148
    life insurance, 145
    major medical, 149
    medical/health insurance, 145
    obligation to employees, 33, 140
    policy, 139
    statutory, 149
    strategy, 33
    surveys, 150
    vacations, 148
    why provide, 140
Canada Customs and Revenue Agency, 4
    form CPT-1, 6
Canada/Quebec Pension Plan, 142
Canadian Labour Law
    and employee involvement, 12
    employment law, 20
Cash Plans, 194
CD-ROM, 337
Checklists
    benefits, working conditions, work/life balance program, 284
    classification structure, 270
    conducting your own survey, 276
    developing a step-rate system, 278
    developing a 3M system, 280
    large group incentive plan, 282
    performance appraisal system, 286
    salary information from published surveys, 274
Classification Structure, 58,113
    checklist, 270
    example, 84
Coaching Employees, 237
Combination Plans, 195
Committee. *See* Design Committee; Job Evaluation

Communications, 259
    after implementation of program, 262
        cheques, 265
        employee meetings, 265
        group incentive plans, 264
        internal job postings, 263
        orientation, 264
        pre-retirement planning, 266
        recruiting, 262
        supervisory training, 264
    during design, 261
    media, 266
    what to communicate, 260
Compensation Policy, 25
Competency-based Pay, 26
Competitive Advantage, 3
Compressed Work Week, 9
Confidentiality
    focus groups, 14
    job evaluation committee, 72
Contribution Formula,196, 198
Costing
    annual or hourly costs, 141, 153, 164
    benefits, 165
    new salary program, 163, 166
    step-rate, 166
    3M system, 168
    work-related pay, 165
Deferred Profit-Sharing Plans, 194
Demotions, 135
Dental Insurance, 147
Design Committee, 14, 53
    members, 15
    size, 15
DPSP. *See* Deferred Profit-Sharing Plans
Employee Attitude/Opinion Surveys, 10, 17
Employee Involvement, 6
    consultant, 18
    employee committee, 14
        characteristics of members, 15
        responsibilities, 16
    focus groups, 14
    literature, 7
    management authority, 13

Employee Involvement — *continued*
    methodologies, 13,14
    opinion surveys, 10, 17
    personal experience, 8
    rationale for, 7
    unions, 17
Employee Profit-sharing plans, 194
Employee Share Ownership Plans, 211
    disadvantages, 214
    effectiveness, 213
    types, 212
        stock-grant, 212
        stock-option, 212
        stock-purchase, 213
    why have, 213
Employees
    Canada Customs and Revenue Agency, 4
    groups, 28
    who are they, 4
Employment Law in Canada, 20
EPSP. *See* Employee Profit-sharing Plans
Equity
    internal, 27
    theory, 18
Expectancy Theory, 18
External Competitiveness, 27
Factors
    weighting, 76
Group Incentive Plans, 171
    allocation formula, 179
    comparison of plans, 184
    conditions required, 172
    dividing the bonus pool, 179
    employee share ownership plans, 211
    generating the funds, 178
    membership, 175
        category of employment, 175
        commissioned sales staff, 175
        illness, 176
        laid-off employees, 176
        length of service, 176
        terminated employees, 176
        union status, 175
    productivity gainsharing, 203

Group Incentive Plans — *continued*
  profit sharing, 193
  team-based, 185
Groups
  employee, 28
  incentive plans, 171
  occupational, 28
Hours of Work, 156
Improshare, 205-206
Indicators of Problems with Compensation, 2
Inflation, dealing with, 114, 116
Information, sources of, 289, 293
Internal Equity, 27
Job Descriptions
  formal job descriptions, 68
  job description questionnaire, 62, 319
    distribution and completion, 67
  other formats and uses, 68
  questions in a JDQ for point-rating, 64
  types and uses, 61
Job Evaluation, 39
  committee, 53
    rules for the committee, 71
  conducting job evaluation, 71
    rules for conducting, 74
  factors, 44
    effort, 45
    responsibility, 45
    skill, 44
    working conditions, 45
  market pricing, 56
  point bands, 48
  point tables, 47
  selecting a plan, 54
    buy, build or adapt, 55
  types, 40
    advantages and disadvantages, 51
    classification, 48
    factor comparison, 50
    paired-comparison, 41
    point-factor plans, 45
    point-rating plans, 45
    whole-job ranking, 41

Job Evaluation — *continued*
Tyson-Totten Job Evaluation Plan, 55, 307
adapting the Tyson-Totten plan, 329
Job Rates, 108, 115 (*See also* Salary Ranges, control points)
Jobs
benchmark jobs —
functions of, 74
selecting, 74
changes in jobs, 133
methods of obtaining information about, 59-60
new jobs, 134
to include in surveys, 100
Labour Market, 29
geography, 30
industry, 31
occupational groups, 30
size of company, 31
sources of information, 293
Legislation, 3, 20 (*See also* Pay Equity)
Life Insurance, 145
Long-term Disability Insurance, 146
Lunch Periods, 158
Major Medical Insurance, 149
Management. *See also* Performance Management and Rewards
by objectives, 221
commitment, 174
Membership in Group Incentive Plan. *See* Group Incentive Plans
Merit
increases, 122
pay, 115
steps, 119
Money Purchase Limit, 144
Motivation
equity theory, 19
expectancy theory, 18
theories, 18
Objectives
management by, 221
profit sharing, 196
Old Age Security Act, 142
Ontario Pay Equity Act. *See* Pay Equity
Organization of Compensation Function, 34
general duties, 35
number of staff, 34

Organization of Compensation Function — *continued*
structure, 35
customer-based, 36
functional, 36
Pay
for knowledge, 26
for performance, 122
skill-based, 26
Pay Equity
history of, 241
jurisdictions in Canada, 242
Ontario, 13, 241
Quebec, 13, 245
Pensions, 142
legislative framework, 142
Performance Appraisal, 217
anchors —
short paragraph, 222, 226, 229, 232
short phrase, 222, 226, 229
checklist, 287
factors used, 230
performance criteria, 230
process, 233
advising the employee, 234
distribution of the forms, 234
review and approval, 234
timing, 234
who conducts, 234
selecting performance criteria, 232
techniques, 220
types of appraisal instrument, 220
behaviourly anchored rating scales, 226
direct indices, 221
employee comparison, 220
essay, 221
management by objectives, 221
rating scales, 222, 227
weighting of performance criteria, 233
Performance Improvement, 237
Performance Management and Rewards, 217
features affected by purpose, 218
appraisal techniques, 220
distribution of the information, 219
role of the supervisor, 219

Performance Management and Rewards — *continued*
    features affected by purpose — *continued*
        timing of the appraisal, 219
    major purposes, 217
Performance Rating Scale, 120
Person-based Pay, 26
Premiums
    lead-hand, 160
    shift, 158
    weekend, 158
Profit Sharing, 196
Point Bands, 80
Point Tables, 77
    methods of building, 77
    selecting a method, 80
Policy Line, 32
Productivity Gainsharing Plans, 203
    characteristics, 203
    comparison with profit sharing, 207
    efficacy, 208
    Improshare, 205
    other gainsharing plans in Canada, 206
    Rucker, 205
    Scanlon, 204
Profit Pool, 197
Profit-sharing Plans, 193
    cash, 194
    combination, 195
    deferred profit-sharing plans, 194
    definition, 193
    employee profit-sharing plans, 194
    group RRSP, 195
    history, 193
    major design issues, 198
        allocation, 200
        membership, 199
    objectives of plans, 195
    strategic issues, 196
    types of plans, 193
Promotions, 135
Publications, for compensation professionals, 298
Quebec Pay Equity Act, 13, 245
Rating Scales
    descriptors of performance levels, 229

Rating Scales — *continued*
  developing a rating scale, 227
  numerical scale, 228
Registered Retirement Savings Plans, 144, 195
Retirement Plans
  company provided, 143
  government, 142
  limits on contributions, 144
  other plans, 144
Rucker Plan, 205
Salary Administration
  single rate, 114
  step-rate system, 115, 116
    advancing a step, 118
    checklist, 279
    number of steps, 117
    size of steps, 117
    steps above the job rate, 119
    time required at each step, 117, 118
  3M system, 115
    administration, 128
    checklist, 281
    expectancy theory, 121
    increases in salaries, 122
    inflation, 122
    number of segments, 121
    salary increase form, 130
    salary increase table, 123
    timing of increases, 124
    variable dates, 125
  updating salary structure, 133
Salary Grades
  point bands, 83
Salary Ranges
  control points, 107, 113
  increments between control points, 108
  single-rate systems, 114
  3M salary ranges, 110
  width, 113
Salary Surveys, 87, 114, 293
  conducting your own survey, 100
    area, 103
    companies to be invited, 103
    information to be surveyed, 101

Salary Surveys — *continued*
    conducting your own survey — *continued*
        jobs to include, 100
        methods of conducting, 104
        report to participants, 105
        survey data to be requested, 102
    consolidating several surveys, 98
    selecting and interpreting published surveys, 91
    types, 88
        custom, 277
        executive, 89
        published, 88, 275, 293
        third-party, 90
    why do, 87
Scanlon Plan, 204
Shift Premiums, 158
Shift Schedules, 157
Short-term Disability Insurance, 147
Skill-based Pay, 26
Starting Salary, 113
Stock Plans, 211
    stock-grant, 212
    stock-option, 212
    stock-purchase, 213
Strategy, 25
    base pay, 32
    benefits, 140
    components of the package, 25
    pay the job or pay the person, 26
    working conditions, 155
    worksheet for developing, 36
Surveys
    benefits, 150, 270
    custom, 100, 277
    salary. *See* Salary Surveys
    work/life balance, 270
    working conditions, 162, 270
Team-based Incentives
    definition, 186
    design issues for teams, 187
    models, 190
    prevalence, 186
Teams
    types, 187

Unions
    group incentive plans, 175
    profit sharing, 199
    variable pay, 200
Updating Salary Structure, 133
Work/life Balance, 251
    checklist, 270
    components, 254
    day care, 256
    dependent care, 256
    employee assistance program, 256
    financial planning, 256
    fitness centre, 257
    flexible spending accounts, 256
    flexible work arrangements, 255
    general principles for selecting, 253
    maternity leave, 255
    other leaves, 255
    rationale, 252
    reasons for, 252
    responsibility for, 254
    special leaves, 256
    volunteerism, 257
    work design, 255
Working Conditions, 155
    bereavement leave, 160
    call-in pay, 158
    checklist, 270
    definition, 156
    hours of work, 156
    jury duty, 160
    lead-hand premiums, 160
    lunch periods, 158
    policy, 155
    reporting to work, 161
    rest periods, 159
    shift premiums, 158
    shift schedules, 157
    standby pay, 159
    statutory minimums, 161
    surveys, 162